UNTIL VICTORY ALWAYS

A MEMOIR

UNTIL VICTORY ALWAYS

ALWAYS

A MEMOIR

Jim McGuinness
with Keith Duggan

Gill & Macmillan

Gill & Macmillan
Hume Avenue
Park West
Dublin 12
www.gillmacmillanbooks.ie

© Jim McGuinness 2015

978 07171 6937 5

Print origination by O'K Graphic Design, Dublin

Printed by CPI Group (UK) Ltd, Croydon, CRO 4YY

This book is typeset in 13.5/17 pt Minion.
Title and chapter headings in Frutiger Light

The paper used in this book comes from the wood pulp of managed forests. For every tree felled, at least one tree is planted, thereby renewing natural resources.

A CIP catalogue record for this book is available from the British Library.

5 4 3 2 1

To my family, the team and all those who shared the journey.

CONTENTS

2011

I carry them with me.

On 28 August 2011, a few minutes before Donegal and Dublin play in the All-Ireland semi-final, there is an unholy shower of rain. It comes from nowhere, clearing the air on one of those heavy Irish summer afternoons. The boys are drenched. I am soaked through. Everyone on the sideline is soaking and you can see supporters at the front of the stands tearing away for shelter. The place actually gets darker. Jesus, I mutter. Is the world going to end here?

Unexpected events, even weather patterns, can unsettle a team on big days. On some days, teams are highly strung, nervous. But the rain storm passes over Croke Park and you can tell that they have scarcely noticed it. They are focused. They are ready. We have spoken about this match. Seventy minutes from an All-Ireland final. For Donegal people, All-Ireland final days come seldom in a lifetime. We have spoken about what we are going to do. We have thought about bringing all fifteen men behind the ball, of leaving no player in the Dublin half. Early that morning, we spoke about the possibility of keeping Dublin scoreless at half time. We believed that there was a fair chance of that happening. We are clear about what we are going to do. We are clear about what Dublin will do. Soon, the ball will be thrown in and then the outside world will fall away. And I am excited. We have studied Dublin's championship progress and they have a deeply talented team. They kicked nineteen points from play against Tyrone. From play! That was a statement of intent. But even so, as we saw it Dublin were essentially a defensive team. For instance, our defenders were free to carry the ball forward if they wanted. But it was clear that the Dublin back six stayed at home. My thinking was simple: If they had six back at all times and we have three or four up, they are going to win that battle. So why should we do it? The winning of the game would come down to our transition from defence to attack. During training in Ballybofey for the last fortnight, that became our mantra. Get up the field. Move at pace. Attack in waves. If we drove out of defence in numbers, we should have an overlap and we should be meeting six defenders in a standing position. It was a numbers game. They only had eight players forward, so they would struggle to score against fourteen Donegal players defending, with six going man-to-man and another seven covering and sweeping. And if we moved sharply once we got the ball, in theory we could score every time. Carrying the ball at close quarters and moving with invention is the Donegal style. That old notion about the Donegal close passing game originating from playing on football pitches flush with the coast, exposed to Atlantic gales and showers, is something I always believed. The running game is how we play Gaelic football.

So the whistle goes.

There would be evenings at team meetings when we would be getting hot and heavy with tactical formations and it would be doing your head in and I would hear Gerry Gildea's voice. Gerry was our manager in Glenties for a few years when we were kids. His son John went on to play midfield for Donegal for a decade. Gerry was priceless and there are about a million stories about him. These Jehovah's Witnesses turned up at his front door one evening and when he answered, they told Gerry that they were looking for Jesus. Gerry just scratched his head and said: 'Jesus, I didn't know that man was missing 'tall.' One evening we had a game, Gerry landed into the dressing room, threw the jerseys on the floor and announced: 'Brendan O'Donnell in goal. John Gildea in the middle of the park, and the rest of yez: spread out.'

There was a lot to be said for that, too. Spread out, go play:

that's the game. But so is what we are doing on this afternoon. After twenty minutes, the sound of boos comes rumbling across the ground. The Dublin fans are frustrated. We are defending out of our skins and are patient and disciplined, and the game is panning out as we expected. There is just one thing. We aren't moving as we should. The boys are bringing the ball slowly out of defence, trying to play it smart and considered instead of just trusting themselves to bomb forward. They are all ball players. They can move on instinct and carry the ball. But we are conservative and cagey. In a funny way, I can understand why the Dublin supporters are booing. It appears as if we just want to defend. Nothing could be further from the truth. The plan was to defend with our lives, then attack, beat Dublin and reach the All-Ireland final. Later that evening, on television, this game will be labelled a disgrace to football and the fault will be squarely placed with us. Donegal will lose and the general consensus will say that football has won.

Kerry and Dublin will contest the All-Ireland, just like it always was, just like it should be, and everyone will breathe a sigh of relief.

Later that winter, I will find myself in the car, driving home, on the outskirts of Dublin, still on the motorway, flicking through the radio channels and happening upon a discussion about the football reform committee. And the presenter asks this simple question: But why does football need to be reformed? The Donegal game against Dublin is one of the reasons given. I can't believe what I'm hearing. Lots will be said and written about this game and in the years ahead I will be asked a lot of questions about it. All except the most obvious: Why did you do it?

But that is the future. Right now, we are lost in this game and you can't keep your eyes off it and, in a vague way, we know the world hates it and we don't care. It is working. It is close to half time and Dublin have scored two points and look out of ideas. Rory and I are standing there and we are both thinking the same thing: There is no way we can lose today. There's no way we can lose this game. If we keep doing what we are doing, losing feels impossible. We head down the tunnel. The scoreboard reads 0-04 to 0-02.

Football is about way more than the game. Why does Croke Park have such a hold on all of us? I can quickly count the number of times I have been on this field in my life and I know that I am privileged. Hundreds of talented football players have never had that chance. Just being here began as a vague, childish dream that tens of thousands of Irish boys and girls have and I have got to live that several times over. Donegal have won and lost matches here but there are moments which keep turning in my mind that are outside of the whistle, beyond the game, outside of time.

There is that day in September 1992, some minutes after Donegal had won its first ever All-Ireland, and I am an innocent, I suppose; a teenager on the fringes of a team toughened by disappointments but still – always – a Donegal supporter and charging in from the dug-out just wanting to congratulate the men who had actually played. The pitch is black with people and the Hogan Stand seems like it's miles away. And then, after Anthony Molloy's speech and his salute that any Donegal person present won't forget – 'Sam's for the Hills' – waiting until it was my turn to walk up those steps towards that cup and to look out at that massive gathering of people from the county and to have that scary and solemn moment of lifting the Sam Maguire. There's that unforgettable dream.

And there is a muggy early evening in the summer of 2002 when we were still in the stadium having a few beers after being soundly beaten by Dublin in the All-Ireland quarter-final replay. A group of us is standing there not talking about how or why we lost, talking about anything else instead, but privately hurting inside. Colm Anthony's mother gestures to me and I come over to say hello, and as I arrive she is getting the attention of someone else. All of a sudden I find myself looking at this girl who makes me forget that this day is another bad one for Donegal, that it marks another season down the drain. She is standing there and I am looking at her and she is looking back at me, and normally I'm not stuck for words but I am in this instance and, worse, I'm blushing. And this is when I first set eyes on Yvonne McFadden.

And there will always be the Sunday evening in 1998, hours after we had played against Offaly in a league semi-final. Donegal had lost but the match itself had soared: Kieran McManus had delivered this extraordinary goal for Offaly and the Donegal lads were moving well and we had a good feeling about the summer ahead. Afterwards, we were in the players' lounge. My brother Mark was with me. He went to every single Donegal game and he was waiting around to give me a lift home. A journalist asked me for a quick interview when we were about to leave. Mark thought this strange: he had never seen me doing anything like that before. I was his kid brother. We were about to leave, and as he said, 'Are you right so?' I happened to look out of the window and the place ... that field. It was an April evening but it was summery and the stadium was empty. It could be ours for a few minutes. 'Do you want to go across the pitch?'

Mark said, 'Aye, alright.'

So we made our way down and walked across at the Canal End around the 21-metre line. We looked up the pitch towards Hill 16 and then we both stopped at the same instant. There were seagulls just floating around over the ground. The sun was low over the city and you could tell that the evening would be cold, but not yet. There was warmth in the breeze. We stood still. And there were sweet wrappers and crisp bags rustling through the stands and blowing about the field. I was a wee bit apart from Mark. I remember him turning to me and saying, 'Jesus, it's some pitch.' You could feel this atmosphere. We were there all alone but you could feel this energy; that there had been a big crowd of people present and that something had happened and even though the day was over, that energy was still kind of moving around, trapped in the stadium. I think that is why we both stopped, because we could feel that.

Now, every time Donegal win an Ulster or All-Ireland Championship, we have this ritual of going back out onto the pitch about an hour or so after the final whistle to take a group photo. It could be in Clones or Croke Park and the crowd would be long gone but that feeling, that atmosphere, is always there. And it transports me back to that moment with Mark. The pair of us looking up the pitch and saying very little. It was just so pure. That will always be a very special moment for me.

———

I became a Gaelic footballer to be like my brother Charles. Mum and Dad had five children: Noreen, Frank, Charles, Mark and me. I understand now that there is an extraordinary sense of security that comes with being the youngest child in a big family. I felt so protected. And we were just very happy. On school mornings, Mum had the bags all packed for us, with lunches made, and left at the door. For a year or so, the five of us would walk to national school together. This was 1970s Ireland, when youngsters actually walked to school. When we were very young, Dad got this stereo into the house, which was a huge thing for us, very extravagant. And we had these records which Mum would stick on. We had this Makem and Clancy LP which we played a lot and we'd all be sitting at the breakfast table singing ballads. 'The Two Hundred Year Old Alcoholic' was a favourite over the cornflakes. 'Oh, it's never too late to start living, / To get out and have some fun. / The sun will be just as shiny in the morning / As the first day the world begun.' We would belt this out at the top of our voices, with that abandon that children have. Mum would just indulge us. We didn't have a clue about what the song was about. It was for the mischief. Being the youngest in the house seemed like a great arrangement to me. But there was one morning when I sort of stepped out of the moment and just sort of felt it happening around me and watched the other four. And I couldn't articulate then what I was feeling but I know what it amounted to: This is great. It's perfect.

I was fierce close to Mark because he was the next one up; we would mess and fight and we slept in the same bed. We grew up in a council house and the four lads slept in two double beds in one room. By hook or by crook, we were going to be close. But Charles was a wee bit older, so he was like a role model to me. There were only four years between us, but that's a considerable distance when you're a child. And as it happened, Charles was a really special boy. Everybody recognised that. He had a beautiful manner about him and the looks to match. He was a brilliant athlete, a natural. In the mornings he got up early and rode this silver Raleigh racer from Glenties over to Ardara and then down to Narin and he'd land home, hop into the shower and be in school for nine. And he had all the gear –

the spikes and leggings and vests and all that stuff. Nobody else was wearing it. He liked to look good.

In my eyes, he had unbelievable style. Not expensive clothes or anything, but things looked good on him and he took great pride in his appearance. Adidas boot runners were the big thing when he was a teenager. On a Friday night the whitener would come out to restore them to past glories. Even the laces would get a rub. So Charles wore those a lot, and stonewashed jeans and a grandfather shirt, and his pride and joy was one of those vintage army jackets everyone had with the West German flag on the arm. He didn't wear the fur lining, though. That was him. I'd see this ... apparition coming down the stairs to head down the town and think, What a cool guy.

Ours wasn't really a football house. My father never played so there was never that domineering, go-to-every-game-in-the-county attitude in the house. We just found our way into it. There was no big indoctrination. We had a café down the town which was wild busy in the summer – Glenties seemed to be a big draw for bicycling German tourists in the mid-1980s. And we ran buses. Frank started working in the café at the age of thirteen and he has been there every day since. It was a busy time. I'm not sure what Charles's intentions were after he finished school, but my mother would say he'd wear out a yard brush in no time. He had this unbelievable work ethic. He'd be up early, cleaning out the shop and the yard and was forever hoovering and polishing about the house. He was a really good boy. Sport and horses were his two big interests. His birthday was 12 September, the Harvest Fair day in Glenties, and Dad bought him a horse one year – even though we had nowhere to keep it. We had to keep him in this field out near where the Gildeas lived. Once, we actually had him in the shed at the back of the house until our parents came home and worked out very quickly what we were up to. But Charles loved animals. John Roarty was a very good friend of his and his family kept horses, so they would spend weekends cleaning out stables and brushing them down and going to shows and riding out. He was a blackguard, too, Charles, but in a good way. He was brilliant fun and had a good gang of friends. They all wore those green army jackets. A lot of his gang are still around Glenties. He was always so positive and glowing. He played full back for the Glenties senior team just a couple of weeks before he died and he was a very good operator on the field. I can still see him ... the size of his chest and his legs and how athletic he looked and ... how beautiful he looked, to be honest. He had dark, really clear skin, dark features and a big mop of curls. He was just ... he was somebody I really looked up to. He was my older brother. He was cool, in my mind. I found out later that he had a fair few fans among the girls.

Charles's death came completely out of the blue. It was Friday 13 April 1985. He got showered up because they were all heading to an underage disco in Ardara. Frank drove a pile of them over in the bus. Noreen had been over in Jersey with a friend and she had come home, so there was a heap of photographs on the table. I remember we had been looking at those. The older ones headed to the disco. I can't remember if Mark went. I was well asleep by the time they got home. About four in the morning, there's this terrible shout in the room. The light goes on. There is mayhem. We thought Charles was having some kind of a seizure. It turned out later that he had an enlarged heart. Nobody knew it. Mum came racing into the room screaming his name. There was no life in him. It was all happening so quickly. She ran out of the house onto the street and just started shouting for help. Neilly Bonner, a neighbour, stuck his head out of the bedroom window. 'What's wrong,

Maureen?' He came racing across the street, up the stairs and started doing CPR. I jumped into the bed beside Charles. His leg was warm. And I thought: He can't be dead. Sure his leg is still warm. So Neilly was working away on his chest but there was no reaction. The doctor was called and it seemed like an eternity before he arrived. Then he was in the room too and started working. I just kept watching Neilly all the time, studying his face. And there was this moment when the doctor turned to Neilly and just shook his head. And I was thinking: No way. No way. No. No. No. No. No. No. No. No. No. No.

The doctor then started to confirm it just in his body language. Nothing-more-we-can-do-here sort of resignation. And in that single moment your life will never be the same again. We had all been asleep, tucked up for the night. You actually start to believe you are in a nightmare and that you are going to wake up. Except you don't. It is just reality. You are sitting in this bedroom and it is really quiet and people are moving through the house. I didn't leave the room. I stayed there just saying to myself: He is going to wake up.

He is going to wake up now in a minute.

Then Father Con arrived. I knew Father Con because he had started doing a bit of coaching with us when we were playing under twelves. And he sat down beside me and I put my head down in his lap. He had his hand on my head and was just saying over and over, 'It'll be okay, Jim. It'll be okay.' I was in shock, numb, but for those few minutes I felt secure and I actually fell asleep. Fast asleep. Then I woke up again and everyone was still in the house. And it was then I understood that this was real.

Yet I wasn't allowing it to happen in my mind and from that moment, I started bottling things. I was in denial and I was searching ... I was desperate to find any kind of solution so I could make things better for Mum and Dad. I just wanted to remake everything the way it was in the house because it had been perfect. Then this pain hits you. It was a vicious circle. You go to bed at night and you are just pining. It is like freefalling ... as if you have jumped out of an aeroplane and you are plummeting. That feeling over and over again from your chest down to the pit of your stomach. You are dropping and dropping and dropping and you can't get a handle on yourself. And there is nothing you can do about it. Then you fall asleep eventually and you wake up and there are a few seconds when it is a dream and then you realise that it is real and it feels like a knife going through you again. That goes on for years.

The whole town was in shock about Charles. Our house was packed for days. There was consolation in that. It was all comfortable and there was a sense that we were all in this together: family, cousins, friends of Charles, boys from the club. But I will tell you one thing for nothing: when the funeral is over and you end up back in the house and you end up back in the room where the coffin was and there is nothing at all in the room now except the metal stands where the coffin was sitting: that is a moment that doesn't leave you. That feeling.

That emptiness at that moment.

After the funeral, we had dinner down in the Highlands Hotel. As it happened, there was a circus on in the town that day. Everyone was knocking about the hotel and some people were having drinks. So I was there with my cousin and I asked could I go. My mother was so far through that she just looked at me and said: 'Do if you like, darling.' I knew it wasn't right, what I was doing. But I couldn't take what was happening around me. I just wanted to be away from the hotel. So we headed up to the circus and paid in and we climbed high up on the seats. I had this grey suit on me. We were sitting on these wee orange and red boards. And I felt like everyone was looking at me. People knew who I was, they knew what had happened and they must have wondered what was going on. They might have been thinking: How can that be allowed to happen? Why is that young fella here? Or maybe they were thinking: It's totally understandable why this would happen. I didn't know. I was twelve and I had lost the person I adored most in life. I didn't know what to do. I looked across to meet the looks, and the faces would turn away and then I would look back at what was happening in the circus ring, the costumes and the face paints and the trapezes, and there was a wee minute or two when I was able to believe that everything was okay. I was able to pretend that nothing had happened. That is where the escapism started. And from the moment when Charles let out that shout, the absolute rawness of life – or in this case death – hit me like a sledgehammer. I was sent spinning in a completely different direction, away from the boy I had been. Life was never going to be the same again. I felt that without being able to articulate it or make sense of it. Every single day I felt kind of off balance, like I couldn't trust the ground beneath me. I went from a happy-go-lucky child – the youngest, the rascal who gets away with it, not a care in the world – to a very, very vulnerable person in the blink of an eye. And our entire family was in the one boat. It changed us all. There was just a constant, deep sadness that we all had to cope with. You feel lost and isolated and helpless, which is the worst part. I still have that feeling. I have never lost it. I have carried that with me every moment of my life. And the weird thing is, I laughed a lot in the weeks afterwards. The more I hurt inside, the harder I laughed. At school, I was the joker, I was with the messers, and by laughing I was telling everyone that things were fine.

Then the month's mind comes around. And the kettle is

going non-stop and the house is full of people and you live it all again. I am thinking: What is life all about? Why has this happened to us? No twelve-year-old should have to think about this stuff. But I am thinking about my mother and father and Noreen and Frank and Mark and I'm trying to figure out what it is that I can do to make this better. People kept calling for ages afterwards. They'd call the odd Friday evening or Sunday afternoon and their visits would give our parents a great lift, we could see that.

So one evening a group of Charles's friends arrive into the house, which can't have been easy for a group of teenagers. Like, from when they were wee bucks in national school, Charles was with them and he was a vital kind of presence. They'd heard him laugh and had had the craic with him and kicked ball with him and knocked about the town and then he was gone. They were hurting too. Charles was missed by a lot of people. Everyone was on the couch and the chairs chatting away and Mum was bringing in tea. I was about two feet away from the telly, sitting in the hearth of the fireplace. I used always sit there. I was always being hunted away from the fire because of the smell of singeing coming from my clothes. We had this coal-box that was gold and it was polished with Brasso. Charles did it for Mum every Saturday and the briquettes and coal would be in there. So I would sit beside that box with my arm resting on it, looking at the telly. They are all chatting about Charles. I was kind of paying attention and kind of trying to concentrate on the television because I was thinking: It is great that we are all here remembering him. But Charles isn't here. And there is nothing anyone can do about it. So in one way I am happy and in another way it is killing me because we are all so powerless. I think it was Eoin, then, who said: 'Ah, it's a wild pity. He was guaranteed to be a county minor.'

So my left ear cocked up at this. And the chat goes up. 'Aw, he was a cert.' 'So strong and a year to go.' 'He'd a walked onto the team.'

I am staring at the telly and I am listening hard now. And this voice in my head goes: I am going to be a county minor. I am going to be a county minor. I'm going to be a county minor. I am going to be a county minor.

And from that moment on, I wasn't playing football anymore. I was doing that.

———

I used to walk around the huddle asking the same question.
— Can I trust you?
— Yeah.
— Can I trust you?
— Yeah.
— Can I fucking trust you?
— Yes.

So one night I say to them: This is just lip service, boys. This is nothing. Here is what we do. On the whistle. Roar at the top of your voices. For one minute flat. Scream from the bottom of your lungs.

We were in the hall of the Aura Leisure Centre in Letterkenny. Thirty pairs of eyes looking back at me, doubtfully. Thinking: This man is off his head. This is just before Christmas in 2009: record lows and the countryside frozen hard and sparkling. I got the Donegal U-21 job just when I began to doubt I would ever get to coach a county team. The way the competition was structured meant we had just ten weeks together before we played our first game. I remember being at home when the phone call came through telling me I had it. Yvonne was delighted for me and she said: 'Whatever you have to do now, go for it.' But I was reeling for a few seconds. I knew I had to make this count and that we couldn't hold back. It felt like an important moment. The very first thing I did was ring Michael Murphy and ask him to be captain. I didn't have a relationship with Michael at that time, but I knew enough to know I wanted him as captain.

One morning after one of our first training sessions in Letterkenny, I held up a photograph of the Cork U-21 team that had won the All-Ireland and told the players that that is who we are going to be. James Carroll gave a laugh. He wasn't being disrespectful, it just sounded outlandish to him. It sounded daft to them all. And I lit up, not at James but at the mentality. We had to try to break this pattern of underachievement and lack of belief and we had a really short time-frame to do that.

'What are we laughing at? Do we want Tyrone to win it again? Because we aren't good enough in Donegal? Is that it? We will just fuck around for a few weeks? If we stay in this place where every other team is stuck, nothing is going to change.' They were silent and respectful but nobody believed a word. Not at first. How could they? They didn't understand where this other place was.

We made small steps. We arranged a challenge game against Sligo in Ballyshannon. Michael Murphy had a family confirmation on the same day and asked to be excused. I told him that we needed him, that he had to be there. His dad drove him down and waited for him. Michael came into the dressing room in his suit. It was hard on him and we could have played the game without him but it was important that there be no excuses, not even from him – especially not from him. I was fired up that day before the game, talking to the boys about other teams, about expectations, about what we wanted out of the game.

Tyrone and Armagh had been driving me demented for years. I was sick of listening to it and watching them winning Ulster titles and hearing about the Six Counties and the great players and the coaches and the facilities. I was tired of it. And I admired them. I admired them so much because they were smart enough to put systems and structures in place to make things happen. But they weren't gods. They were not superhuman. People in Donegal thought they were. We elevated them in our minds and they regarded us as a joke. They knew we would always buckle in the minutes that mattered. The inference was always there: You haven't got it. You are soft. We hadn't the courage to look them in the eye and take them on and keep going until the final, final whistle. They knew that and they played on it. That pattern, that oppression, may have started happening as early as 1993, when we were still All-Ireland champions, when we had a chance to put back-to-back Ulster titles together and we missed it. After that, Donegal teams had become progressively softer.

I told the boys about a particular day that always stuck with me playing U-21 football with Donegal. Hughie McClafferty was manager and we had a good team. He had me at full forward. I had been minor the year before. We were playing Tyrone in Castlederg and from the beginning they were in our faces, mouthing and intimidating us. They marked tightly and they did anything to put you off – stamping on toes, pawing at you. They played on the front foot and made us react to them. It was effective because it spreads a message. They looked the part, with their white jerseys and white socks. They carried themselves with a real sense of certainty and an attitude that let us know: We are Tyrone. Youse … are nobody. There was that old Six Counties element to the Ulster teams; it was an undercurrent associated with the Troubles, a sense that 'we've seen shit that you have never seen'. It all communicated to us the idea that they were tougher and just better. Early in that match, the ball came into the square and I ended up on the ground going after it. The man marking me put his foot on my face before I had a chance to get up, and he turned the ball of his foot so I was left with a ring of studs circling my eye. I was marked and cut and probably a bit shocked. The referee did nothing. He either didn't see or pretended he didn't. The full back just laughed. This was in an empty football park in the middle of nowhere.

So years later, I tell the boys that story. The point was that we held Tyrone and teams like them in the height of respect and they regarded us as players to be toyed with, to mash down with the soles of their shoes. What I wanted to do was to change the mindset of this Donegal team and to send them out onto a field with just this single belief: I don't care where you are from. I'm from Donegal. I am ready. I am taking you on. If a team has that attitude at least, then you can be at peace with the result. That was the thrust of the message that day in Ballyshannon. When we came out of the dressing room, there wasn't anyone about except Pat from the local club, who had opened up and made us tea. I'd be fairly certain he heard every word and he gave me this look coming out; one of those quizzical Irish looks which contain about a hundred different meanings but which ultimately say to you: Jaysus, you've your work cut out. But I was passionate about us. If we had a theme in those early weeks it was: Why not us?

So we are in the hall in Letterkenny and outside it is minus whatever. There was a public gym just down the corridor and it was always crowded in the evening with students and yoga classes and whatnot. We are going to give this collective roar a go. I blow the whistle and there is this unbelievable din, the sound of thirty ramped-up young fellas roaring and screaming their heads off. They are screaming and laughing through it but after forty seconds, the noise begins to lessen. I blow the whistle and call a halt to things. I get them in a huddle. I look every one of them in the eyes. 'Can I trust you? Can I trust you? Can I trust you? Can I trust you?', as I make my way around the huddle.

'I need to fucking know that I can trust you. Forty seconds is not sixty seconds and forty minutes of a game is not sixty minutes. I need to know that I can trust you with my life. Can I trust you? I need to know that you can do this.'

Then we went again, at the whistle. And every single one of them just scream from somewhere deep inside and their faces are turning red and their eyes are bulging and they take the roof off the place for a minute solid. I'm delighted. We hadn't played a second of meaningful football at that time. But they were willing to do this. I know it sounds stupid now, but at the time it seemed important. Nobody knew anything about us. We hadn't done anything. We were just a group together trying to change the pattern of defeat and disappointment that we had inherited. And we had to go headlong over the cliff. We would leave ourselves no excuses.

Michael rang to say that the boys who were based in Dublin would find it impossible to make it up to Donegal two nights a week for training. That seemed fair enough to me. 'Grand,' I told him. 'Sure I'll be up.'

I trained the Dublin crew each Wednesday evening in Dublin City University. There were just seven of them – Michael, Danny Curran, Antóin McFadden, Michael McGinley, Declan Walsh, Conor Classon and Eamon Doherty. I usually arrived forty-five minutes before them and got the pitch organised and lined out with cones for whatever drills I had prepared. It was wonderful: dim lights and fairly quiet, the odd student kicking around, but it was like a private little world. And we started at the beginning, just doing simple passing and kicking drills but at a hundred miles an hour. The main sound was of the whistle and then questions.

'Didn't we agree to go all out? Then why are we going eighty per cent? Is that as hard as you can run? Are you telling me that's as hard as you can run? No. Then what is holding you back? Why go at eighty per cent when deep down you want to go at one hundred per cent?'

Then we would go again and we would keep stopping and starting until we all knew that they were moving at the absolute maximum their bodies would permit. Part of it was to improve fitness but, more important, it was about getting them to see that they could shake off their inhibitions and just go for it. People are afraid. People are afraid just to leave it out there in case they are judged negatively. It is human nature. We hold back even though the most exhilarating and liberating thing you can do in your life is to just put yourself out there. So in DCU and in Ballybofey and on the beach in Dunfanaghy, that was the question the boys began to address for themselves: What is holding you back? People aren't often asked that question in life and it is a simple one. It is at the heart of so much.

Those ten weeks with the U-21s were about as pure as coaching gets. They were a wonderful, honest, receptive group of young men. It was fun. Conor Classon needed to do extra running on the treadmill because he was a big guy. I used to run the same programme. After the warm-up, we'd do thirty minutes at 11.7k, jump off, stretch, and start again at 12k, before moving up a few notches every five minutes. We'd finish at 15k speed. He hated it and all you would hear was this broad moan: 'Ah Jim, I can't feel my calves. I can't feel my calves.' Or 'This is boring. This is so fuck-ing bo-ring.'

At training, we ran simple drills, kids' stuff, fundamental stuff with the boys running as hard as they could and trying for precision passing and kicking. Mistakes didn't matter. Mistakes were good. On the first evening in Dublin the boys were all hanging after just three minutes, hands on knees, tongues out, panting. Michael was sixteen stone and ten pounds then, nothing like as mobile as he is now. What he has done with his body since that time is incredible. He looks like an athlete who happens to play football. After the first twenty minutes, there was silence: just the sound of the boys running hard and kicking the ball and concentrating. If anyone wasn't going all out, we blew it up and started again. There was never any dissent. You'd praise them. 'This is good. You are close to passing your threshold. This is what you want.' We trained for about an hour and three-quarters each evening, just a small group doing ball work and sprints. I'd have brought sandwiches and fruit and water up with me in the car and afterwards we would sit down in this wee dressing room and just chat. As soon as the session was over, any authority I had over the players disappeared. I liked to think of it as a moving triangle. When decisions had to be made, or when we were at training, fine. I was at the top of the pyramid. But after that, we were all level. And we would chat about stuff. We were all just people from Donegal, trying to do things for the county. And the players were the ones who mattered. My job was to try to help them get the best out of themselves. It was a pleasant feeling, knowing that we had given everything for that night. Then I would get in the car and drive home. I'd rarely put the radio on. There'd be very little traffic on the roads.

Tuesdays and Thursdays, we trained in Donegal. Saturday at nine a.m. we were at the dunes in Dunfanaghy. If we didn't have a challenge match on Sunday, we were there again.

Through December and January, the dunes were all covered in frost and the air was as raw and fresh as it could be. Once the first week or two passed, the boys began to feel good about themselves. People want to be pushed. They need to see you pushing too, and that is when the buzz comes into it. People are conservative by nature so they sit in that place where they don't really risk looking foolish but are still hoping they might achieve something. The journey for us was to shake that off. Day by day, we would see them pushing themselves harder, running even further and faster and without inhibition, challenging themselves mentally. Sometimes they would take what you said literally and push past the threshold so their stomach turned and they got sick on the spot. That was just the body pushing past a point where it can't give any more. And it is pure, that. So I'd never let anyone laugh when one of us got sick. It showed that we believed in what we were doing here.

Those weeks flew by. The date of my first game as manager of Donegal was 24 March 2010. We were playing Armagh in Brewster Park in Enniskillen on a Wednesday night. That was the centre of the turning world for us. Everything we had done over the ten weeks was about getting them ready to face the challenge. Hours to go now and it is a pure disaster. We had taken a bus from the Abbey Hotel and arrived at some place in Enniskillen. They weren't ready for us. They ran out of food. Mark McHugh and Leo McLoone had come from Galway and there was nothing left for them to eat. We had asked for a room to be set aside for video analysis and what they had for us wouldn't hold a primary school class, let alone a group of men. This was about five o'clock with throw-in at eight. The projector wouldn't work. We weren't even surprised by this stage. Maxi Curran had to leave and get a loan of a projector from another hotel. The heat in the room was ridiculous and

I was sitting there thinking: This is a shambles. This is going to fall apart. When Maxi came back, he had to sit down on the ground in order to get the projector to work. We went through the game plan but the heat in the place was stifling. On the bus on the way over to the park, I stood up and said to the boys, 'Don't get off this bus if you are not absolutely ready because you will be untrue to yourself. If you decide you are getting off the bus, you have to go stronger and harder and faster than you have ever done in your life.'

I turned to Pat Shovelin in the seat beside me then and asked him, 'Are we ready?' Because I didn't know. I just didn't know. This was knock-out football and there was one certainty: if we lost, I would never manage another Donegal team again. That night was one of the few times when I was ever really nervous. And Armagh were hotly tipped. They were a strong team and had a good coach in Jim McAlinden.

It is important that players go through a ritual before games that becomes a sort of comfort to them. Because the match was at eight, we arrived at the ground at 6.30 and they had half an hour to get organised and relaxed. We warmed up on the field at seven and were back in the dressing room at 7.30. Then you'd just walk around reaffirming the key points: kick-out signal, first to every ball, double ups. The boys would close their eyes and visualise what we were going to do – see the work rate, the tackles, the double up. Paddy McGrath was detailed to get as tight as he could on Jamie Clarke with Mark McHugh or Thomas McKinley tackling back all the time.

And it wasn't perfect, but they played. After each game, every player filled out an evaluation sheet listing where we did well and where we fell short, and our shortcomings were glaring. Our timing was poor, we hand-passed to the feet too often, we didn't push our boundaries, didn't support off the shoulder enough, gave backchat to the referee. But they had played. Leo broke out of defence and delivered a long ball towards the square. Michael drifted off the edge of the 14-yard line. The pass was coming in at a bit of an angle and before he had even begun to leap for the ball, most people in the stadium were thinking 'goal'. James Carroll ran off his shoulder and Michael slipped him the pass. He was through. James's finish was emphatic. We had serious energy and courage and it was a good buzz, playing under lights. Armagh took Jamie Clarke off with fifteen minutes to go. We won by 1-09 to 0-09 and it felt like a night that would fuel us. The thing was rolling now. We had momentum. Everyone was quietly happy when we sat down for dinner afterwards. I have this absolute craving for sherry trifle, and I have to admit that for all of that U-21 season, the dessert was sherry trifle every night. It was about the one thing they complained about.

———

In the September after Charles died, I started first year at the comprehensive. Our street was just two hundred metres from the school so we could leave the house at nine in the morning and be at the desk at ten past. School was a world I didn't fully understand. I was punctual and I hope I was mannerly enough. I know I was a chatterbox. But I wasn't there. The seats; looking through the big metal-framed windows; the bell ringing; the shuffling down the corridors; the lunches ... I sleepwalked through it all. It was a place I never felt I belonged and my real life began as soon as the bell rang at twenty to four. Most days I was first out of the classroom door and I knew the escape route: through the double doors, race across the football field, duck through the hole in the fence, around the back of Ard Patrick and into the house. Through October, November and December of that year, I had my bag ready to go. Race up the stairs to the bedroom and throw on my gear.

— I'm grand, Ma, sure I'll have something when I get back.

— It's only a shower.

— Just for a wee while.

— I'll do it after dinner.

I had a key to the football clubhouse, where we had six footballs stored in a net bag, and once I ran out onto the field, I completely lost track of time. I was in my own world and it was a place that never let me down or held any surprises. I dreamed up little drills for myself. I did this thing of just lamping the ball as high into the sky as I could and watching it rise and rise and then slowly fall and I would catch it. Then I'd turn, sprint into the 21-yard line and drive it over the bar. Or I'd place a line of balls along the 45, sprint out, collect one, solo back and fire the shot. I did that flat out with the six balls, over and over, and I wanted every shot to go over the bar. If I missed – and I missed plenty – I would be overcome with this fury. There was nobody else around so I let myself go. Let the frustration out. Just standing screaming at the top of my voice.

— Fuuuuuuck!

— Fuuuuuuck!

— Fuuuuuuck!

Then I would start again.

Our pitch was like a refuge to me. Weather didn't matter. The wilder the better. At that time of year in Donegal, it gets dark so fast that you can nearly see the daylight leaving. The wind and the rain were like a protection, a disguise, because you know the whole town is hunkered away indoors, with the fire on and the telly on and nobody is going to notice you or even think of you here on this pitch. The wilder the afternoon was, the less chance there was of someone coming along to distract you, to annoy you. So you are there to let yourself go, to forget yourself and who you are and everything else.

And this was where I got to be with Charles. This was where I could honour his memory. Sometimes it would rain so hard the surface of the pitch would be flooded. And sometimes the wind would be screaming in your ears. You'd run so hard you could feel your legs go, you'd hardly be able to feel your fingers with the numbness. You could see your own breath in the air, bellowing. Your boots and socks became so saturated with rainwater that you couldn't hope to kick properly and any time you'd connect with the ball there'd be a ferocious spray of water. That feeling of the rain and the elements and of being there on my own meant that in later years I loved training in those conditions. When it was raw and the pitch was muddy and the wind was completely sharp and clean and everyone sliding about and it was bitterly cold: I still love that feeling. It makes me feel engaged with the world. So I gave myself up to it on those evenings. A friend of mine whose dad had a digger later told me that his dad was digging stones out of the river behind the pitch one evening. I must not have even noticed him but he saw me at this craic that night; alone on the field, head thrown back and howling up at the sky. He told my friend: 'That young fella's mental.'

———

A knock at the door. It's some boy from the Ulster Council. 'Match is delayed,' he says. Matter-of-fact. 'Crowd's late. Stay where ye are.' Off he goes. No apology, nothing. We are five minutes from taking the field in Brewster Park. We have been waiting for this date, 7 April 2010. The Ulster U-21 final.

Another Wednesday night in Enniskillen town. This place had become the centre of our universe. We are crowded into the dressing room and outside the evening is cold and crisp and all the boys have families and friends and girlfriends in the stands. This is a huge moment in their lives and we have synchronised everything, from the meal in the Killyhevlin to speaking clearly and honestly about what this night means, about the importance of Donegal not losing another Ulster final, about not imploding, about not feeling that hurt.

Cavan are in the other dressing room and they are expected to win. We have to step out of that shadow and we have gone through the key points over and over – sideline is the enemy, recycle the ball, run hard lines, keep possession, look for the diagonal ball – and everyone is on the same wavelength when this rap comes on the door. The boys look up at me. They are reading me, trying to figure how I am taking this.

We were all learning as we went. The semi-final against Derry had revolved around the red card given to Peter McGee, our full forward. We had figured that with Carlos McWilliams out injured, Derry would have a small full back line, so we named Michael and Peter inside as a two-man forward line. Peter is the youngest of the McGee brothers and touching six foot six, and on the field the height disparity looked shocking. Within minutes, Derry had Caolan O'Boyle back inside to cover them and he was one of their strongest outfield threats. We had spoken to the boys about that: watch for O'Boyle going back. Once that happens, it means they are reacting to us. Leo McLoone was marking James Kielt (and he got man of the match), and with the two boys inside it was just very exciting because it was a chance to tinker around and try a few things.

And then Peter had a rush of blood and got sent off in the first half. I was furious.

This was everybody's future. Everyone, including Peter, had absolutely spent themselves night after night at training. They had purged themselves. I could see that Peter felt terrible and I didn't want to add to his distress but I needed us to see how vulnerable we became through indiscipline. 'You lift your hand? What's so hard about that? If you want to be hard, you put your body on the line and you stay disciplined. Now we're down to fourteen men and Derry are back in it.'

They were all listeners then, a quiet crew of boys. This was a grave moment. And we won the match. Michael scored 1-3 and we remained dominant. Afterwards, Peter apologised to the squad in the dressing room, which was a courageous thing to do. It was a hard evening for him but he absorbed the lesson. They all did. Even though we had won, the atmosphere on the bus was unusually muted.

Naturally, they all wanted to start but regardless, they just bought into what we were trying to achieve as a collective. They were extraordinary to work with. Every single session was fun because they were so wide-eyed and receptive and wanted more information, more training, just more. So the idea of them experiencing an Ulster final defeat, of them having that crushing emptiness at three in the morning that I already knew, was hard to think about.

Then some official knocks on the door and tells us to stay in our dressing room and all of a sudden the boys are out of their zone. So we just go through breathing exercises and repeat the key points and make like it's no big deal, but inside I'm fuming. I can't believe just how casually the GAA can mess teams around like this. We're killing time when another bang comes on the door. They have sorted out the crowd and now they want the game to start. Another voice comes through the door: 'C'mon, boys, out, out, out, let's go.' It's like an order. Our players jump to attention but I ask them to sit down. I open the door and tell the official that we will be out in fifteen minutes and he isn't happy. He says we have to be out on the field, that they need to get the parade going. 'We'll be fucking out when we're ready.'

I just wanted the boys to see that it doesn't matter when we go out. The game won't be played without them. They're the reason people are here. The Cavan team can wait for us now. The parade can wait. Everyone can wait.

All that mattered was that the boys felt okay, they felt ready, that they knew that this was their night. People felt they could delay the game at a whim and then rush us into getting started? No. That wasn't good enough. If the Ulster final wasn't going to start when it was scheduled to start, then we had to control when it did. I think the ball was eventually thrown in at 8.25 that evening.

It was a game I had been waiting for. The memories of the Ulster finals we had lost and all those hollow journeys back to Donegal Town were floating about that evening. If we lost, everything we had spoken about and worked towards would have counted for nothing. We would have been back in the same place. And the boys just played. Cavan were very confident and they had lightning-quick players, so on the sideline we were always on tenterhooks. All it took was one slip or one missed ball. But it never happened. It finished 2-08 to 0-07. Michael scored 1-5 and he was just mesmeric to watch. He frightened other teams. He went up to get the cup with James Carroll. And the feeling wasn't so much exhilaration as this overwhelming warmth coursing through the players and their families and the supporters and everyone mingling on the field. When the whistle goes after a special victory, you almost want to be invisible so you can melt into the crowd and just be close to their joy. I was standing on the pitch watching the boys up on the podium when I saw Yvonne coming through the crowd with Toni-Marie, who was just three at the time. It was dark and they were fairly close to me before I could make out their features. Earlier in the day we had been chatting in the house and I'd said it would be lovely if Toni-Marie could be there. Yvonne said it was a pity the match was so late because she's always in bed by eight. But she had obviously planned to bring her along to surprise me. Toni-Marie had this wee purple bomber jacket on her when she ran towards me.

———

We are sitting in a room in Altnagelvin hospital and as far as I'm concerned I am here to console Paddy McGrath about the fact that he won't be playing in the All-Ireland final ten days later. Above all players, Paddy had come to embody everything the team was about: pace and strength and directness and intensity. He was a good man-marker and was aggressive and attentive and so eager to learn. And he had clattered into a Tipperary player in the semi-final and had broken his jaw. It was entirely accidental, but that didn't make it easier to accept. It was news he didn't want to hear, so he came to Derry for a second opinion, where they told him the same news again. It's a common trip for footballers: if you break your jaw in Donegal, you get it wired in Derry. So his mum is sitting there and I am beside Paddy and I'm so disappointed for him but trying to put on a bright face. 'You're going to be a huge loss to us but we have to just focus now on getting ready and back to it.' Paddy doesn't blink. 'I'm playing that game, Jim,' he says to me. And he is so adamant about it that I start laughing. He's eyeballing me, daring me to contradict him. 'Paddy, you have a broken jaw. And I've a duty of care to you. We can't be reckless here. There is more to life than football.' He doesn't challenge this, but the conversation is still hanging there and we are just sitting around yapping, waiting to see what the doctors say. Eventually the surgeon who is scheduled to wire him up comes into the room and Paddy enquires: 'See this jaw here, doctor? What is the worst that could happen if I play a game of football with that?'

The doctor explains that it would be dangerous.

— Aye, but what's the worst that could happen?

— Well, obviously, the worst that could happen is that you break it again.

— And if I break it again will you fix it again?

Now my jaw drops. And to my amazement the surgeon just nods and says, 'Yes, I will, Paddy'. And his mother hasn't said anything. Now Paddy turns to me and looks me in the eyes and repeats himself.

— I will be playing in that game.

He says this in a way which makes it clear there will be no debate.

They took out two of his teeth and put a steel plate into his jaw and screwed that into the gap where his teeth were. In the very first minute of the All-Ireland final, he came tearing out to chase down a loose ball and threw himself on it head first. I turned to Peter McGinley and said, 'He's going to be all right.'

Paddy's fierceness is about the one happy memory I could take from that night, 1 May in Breffni Park, May Day in Cavan town. It was a balmy Saturday evening and we had a terrific Donegal support. Breffni is shaped like an amphitheatre and the night should have been perfect. But we should never have played that evening. We weren't fit to. It was my mistake. It remains my big, irreversible regret. From the very beginning, the team was getting stronger by the week. They beat Armagh by three points in the first game and ended up winning the All-Ireland semi-final against Tipperary by 0-12 to 0-04. James Carroll didn't play that game: we went with three midfielders to double-mark Peter Acheson, who was a huge figure for Tipperary. When I explained the decision to James he just shrugged and said: 'If it's tactical, that's fine. Whatever you need to do.' I couldn't believe his attitude. No moaning or protests. I'm not sure I could have taken it like that at his age. But they were a very special crew, that team. There had been inklings of what might happen from the very first weeks. We had arranged to meet Kerry in a challenge match on the Friday evening of the weekend when the Donegal senior team were to meet Kildare in the league. It was exciting because it was the first team overnight trip and we stayed in Newlands Cross and everyone had official gear and the players felt as if they mattered, as if they were worthwhile. We knew Barry John Keane was playing with Kerry and had warned the boys about him. And he didn't disappoint – kicking points, catching ball, back on defence. All you could hear were these Kerry accents: Good man Barry John! Go on Barry John! Again, Barry John! Myself and Peter couldn't figure it on the sideline. 'This guy is fucking everywhere,' Peter said. It wasn't until afterwards that we found out there was a Barry John Walsh on the team as well. That was a comical moment.

We drew that game, which was encouraging, but on the Sunday morning we played a challenge against the Athy senior team and we were up 2-10 to 0-02 at half time. The boys were sensational and I was shocked by them, to be honest. There weren't many people at the game but the performance made a big impression on anyone who saw it. It felt as if we had made a breakthrough that morning. And once the championship started, the self-belief seemed to surge through them. John Evans came into our dressing room when we had beaten Tipperary. He is good value, John, a real football man with a theatrical touch in the way he speaks. 'I tell you now, lads. I have been trying to play football like that for twelve years. You have a long ball game. And you've a short ball game. Hard to beat.'

It was true. We had reached a stage where we were extremely difficult to beat. Yvonne and I stayed in the Skylon on the night of the semi-final because the match ended late. Everyone was just talking about the final. I remember going up to the room and Toni-Marie was asleep in her bed and the curtains were drawn so it was pitch black. And I sat on the edge of the bed just thinking to myself: we are in the All-Ireland final. It was that basic, just repeating those words in my mind over and over. Because it was hard to absorb.

We were playing Jim Gavin's Dublin team in the final and we knew they were a terrific side. On the Wednesday evening before the match, we trained as usual in Dublin. The boys were doing a ball drill and all of a sudden my head felt wild dizzy. For a second I thought it was just from concentrating on their movement because they were at full tilt. I was staying with JD McGrenra, my friend who has been with the team as physical therapist from the beginning. JD lives in Swords and I sometimes stayed over with him if it was too late to go back to Donegal. The next morning I woke up in his house and wasn't fit to leave the bed for twenty-four hours. I was destroyed. Then the phone calls and texts started coming through. Conor Classon wasn't feeling well. Danny Curran was sick. Kevin Mulhern and Daniel McLaughlin reported the same symptoms – headaches, dizziness, fevers, stomach sickness. Yvonne said that Antóin, her brother, had the same thing.

Charlie McManus, the team doctor, ended up doing a tour of the county checking up on the players. It wasn't known officially but word went around within hours. I got on the phone and told Aodh Máirtín Ferry, the county secretary, that I didn't think the game could go ahead. He was aghast at the notion and kept saying that it was being televised live, that we would be thrown out by Croke Park if we refused to play. I should have just refused point blank. I should have said that we were unable to field a team. Because that was the truth.

They were completely drained on the field, and Mark McHugh ended up in hospital on Sunday evening. By half time they had nothing left. They were on antibiotics and I always remember being in the dressing room at half time and not being able to hear my own voice for the fit of coughing around me. And it became one of those moments where you are just managing a situation instead of a game. Except this was their All-Ireland final. Daniel and Antóin weren't able to continue. They were two of our major workers and everyone fed off their energy. The boys who were out there ran their hearts out and I still have no idea how they stayed with Dublin for so long because we weren't pressing or turning the ball over the way we had been all season. My head was buzzing all through the game and I just had an ominous feeling. In the last minute, we were trailing by 1-10 to 1-08 and we won a penalty. Michael was bent over the ball, teeing it up. Maxi Curran was standing beside me and I turned and said: 'We're not going to win this game.' It was a funny one. I don't know where it came from but I had this feeling.

And then we watched Michael running up to take the penalty and he connected beautifully. We had watched him do this time and time again. He hits the ball with such power and accuracy and without any fear. He never hedges his bets. Nobody knew anything about the shot until it came clattering off the crossbar and it travelled so far up into the sky that by the time it came down, the Dublin defenders were back in position. Then the whistle went and it was over and the Donegal boys collapsed on the spot, right across the field. It is a devastating sight, that. You want to just pick them up, help them and console them.

I walked down the sideline to shake Jim Gavin's hand and I had to wait a few seconds because he didn't see me. So I watched him celebrate with the other Dublin boys, stood just a few feet away, close enough to hear and feel their absolute delight, wondering what that must be like. The end of that match left everyone completely stripped of any energy. I went around the boys talking to them but they were all in their own wee world. It is a form of grief, losing a match like that. The U-21 competition is strange because it is fleeting. As a player, you only get one shot at it and then it is in your past. So there was a real heavy sense of finality just minutes after the final whistle. This group would not be together again. I sat down beside the dug-out and people were coming up saying 'Hard luck'. Yvonne made her way over with Toni-Marie. And we all just went through the motions of getting showered and changed, saying a few words and then heading back to the Abbey Hotel on the bus. It was very quiet and sombre. We tried to eat dinner and everyone stayed around for a few drinks but it was very hollow. It was too hard. I felt so proud of them. Nothing had been expected of them at all and they came within a penalty of winning the All-Ireland. Their attitude and their willingness to do whatever was asked and be whatever was asked was humbling. It was kind of innocent. Nobody wanted it to be over. They were such fun to work with. At about half-two in the morning, I headed out onto the Diamond and got a taxi home. I didn't want to leave the boys but I just couldn't stay any longer.

If you've never been to Glenties, try to imagine a small town, set away on its own, in the middle of a mountainous, coastal county. It didn't feel isolated, not to us: when you live there, it is at the heart of everything. New York or London: they are the remote places. I'm not sure if geography was a factor, but Glenties fielded an intermediate team, always and ever. It seemed to be our accepted role. We tried hard and plenty of boys loved the game, but deep down we knew that the game, the real football, was being played elsewhere – by Aodh Ruadh, by Kilcar, by Killybegs. We were in the wilderness. We were Glenties. Nobody gave us much of a thought.

And this plays on your mind when you are trying to present yourself to the outside world as someone worthy of a place on the county minor squad. When I was 15, I was sent along for trials on the divisional team. All of the other players seemed to know each other. I ended up a substitute. So I am sitting there trying to figure this out: how am I supposed to get from being a substitute on a divisional side to being a full county minor in the space of a year? Only the best divisional players get asked along for county trials. I was nowhere. I wasn't going to make it. I wasn't in their thoughts. They didn't even know who I was.

I was going to have to work harder. So the hours by myself at the pitch became longer. I started turning up to watch the senior boys train, standing behind the goal and kicking the ball with them until one evening I just ... joined in. Nobody asked me to. I was there so often it's possible that they didn't even notice. And to this day I've no idea what any of them thought about it because I've never spoken about this before.

The other thing that happened in those years was that I went from about five foot four to six foot three over the space of four years. A few days after we started at the comprehensive, a

notice went up on the board about first year basketball training.
I had never played basketball before but knew that our teacher,
Manus Brennan, was into the game. We hadn't a clue what we
were doing at first. One of our forwards, Marcus Flannery, had
this habit of grabbing a rebound, forgetting for a second that we
were on defence and going straight up and sticking in a lay-up.
Marcus turned into a good strong player, but in his first year,
scoring own-baskets was his thing. Manus would go spare on
the sideline. We'd fall around laughing. That happened game
after game, eventually getting to the point where we'd be ready
for it, primed to send him running in the right direction. But
Manus was dedicated and he made us dedicated. He trained us
twice or three times a day: eleven, lunch and after school.

We won our first ever game 8-6. The team we were playing
didn't have an indoor court so we played on the tarmac court
outside. Sometimes it was so windy that the ball would change
direction after you shot it. And sometimes that was a help. Four
years later, we won a Donegal county final down in Falcarragh
100-30. The transformation of that team over those four years
was one of the key lessons that I learned in my sporting life.
And in my life, full stop. That was the power of coaching and
the power to articulate a concept and the power to teach it, all
laid out so plainly for us. We got to live it. It has played a very
important part in teaching me the way to go as a coach. If you
score 100 points at schools level, even against a weaker side,
you are doing something right. In 1988, a county senior men's
league was revived and Manus entered us into that, so we played
against Donegal Town and Kilcar and Ballyshannon as well as in
school. We played a lot of ball and my hand–eye co-ordination
was getting better and I found myself moving with more agility,
more instinct. When we started in first year, I was a guard and
the smallest player on the team. Four years later, I was the tallest.

Manus entered us in the All-Ireland competition and we got to the quarter-final where we were beaten by some school from Tallaght who were really slick and smooth and you could tell they'd had a ball in their hands from day one. We lost narrowly and played as well as we could have played and we felt like a team then.

Manus taught us discipline, he gave us skill sets and, most of all, he showed us the power of repetition. Kieran Lynch takes the ball up the court, shows four fingers and we run this drill – ball at the top of the D, he makes a cut, peels towards the high post, ball inside, worked back out – over and over, so many times that nobody even has to think about it. When everyone did what they were supposed to do, it worked. If somebody strayed away, the whole thing broke down. At that game against Tallaght, they presented us with these t-shirts with the logo of Green Giant, the frozen food company, which was sponsoring the competition. We were all fierce proud of them. Of course, it was only a matter of time before Mark was wearing mine to football training. It was too small on him. Like, it was too small for me and he was bigger than me. Mark was six foot four and broad. It looked sprayed on to him. Connie Doherty spotted it as Mark made his way to the dressing room, declaring, 'There's the jolly green giant coming.' And from that day on, Mark was always known as 'the Giant'.

———

In 1990, I made the Donegal minor squad and ended up being named on the team to play Cavan. Your heart is thumping so loudly that you are convinced that the whole room can hear it when they are calling the names out. It was a strange moment.

You are happy and relieved and disbelieving all at once and it passes so quickly. It's your name for a second and then it moves on. So even though I heard my name and the other boys were saying 'Well done', I didn't accept it or believe it until I had my hands on the jersey. I had to wait until the Sunday afternoon in MacCumhaill Park. In your head, getting your first Donegal jersey is an elaborate ceremony. The reality is different: thirty teenagers in a dressing room and nervous energy pinging about the walls and the mentors trying to keep us halfway sane. I was sitting on the bench just waiting. I already had my shorts and boots on, and the next thing the zip on the gear bag is opened and these folded jerseys come out and once the number is checked, they are thrown across the room to the relevant player. I was number 14. The jersey flew across the dressing room in slow motion and I grabbed it with my left hand and didn't say anything. I just slipped into the cubicle in the toilets and I got down on my knees in there and said a prayer to Charles. Then I put the jersey on, went out, and told myself the words I had been waiting to hear four years earlier in our sitting room.

You're a county minor.

It was the first time I had felt good, genuinely content and at ease in my own skin, since the night Charles died. And, of course, I missed him like anything at that moment. Bereavements get you every way: on your worst days you want the ones you love to be near you; but even on your best days you want them there just as badly to share in it. Nothing means as much without them. So they are always there.

Of course, the thing about wearing a county jersey is that it usually means you have to play a match shortly afterwards. We were awful that day, to a man. Thankfully, so were the Cavan lads. I think now that every single one of us suffered from an overwhelming collective stage fright. People probably don't rightly understand what a jolt it is to the system for seventeen-year-olds to play their first ever game in front of fifteen thousand people. My legs felt heavy and I could sense a sort of lethargy coming from the other boys, who were normally buzzing around the place. Going for every ball was an effort. I couldn't run. I felt nauseous. I was waiting to be called off but it was hard for the manager, who probably couldn't decide which of us was the worst. It was a terrible experience. The match ended in a sorry draw. And I had spent the Saturday night trying to do everything right, eating early and then going to bed. Naturally I then spent the night staring at the ceiling, tossing and turning, looking at the clock and playing this fabulous game in my mind.

Before the replay, I made a promise that I wouldn't do that again. So on the weekend of the replay I did what I would do on a normal Saturday night: went up the town, met the lads and landed home late. I met my father on the landing. He'd heard me coming in. Ours was one of those houses that only creaked after two in the morning. So we met each other in the dark. I looked at him. He looked at me. Then he put his finger to his mouth and just went 'Sssssshhhh', as much as to say, 'Don't waken your mother, this will be our little secret.'

I played well the next day. We beat Cavan and then, against Derry in Clones, I scored 1-3 and was taken down for a penalty. The supporters have this tradition in Clones of giving the minors an ovation when they come out to watch the senior game. I could hear these shouts coming from the stand. 'Good man, McGuinness. Good man!' It was shocking to hear that. I couldn't figure out how the hell they knew who I was.

———

Another leafy autumn morning, in the car again, and I'm nervous. Good nervous. Some dates leap out and hold a special significance, and 6 November 2010 will always feel weighted for me. That was the day the Donegal panel met formally for the first time in the Rosapenna Bay Hotel, Downings. It felt really important to me that everything was perfect. Myself and Yvonne and Toni-Marie had done a quick tour of the place the week before just to see how it would look and to figure out how I could best arrange the day. So on the morning of the meeting, we arrived there very early to put everything in place. When the players began to arrive, there was a tea and biscuits reception in the foyer. In the main meeting room, we had forty chairs laid out and then chairs for the support team set out in an arc. We had tables set up so we could break into groups. The atmosphere and the way the room was laid out was intended to make the boys feel as if they mattered and as if we were all here to decide on something important. The one thing I was fully certain of was that the panel would have their opinions of me formed in the first half an hour. We needed to create an immediate focus and clarity. I felt that in Donegal squads, that sense of one hundred per cent honesty was missing and that was why we couldn't win Ulster championships. It was time to be true to ourselves.

So we're setting up chairs and I'm rehearsing what I want to say and at the back of my mind is this voice saying: I don't know where we will end up. I don't know if we will win a thing. But what I didn't want was regrets. I wanted honesty in our group and to communicate to them the idea of everyone in this together, trying to bring Donegal football on, everyone sacrificing. I had to try to sell them a vision. It was that simple. I knew what I wanted, but the players had to want it as well. So there was that gnawing question: Do they?

The way the Donegal senior position fell to me had caught me unawares. Like a lot of supporters, I had travelled to see the senior team playing against Armagh in Crossmaglen in the championship during the summer. The job was nowhere on my mind then. I was actually just excited because Paddy and Mark were named in the starting team and I was tracking them. This was just a few months after the All-Ireland U-21 final so I was still emotionally attached to that campaign. Watching the seniors was a form of escapism. Crossmaglen is one of those great provincial grounds where the supporters are looming over the pitch. You get to watch the match close up, in real live higher definition and it is loud and claustrophobic. There is nowhere for anyone to hide. When I was walking along the wire I heard a shout from a guy called Martin McCaughey, an Armagh man whose family Yvonne and I had met on holidays in Turkey the previous month. We became friendly. He was great fun. Whenever he would see us in the lobby, he would shout 'Up the orange!' None of the other guests could figure out what he was on about. He didn't give a hoot. So I ended up watching the match in the company of about thirty Armagh supporters. It was a beautiful day, sun belting down and the crowd was bubbling. It was the essence of summer. But from the very beginning, the Donegal boys just weren't there. The Armagh players were travelling hard and tipping over scores and the local boys started letting me know about it. It was all good-natured and I was standing there hoping Donegal would come to life. But the longer they went on, the less the Armagh boys said. It became staggeringly easy for the Armagh team and then, for Donegal, it became embarrassing. At one stage, Martin said, 'It's just an off day' and some of the other Armagh lads made similar excuses for us. Sympathy is about the last thing you ever want to receive. It was saddening and angering to watch and the boys were just lifeless out there. Paddy McGrath had completely overshadowed Jamie Clarke in the U-21 championship, but Clarke was putting on a show here and scored 2-2 in the first twenty minutes. Paddy was pulled off soon after. They were just cutting through us all over the field.

It was difficult to watch. Those days are so deflating because they bring the sense of another year finished and wasted, another irretrievable year. I felt bad for the players but I felt really bad for John Joe Doherty, the Donegal manager. I had always liked JJ and he was a huge figure in 1990s football in Donegal. The thing about JJ is that he is a very tough customer and he played the game hard and fair. He was a quiet kind of leader in that he won balls that he had no right to win and then he would drive out the field and he was so strong and certain on the ball that he would inspire players around him. He had that rare capability to turn the momentum of a match into reverse thrust. So he hadn't sent out a Donegal football team for this to happen to them and I knew, watching him standing on the sideline, that this day would hit him very, very hard. JJ is from Glencolmcille. He came from a very small parish that produced teams capable of contesting senior finals against Ballyshannon and Killybegs and these kinds of teams. I knew what championship football meant to John Joe. It was a sacred thing to him and he was steeped in it.

As I was leaving the ground, I came across Donal Barrett from Milford, who was just sitting in his car completely flummoxed by what he had seen. Neither of us could understand it. Donegal football seemed to have drifted to a place that nobody could fully grasp or reach. The Donegal people leaving Crossmaglen that afternoon were just very quiet. Nobody was scolding, which was eerie. It was as if everyone was silently trying to work out a puzzle they had been presented with. I gave a lift to a couple with a child whose car was parked on the edge of town. They didn't know what to make of it either. And that was the mood, leaving Armagh on a gorgeous July evening. It was all questions. The radio carried reports of the match, all faintly incredulous at the scoreline, 2-14 to 0-11.

On the drive back, I realised that JJ would probably step down and the job would become vacant. Would anyone want it? Some instinctive part of me believed that even after this low, there was substance and potential in this generation of players. But another part of me doubted. What if they were somehow broken? What if all I was hearing all the time – they had no heart, no honesty, they didn't care – was completely and irreversibly true? That didn't tally with what I knew of those boys as people, but still. The whole way back to Creeslough I was trying to piece it together. I knew that this time I might have a realistic shot at getting the senior job, but I was more bothered than excited. And anyhow, I was so suspicious of the political lobbying that went on for these jobs that I still didn't fully believe I would ever be offered it. I was never going to phone anyone or lobby anyone to ask them to put a word in for me with the county executive. I was never comfortable with that. So when I was offered it, after going through a tortuous and pointless interview process on two previous occasions, it came about with bizarre simplicity. It was a quick phone call and the rest was just a formality. I was dazed. And again, Yvonne sort of cleared the path for the months ahead. She implicitly understood what it would involve in terms of time and sacrifice and commitment if anything was to happen. She just said, 'You have it now. So make the most of it.'

The weeks afterwards were just a really exciting and furious cycle of endless phone calls and meetings and planning. Everyone I met on the street had a strong view on the task ahead of me. I lost count of the number of people who promised me that the job was a 'poisoned chalice'. I met Eileen Gallagher, a Glenties woman I have known all my life, and she put it to me plainer. She was heading into Sean Boyle's house one afternoon and shouted over to me.

— You are off your head! You are off your head!

A few days later I met Billy Boyle outside Lafferty's shop in Creeslough. Billy spent a good few years on the oil rigs and there is a class touch of Texan drawl in his accent. You could listen to him all day. He was talking about the Donegal job like I had inherited a serious problem.

— Jesus Christ, Jim. What are you gonna do? What are you gonna do?

The pair of us were facing the Cope up the road so I turned to Billy and he was roaring laughing by the time I was half way through the answer.

— It's very simple, Billy. I'm going up the Cope there. I'm going to get three feet of Wavin pipe and I'm going to beat them around the back of the legs. That's what I'm going to do.

I wanted a back-room team made up of people not so much with decades of football experience but with an innately positive attitude. Who hasn't been in a dressing room where someone will come in, survey the scene and then remark, 'Jesus, it's wild flat in here'? I've heard that countless times and always thought, 'Well, it is flat now because you just said it is.' So that mood-dampening was not going to be for us. Ever. The support staff were given very clear instructions on that. They had to be absolutely respectful of the players at all times – and they would get that back. There would be no bitching. Our role was to encourage the players to become better and better. So many people who got involved with us were there on a voluntary basis.

I was trying to order training gear, meet with dieticians and selectors and strength coaches, and meet the county board people to talk about budgets. I think the county board saw me as expensive. Anytime they met me, they were thinking: How much is this going to cost us? This wasn't an aspect that appealed to me but we had to fight to establish small, vital concessions – like gym membership for the players during the training ban months. I felt the county board believed that the Donegal football squad was there to exist rather than to win. It was a culture of mediocrity. And I always felt that other county teams knew that and they were laughing at us. They were secretly laughing at us. Having so many volunteers on board meant I could go to the county board and explain that this wasn't costing a penny. But we needed more. Not long after I became manager, I began doing something that I had never done in my life. I lifted the phone and asked people for money. In the beginning, I absolutely hated it. But the response was extraordinarily generous and positive. Not one business person turned me down. They contributed well over a quarter of a million euros over the seasons. The one thing they asked is that they weren't named – and that they knew how the money would be spent. So if we stayed overnight or on a weekend and the bill came to €8,000 we would advance the receipt and they would pay it directly.

We held a series of football trials on 9 August and 20 September. I had a good read on the younger players at this stage but began holding meetings with the senior players upstairs in the Clanree Hotel in Letterkenny. There is a couch in the foyer there which became a sort of unofficial psychoanalysis office for Donegal football. There was a common refrain among the senior players, whatever their personality, in those first weeks.

— I know I'm not going well meself.

— I know the team isn't playing well.

It was downbeat and consistent. At first, I didn't even want to talk about football with them; I'd rather just tease out any issues in life they might be fretting about. Players have families and relationships and job pressures, and the premise of being a county footballer is based on such single-mindedness – selfishness, really – that I wanted them to know we would do anything in our power to try to make it easier for them to train and play. Those conversations were about trying to make the players feel valued. Anyone could see that the self-confidence had been absolutely battered out of them. They were apologising about themselves as footballers. But they weren't ready to quit the game. That was the one spark of optimism. They weren't quite beaten inside. Still, I was apprehensive about bringing them to the point where they would actually take a breath and go deep inside themselves.

It was never a question of their football ability. For instance, I had played against Rory Kavanagh many times and had watched him play for years. At his best, he was breathtaking. He was athletic and outstanding in the air and had a venomous ability to accelerate away from players. He was like Karl Lacey in that he could kick a point from the same area of the field but from greater distance. He was a passer. He could be physical and even though he usually played it cool he had a flashpoint temper. He was a true ball player, as I saw it, and I wanted him as our midfielder. The big problem was that he didn't have the strength to play there. I had watched him in the 2009 quarter-final against Cork. He scored a goal but he was shoved around the place. Over seventy minutes those hits take their toll, and you need to have the physique to stand up to it in the last twenty minutes. So when I sat down with Rory on that couch,

I gave him my vision for the team. I told him we would win the Ulster final and that we would push on from there. I didn't mention the All-Ireland because that would have seemed like lunacy to them then. Making them believe we could ever win Ulster was a tall enough order. So I told Rory about how much I admired him as a player and how he needed to be stronger to fulfil his potential. He was twelve stone twelve pounds the day we met and he needed to be a minimum of fourteen stone four pounds by the championship. To do that, he would have to commit to a different way of life. It was a short, frank chat and then we shook hands and Rory kind of half smiled as we said good luck. It was just a blink-of-an-eye expression but even as I was walking to the car I realised that Rory hadn't fully understood what we had been talking about. He had absorbed it as just another conversation. So I waited a few days and then called to ask him to meet me again and naturally enough he was confused. We did meet a second time but it took a further phone call before I explained myself fully. He was too polite to say it but you could sense it down the phone. I told him that I felt he could be midfield in a Donegal team that was going to become very successful. 'But if you want to do that, you are going to have to do certain things.'

Within a week, he had started a hypertrophic weights programme we devised. Adam Speer had yet to come on board as our strength coach, so I drew it up. It incorporated ten exercises with ten repetitions completed six times. That meant six hundred lifts per session. He went on an intensive protein and carbohydrate diet. Nobody subsidised it: he told me later it cost him around seventy euros extra a week. Rory is a teacher at Scoil Colmcille, so he would get to the gym at half past six in the morning, then he would teach, and he'd train with us in the evening. I would be at him to eat chocolate and ice cream on the odd evening he had sitting on the couch just to keep his calorie count up. And the transformation was dramatic in terms of what he did on the field. At six foot two and fourteen stone, he gained speed and power. It took a while but by the following May, when the nights were warm and it was near twilight, to see him solo and shimmy a defender out of it at full speed was really something. He glided over the surface of the field. There would be nights when Rory would do something and everyone's jaw would just drop. We didn't want him stronger so that he could go around bashing people; it was the opposite. It was to enable him to do the things that he did brilliantly. And Rory just took off. You could see then that if we fulfilled our potential Rory was on his way to becoming an All-Ireland-winning player in the middle of the park – which is a very prestigious thing, in my opinion. He had all these subtle attributes, too. He could read the tempo of a game and knew when to make a move. He was feisty and could punch a hole in a defence or drop back and be the transition man between backs and forwards. He had an appreciation of the overall game and was intelligent. And what I liked most about him was that he was very stylish. He was a Donegal player in that old sense. Rory Kavanagh looked good with a football. But now he was becoming the real deal.

And there were other talks too. I was forced to tell Colm McFadden that the Wednesday night darts games would have to go. Whenever I think back to the humiliation in Crossmaglen, what immediately springs to mind is what happened to Colm. Above all players, his reputation was completely besmirched after that loss. Several players were judged – inside and outside Donegal – as categorical failures by the end of that day. There had been episodic bursts of criticism before but the nature of that defeat led to a number of calls for that entire generation of

players to be let go, almost in disgrace. I remember a number
of pundits saying on the radio that, for whatever reason, they
had never done it for Donegal. The general view was that it was
time to cut them loose. That idea still agitates me now; that
people can be so flippant and critical and feel as if they have the
right to dismiss the worth of another person. The players were
aware of it. It was impossible not to be.

That day in Crossmaglen was Colm's one hundredth
appearance for Donegal. It was cosmically bad timing. As it
turned out, Eamon McGee would get to play his one hundredth
game in the All-Ireland final. Karl Lacey reached his century of
appearances against Cork in the All-Ireland semi-final and it
was a fabulous moment for him. But Colm's fell on that sorry
day in south Armagh. Aodh Máirtín Ferry was county secretary
and he was sitting in the dug-out when Colm was substituted,
close to the end of the match. They had this ceremonial plate
to give him and Colm saw it sitting there and said, 'There'll
hardly be any need to get a photo taken after this.' And he
smiled because it was a really bitter keen moment for him. He
was sick to his stomach. And at that very second, the television
camera happened to pan in on him. It looked to all the world
like he was laughing and couldn't care less. People immediately
concluded that he had no respect for Donegal.

I knew a different man. Colm Anthony is my brother-in-
law. We have never lived in each other's ear but we would
be close. I knew how much he worked on his game. When
I was recuperating from a broken leg in 2006, we devised a
speed programme. We met at Dunfanaghy three times a week
for speed and stamina sprints. He was always down at that
pitch. For years he has had this routine where he starts at the
fourteen-yard line and kicks a free and then moves right across
the line and then on to the lines further out. His father would

come along and blow the whistle and Colm's routine was so deliberate and automatic that nothing ever changed. He places the ball on the ground, picks it up and looks at the posts. He stands with his back to the posts looking over his right shoulder and then his father blows the whistle and he kicks the point. He has done that on his own tens of thousands of times. So to have him depicted as not caring was hard to take. Colm has a laid-back manner and an easygoing way of playing that could be interpreted as indifference. And so many people were saying that one of my biggest problems would be Colm McFadden because he wouldn't perform and he was my brother-in-law so it would be a test of my fortitude. But Colm had never been asked to do what we wanted him to do. And he just embraced it. He went from being a conventional laissez-faire corner forward to a very strong, powerful guy with these phenomenal kicking skills and an absolute coolness in front of goal. I don't know if he was ambitious in his younger years. I have never asked him. My feeling is that they were all quietly ambitious but didn't dare voice those thoughts because they never felt as if they could be winners. So when we met I told him we needed him to be more dynamic and to get out and win ball in front of opposition corner backs. Conditioning would be vital. From that week, he met Adam Speer four mornings a week for strength and speed sessions before going to teach in St Eunan's. He would be out the door before half six in the morning and on nights we had training he would arrive home after eleven. Then up again for more training. It was a radical and sudden shift in his life – and for his family. But he did it. He took to the weights. Neil McGee used to call him 'the Bull' because he developed this massive set of shoulders. He was a pure ball player and has the sweetest strike of a ball you could hope to see, so effortless in his motion and the ball just rising higher and higher as it travels. But he added work rate and became an accomplished tackler. His darts game suffered, no question.

The only trouble I ever had with Colm was on nights when we were celebrating. If the bus stopped on the way home, you could be sure that you'd have to send a search party for Colm. He was like our Mark in that regard. He would wander into some bar and find some auld buck at the counter and fall into chat with him. And he'd lose track of time. He might have kicked a number of points in an Ulster final a few hours earlier but he'd be quite content talking to some boy about anything but football. He is a wild traditional kind of buck in some ways. He is a school teacher like Frank McGlynn and he married young and has strong family values. But he enjoys the odd pint and has this dry sense of humour. He'd be on the edge of a conversation and then he'd just add this one wee sentence which was like a grenade. It could change everything. He was a bit like that on the field too. One of the unspoken joys of being a coach is that you get to immerse yourself in the minutes when players are doing what they do best. And to watch Michael and Colm just kicking points and practising frees on a warm evening in MacCumhaill Park, the repetition of the clear echoing thump and the flawlessness of their striking and their silent concentration: that was a privilege.

So I had met most of the players individually but that morning in Downings was about the collective and as I stood up to speak, my heart was racing. It was pure excitement. I had always wanted to manage Donegal and this was the beginning. I had nothing written down. I know I told the boys why they were in the room. 'We believe you are the group of people that can bring Donegal football forward.'

And after that, I just spoke. The room we were in had huge glass panels looking directly onto the ocean. It was a rough day and the sea was a real vivid blue mixed with turquoise and a lot of foam racing about the surface. It was untamed and clean and mesmerising. The sun was shining and it was catching the water and the whole panorama was really beautiful. I was pointing out of the window. I kept saying: This is where we are from. It was so rugged and so breathtaking. And it was our county. It was Donegal. The place was in all of us. You could see houses along the coast, and you'd think of who might be living there and of people all through the county. 'Them people are waiting for a team for a long, long time. They are waiting for a team to be proud of and we are going to be that fucking team.'

The hours flew by. Mr Kevin Moran, the team surgeon, and Charlie McManus, our team doctor, gave a presentation on alcohol and how long it takes to work its way out of the body. This got a few dubious looks. Months later, the night we won the Ulster final, Kevin got on the team bus with a few bottles of beer in his hand. Neil McGee was sitting near me. Neil and Kevin became very close over the seasons. But Neil leaned over to me that night and said, 'Jesus, I thought that boy was an awful fucker altogether that day in Downings.'

I hauled out the *Irish News* supplement from the folder. It had the full rankings of football counties and I wanted to get the thoughts of the boys. We were nineteenth. 'Lads, I want to get your opinion on why you think we're nineteenth in the country.' We broke into groups for ten minutes. They kept asking for more time. You could hear the debate. They were thrashing it out and I was slightly taken aback by just how honest they were with each other. It took a full forty-five minutes and everything was up for discussion.

For all the infamous drinking sessions and partying, they had never misbehaved before matches. What happened was that after they got knocked out and headed off to drown their sorrows, things became messy. They might go on a tear for a couple of days and it might become rowdy and singing would start. There were a few nights when boys were walking around with no tops on, that kind of nonsense. The odd petty row broke out between them. So we talked about how we were going to conduct ourselves. I actually wanted them to have a social life. But there would be no hammering shorts or downing shots. No stuff like pulling your top off or roaring and shouting or being disrespectful to people. Those were offences that merited the sack, instantly. We agreed not to let the flag down. We decided that our nights out would be on a mutually agreed basis, but if players had a reason to want to go out apart from that, they could ring me. It might be a family party or a wedding or they might just want a few pints. They had my number. They did call. Most of the time, I would say yes to whatever was requested. They were adults. They had to feel as if they owned their lives.

We ate lunch in a part of the hotel that was closed down for winter. Then, in the afternoon, we spoke about what we would have to do to become the best football team in Ireland. That was the hour or two when we shed our skin. That was when we left the old habits and preconceptions and limitations behind us. This was a new time and you could feel the honesty in the room. People were ready for this.

After that, I presented them with the confidentiality agreement. It was quite lengthy and detailed and I gave them time to read it and think about it and the provisos it contained, because they were deadly serious. They weren't just words in ink for the sake of it. When I played for Donegal, the team was called out at training on a Thursday night and my brothers would know it by the time I got back to Glenties. The whole county would know it. That had to end. And telling people what was going on at training had to end. People want information from county players just so they can carry it to someone else, just so they have the story. What we were embarking on was going to be very special and full on and real. It was too important for casual gossip. To be involved in something utterly real and meaningful is very rare in life. We all had to understand that. We had made a pact among ourselves to become the most honest and hardest-working team in Ireland. And now we had to go and do that. It wasn't just pub talk, one in the morning and the songs are playing and you're buzzing and you can convince yourself of anything. This was mid-afternoon with the sea bashing outside and the daylight bright. We had faced up to ourselves.

They signed. They all signed. And that was it. I thanked them. I told them I was excited. A few boys hung around chatting and a few came up and said thanks. They drifted away in twos or threes. I was the last to leave. When I got home, I had a very warm feeling about what had happened. I told Yvonne that the day could not have gone any better.

———

We would meet at Leo McLoone's Rainbow Bar before games. This was how a typical Sunday went playing for Glenties in the late 1980s. You'd go to Mass at eleven o'clock and after communion, the boys would walk down the aisle, heads bowed and hands folded, vanish straight out of the door of the church and across the road into Leo's place. On some mornings, me and the other younger lads would just wait outside if we were travelling to an away game. But there were days when the fun inside was irresistible. This would be at about twenty minutes to twelve and you might have fifteen or twenty men drinking pints. Some of these men would intend lining out for the team in a few hours' time. The feeling was that it was no harm – only a few pints of beer. I didn't really know what 'beer' was then; I thought it was anything in a pint glass. They meant ale. They meant Smithwick's. Leo McLoone was the owner of the pub and the manager of our team. He was forever winding the boys up. So if you walked into the pub, you'd be likely to find Leo going through a kind of mock announcement of our team. He'd introduce a player by name and then he'd be going: 'Between the sticks! He's not very tall! He's not very good! He can handle the odd woman! But not much good on the high ball.' Or: 'Representing Fintown in the middle of the park ... he only has one leg.' It was gold dust. Everyone would be in flying form by the time the official team bus pulled up outside to bring us to wherever we were playing.

Our travel schedule was casual, to say the least. We would be heading off to Mountcharles or some place and everyone would pile in, way more bodies than seats, and we might get there fifteen minutes before throw-in. Boys would be lost in a game of cards and you couldn't see who was down the back of the bus for the cloud of smoke from fags. We were playing intermediate and we were playing division four and it never really occurred to anyone that we wouldn't always be playing at that standard. The boys played because they loved it. Every so often, there would be brief attempts at discipline. So we would be changing and Leo or someone might scold a player who was clearly suffering. But it was all, 'I told you, ye wee bastard, to be stayin' away from the Limelight last night.' And, 'I was nowhere near the Limelight.' 'So how come you were seen leaving there at half three in the morning hanging off a woman?' And on and on. It was wonderful fun.

Because there was nothing really riding on those matches, they took on an absolutely ferocious intensity. There was no grand plan or ambition, so every match and every day was an end in its own right. Boys played as if their lives depended on it. As a youngster, it gave you a fast and hard football education. In the 1988 championship, we played Burt and it was lethal. The match finished in a draw. In the second half, I managed to score a goal and as I turned away, I waved my fist in celebration. Some Burt buck came from nowhere and absolutely decked me for my impudence. I never saw it coming and discovered that you do actually see stars when you are punched like that. It was an interesting sensation for the split second before the pain kicked in. By the time I knew what had happened, a full-on brawl had developed around me. My distinct memory is one of the Glenties boys who was just up watching because he was on crutches whaling all around him with the sticks. Junior football was comprised of young players on the way up, auld lads on the way down and those at the mezzanine level who were simply never going to make it, who just loved the game.

The match was the centrepiece of the day but it was important to honour the full ritual. No matter how fractious or bitter the match had been, there was no question of not stopping in the local pub afterwards. The more seasoned drinkers would resume where they had let off after Mass and swallow another five or six pints. We younger lads would make do with Coke and Tayto, looking over the bottles at the craic. Then back on the bus and away to Leo's to discuss the merits of the day.

Every outing was an adventure. We played Pettigo one day. Conal 'the Butcher' McLoone was about sixteen at the time, a big strong lad, and we had him in at full back. Pettigo had this guy playing full forward who kind of fascinated me. He had a big head of hair and wore this really conspicuous headband like Björn Borg. He was like a hippy who had somehow become embroiled in junior football. So he was full forward, but at the other end of the field, his son was full back. And his son was marking Conal's dad, auld Butcher, who was our full forward. So it was a father marking a son at both ends of the field. And all we could hear all day were these threats travelling up and down. Any ball that went in where Conal ended up on the ground, Butcher would shout up: 'If you lay a hand on that young fella, I'll break your neck.' And from the other end: 'If you touch that lad, you'll be a sorry fucking man.'

Another day, we were out against St Nauls. Mark was playing corner back and I was up at wing half forward. If you were playing any way decent at all, it was only a matter of time before someone on the other team lost patience. You would hear the chat going around among their defenders. 'Is someone going to sort that buck or what?' And shortly afterwards, you would get lamped. So I went for a ball and the next thing I knew I was on the ground and there was blood coming from my mouth and there was this boy standing over me glowering as if to say: Are you getting up? I turned to try and get back on my feet when your man ended up in a heap beside me on the grass. The Giant had come sprinting up the field, faster than he had ever run, just to deck this guy. That happened shortly before half time. Once we got back in the dressing room, Leo waited until he had full silence and then he took a really grave look at the two McGuinness boys and he said slowly: 'Ah Jesus, boys, isn't that lovely to see? Nothing like a bit of brotherly love.'

The weird thing is that we cared so much about those games. Our lives revolved around them. One year we ended up in the Shield final. What the 'shield' actually was, I still can't say. But it took on this magnificent importance in our minds. We could win the Shield, boys! The Shield! The fucking Shield! So we played the final in Glenfin on a dark winter's day very close to Christmas. And we actually won. We discovered that there was no divine law against Glenties actually winning a football tournament. There was a celebration in the town. The thing was that because of a series of postponements – bad weather, waterlogged pitches, boys away – the competition had gone on months and months after it was supposed to be finished. So the new competition started about a week after we had won the final. Needless to say, we were beaten in the first round. So we managed to keep the shield for about seven days.

Around the same time, we played this end of season game in Glenties against Glencolmcille. There had been a wedding on the same day. Injured, I was charged with the responsibility of acting as umpire. When I arrived down at the posts and lifted the flag, the goalkeeper looked at me square on. He was swaying a bit and he sounded kind of melancholy. 'Young McGuinness', he said, 'I'm drunk! And I'm the goalie.'

This was my introduction to adult football in Donegal. It was strange and magical. Leo could play about ten musical instruments – all quite badly. One evening he might haul out the accordion and give that a rattle and half an hour later he would produce the fiddle and play something on that. If the mood took him, he would march up and down the bar with the accordion treating his audience to 'The Star of the County Down'. Leo had been half back in '65, when Glenties had played in its only senior county final. That set him and his generation apart. They had been serious footballers who had taken the club somewhere fantastical. We couldn't imagine playing in a senior final at that stage. So if there was any row at all about football, Leo would settle it by hauling out the accordion and saying: 'Did ye ever march behind the band in Ballybofey, boys?' It never required an answer and nobody could argue with the message. Leo had played in a county final. That was an almost mythical thing in Glenties. That team had done something extraordinary. And Leo was a football man. That was clear. He was sharp and he gave good advice. He would tell us to put a runner on one foot and a boot on the other and to kick with our weaker foot. My first memory of young Leo is seeing him kicking a ball behind the counter in the bar, left foot and right foot. Leo senior was watching him, saying, 'He's not bad, is he?'

And that was the point. We were caught in a cycle in Glenties of chronic underachievement and on the surface, those games sound like a complete joke. But playing with that team was the most fun I ever had in my life in football. Crammed into that bus and the togetherness that you felt after playing these games where absolutely nobody was watching, where nobody except the people on the field cared about it, playing football on these half-bright forlorn Donegal winter days: it was everything. Everybody was laughing all the time and that was important. I remember once everyone being in Leo's and we took a fit of laughter at something that was going on in the pub. You know when everyone gets giddy and you're laughing helplessly and you're not even fully sure what you are laughing at by the end? You had every age group there. And you realise that when it comes down to it, all adults are just big grown-up children.

———

One day at school I asked Manus Brennan if there was any chance he could get me a hoop so I could work on my shot at home. He went one better and got me one with a net attached. It was glamorous stuff. So I carried it home that afternoon. The house was empty. It was like that a fair bit in the afternoons. My father would be off driving the bus. My mother and Frank were in the shop and she wouldn't get back until eleven in the evening

sometimes. I was impatient to get this basket up. Ours was a
middle house in a row of six and we had about four square metres
of a backyard. Each house had a shed and there happened to be a
sheet of chipboard in ours. That would become my backboard. I
found this massive box containing six-inch nails in the shed so I
began hammering the ring to the board and then set about fixing
it to the shed using a ladder. I hadn't a clue what I was at other
than wanting to have it up there before nightfall. It was a minor
miracle that I got it up there and a major miracle that it actually
stayed. It was the regulation ten feet off the ground. Roughly.
And I got hours of pleasure out of it. I would be out the back
after dinner playing basketball in the dark. How many nights?
The constant thud of the ball must have driven the neighbours
demented but they never said anything. I developed this trick
where I could dunk if I took a run at the wall and then push
myself off with my foot. Years later, when I had left home, my
mother had decided it was too much of an eyesore and she asked
a guy to come in and dismantle it. The thing was half rusted then
anyhow. It took him hours because, he told her, he had to claw
176 six-inch nails out of the construction. There were so many
nails driven into the roof that it started to leak. To this day, my
DIY skills are no better.

———

Columba McDyer came walking across the pitch. Between
training and coaching, I had virtually taken up residence
there. I was about eighteen at the time and the young lads were
playing a game around me when I noticed him working his way
through them – a lean white-haired man. Peggy, his wife, was
behind him. Columba was the first ever Donegal person to win
a Celtic Cross when he played with Cavan in the Polo Grounds

in 1947. And he was from Glenties. That was enough to make him a revered figure in our locality, but he was also a very loving, open-hearted, wonderful man. I had so much respect for him. Shortly before he died, I did a four-hour interview with him. We videotaped the session. He sat by the fire in his house and we went through his whole life and it was spellbinding. I found out then that he had been keeping a scrapbook on me from when I had made it onto the county minor team. Just clippings from the *Democrat* and things like that. I never actually saw it. He was a unique man, extremely gentle and gracious and always encouraging. I happened upon this film one night, *Finding Forrester*, where Sean Connery plays this writer guy who had been at the top of his game but his time has passed and he has no bitterness about it; he just wants to pass on a bit of his knowledge. It reminded me of Columba. His every utterance was intended to have a positive effect on people: 'Wonderful, wonderful, that's fantastic.' He is buried outside Kilraine, where he grew up. A lot of the Cavan team were there to pay their respects. I was there. Most of the town was there. When he came ambling across the pitch that day, I was actually worried that something bad had happened. He looked very serious.

When he approached, he said: 'I have something for you. I want you to have this. I think you are going to be a great coach.' And he handed me this blue whistle. When someone of his stature takes an interest in you at such a young age, it leaves an imperishable impression on you. I have used that whistle for every coaching session I've ever taken since that day. It is invaluable to me. Sometimes I can be chaotic in my organisation and it has gone missing plenty of times and has been mislaid. I would be rooting through the gear bag and have this surge of panic because it wasn't where I thought it was and there would be five minutes of pandemonium with everything tossed on the floor. But it always turns up. Usually when I can't find it, it is because I have put it somewhere particularly safe. Oil has been spilled on it but it still works. I wouldn't call it a charm exactly because it is much more than that. After Donegal started winning championship games, a fair few photographs were taken when I was training the team at public training sessions. That blue whistle is always hanging around my neck.

————

One week after Downings, we gathered for our first training session on a Saturday morning in Dunfanaghy. It was 13 November and when I arrived at ten past nine for a ten o'clock first whistle, most of the boys were already there. Dunfanaghy is a terrific place to train; right on the Atlantic and nobody except the odd dog-walker and jogger about. Near the pitch, there is a two-kilometre run from the bridge out to Tramore beach where the sand dunes are. It is right off the main road but in autumn it feels very private and isolated. When I blew the whistle, I called the boys in and told them to huddle up. That was the first of thousands of such huddles. We probably closed in like that twenty times a night for the next four years. Arm-in-arm, locked in tight together and bulletproof against the outside world. There was only one message. I asked them to listen carefully. I told them I wanted them to make eye contact with me when I spoke.

Then I said it.

— We are going to be Ulster champions.

— We are going to be Ulster champions.

— I am telling you now.

— We are going to be the fucking Ulster champions.

And they heard that message at every single training session. It had to be a constant in their ears and in their minds. Why else were we here? Why else would we push ourselves beyond our limitations night after night?

The beginning was much like the U-21 sessions. That morning, we did a very simple fist-passing and kicking drill, but for one minute flat out. The whistle went after ten seconds. 'Where are we at? Where are we at?' Not one player said one hundred per cent. So we went back into it and the ball was flying about and there were mistakes galore and they were cursing and getting frustrated and complaining that they couldn't control the ball at that speed. Mistakes were fine. Mistakes were good. After sixty seconds they were doubled over, red-faced, sucking in air. 'That's good,' I told them. 'All we need to do now is replicate that for another seventy.'

It is a really exhilarating thing to say to yourself, 'I don't know if I am going to be able to do this, but I am going to give it everything.' That is called being alive, being absolutely alive for that minute. We trained for an hour on the pitch that morning, then changed into trainers, got some water, walked together to the bridge and jogged out to Tramore. We stopped at the gate by the beach and explained to the boys that we would be running repetitions on the dunes. We did two sets of six sprints over four hundred metres. They were already pretty weary and the expressions were predictable. There were no complaints but you could see it in the looks they exchanged: this guy is off his fucking rocker. And I was happy to go with that feeling. There was a craziness to what we were doing in those early weeks. It was a sudden and probably a shocking invasion of what they had believed training to be about. Adam Speer led the run and I started about 200 metres ahead of the pack and the cardinal sin was for me to finish ahead of any of them. That couldn't happen. Some of the guys were fatigued but there was no sense of reluctance. Barry Dunnion was probably the most enthusiastic about that first session. He pushed himself so hard that he actually fainted at the end of a run. The doctor and physiotherapist were there but it was still scary to see him just collapse like that. It turned out that he hadn't eaten that morning and simply didn't have enough fuel in his body. Barry was half carried back – he had fallen at the end of the final run – and it was a weary slow-jog back to the showers. Everyone was destroyed. But the mood was good. You could hear it in the voices. There was purity of intent there.

We met again at the same time on Sunday morning. Our weeks revolved around those training days: Tuesday, Thursday, Saturday and Sunday. In the first weeks, muscle pain and fatigue were common because we didn't coast in any sessions and all of the boys were doing intensive gym and weights work between them. There was no dissent and I didn't anticipate that there would be because the boys had identified the problems themselves at the gathering in Downings. They were creating their future during these drills. It was their Ulster medals that we were fighting for, not mine or Rory's or Maxi's or Pat's. After a good work out, you might say, 'We've trained harder than anyone in the country today,' and let that hang in the air.

During the drills, there was no talk. The sound was of breathing, footsteps, the odd grunt, or they might name-check each other. When a big number of people are completely absorbed in one task, you can actually hear the concentration. After every drill, we would huddle up and they could relax. In between drills, I didn't care if they were horseplaying or joking or getting a drink. Anything went. Those breaks were light-hearted and fun. Then it was into the next drill. The atmosphere in our dressing room was always light because they felt good about themselves. They knew they were doing the right thing. There was no self-deception or trying to bullshit the guy beside you. They were all in it together. And that brought a sense of joy.

Some days you might get this bubbling feeling inside you that things were flying. And you have to rein that feeling in because it is so dangerous. You can't allow yourself to feel that – ever. So my thoughts were always on what was next. How hard can we go? What can we do better? I still wasn't sure of any of this. I wasn't sure if we could win a game.

By eight o'clock on 5 February, I was even less sure. Sligo were having fun with us in our very first league match in MacCumhaill Park. Saturday night under lights, and for the Donegal supporters who paid in, it looked like more of the same. We had been tense from the beginning because our desire to do well was almost overwhelming. We were nervy and Sligo were a really well-drilled side under Kevin Walsh. Then Kevin Mulhern got sent off after twenty-five minutes, and when David Kelly scored a goal we were 1-11 to 0-6 down with about twenty-five minutes to go. All the old failings were back to haunt us. Our discipline had broken down. Opposition players were finding a way through and dictating the terms. We were never fluid and there were periods when we looked green and clueless, to be honest. I stood on the sideline and I felt the game was gone. But something happened among them after Kelly's goal. It was like a clarion call to them. They found their game and began slipping over a series of quality points and Michael banged home a goal on the second attempt after a penalty. It was very frantic and we were working against the clock but there was urgency there. Leo McLoone kicked two exceptional points. It still disturbs me to think about Leo before he broke his ankle because he was in sublime form that early spring. People never saw him then. Neil McGee pulled a hamstring and refused to leave the field so we dropped him in at full forward to see if he could do something. And he actually scored a goal – from all of two metres out. Stephen Griffin kicked a very late point that earned us a draw. So we got out of there with something to show for ourselves. We had shown a bit of moral bravery. Our desire was plain to see. But we were desperately lacking in composure. We looked so naive at times. Driving home in the car, all I could think about was that we had to go to Tyrone in a fortnight.

On that car journey, this cold, horrible doubt kept appearing. There was no avoiding it. The players had been leaving their souls on the training pitch for the previous three months and we were planting this seed, daring to vocalise the idea of us as Ulster champions. It was based on a conviction that we had more substance in us. But that night, it seemed farcical; all this grand talk about Ulster while, in the real world, Mark Breheny from Sligo was simply hammering through the middle of our defence anytime he chose to. It was hard to avoid thinking that we were going nowhere. The frightening thing was that it forced me to wonder if this was actually our level. If we were, in fact, a struggling division two team, with sporadic flares of talent but fallible and error-ridden. My expectation for the team was high but this performance was a world away from that. A right crowd of Donegal people showed up and can't have expected much. On Highland Radio, Martin McHugh suggested that maybe it wouldn't be bad if we dropped to division three and rebuilt from there. On this evidence, we might not have had a choice. It was as if we had turned up to play with gusto and then had forgotten how to play. They had felt the pressure without question. And they had fought back. There had been a huge deposit of work done and banked. That was one consolation. Life doesn't work in straight lines. But it was our first big day together and it could have ended up a double-digit defeat. We were almost wiped.

We decided to give the boys a week off. Rory and I were on the phone a lot, night after night, talking things through. Somone informed me that a Tyrone player had said: 'Donegal aren't on our radar any more.' It wasn't meant as an insult, he was just calling it as he saw it. But it stung. And it was the truth. For years, Donegal had stood off Tyrone teams, in awe of them and letting them run their game plan.

We played Tyrone on a Saturday night. I had never had many conversations with Mickey Harte, but he was a person and a coach I thought about a lot. Year after year he had shown himself to be very intelligent, articulate, flexible and operating tactically at a very sophisticated level. He introduced new things to the game. He moved players around the field and was fearless and radical in the way he used his players. He made Tyrone a different proposition from most teams because of the way he thought about the game. They were the barometer for Ulster football. They had five Ulster titles and three All-Irelands under Harte and would be going for three in a row in Ulster in the summer. That reputation was enough to intimidate teams.

We had to try to break down what they did on the field of play. Their entire system was based on energy and work rate and a running game dependent on off-the-shoulder support. You could identify the patterns fairly clearly. They were slick and methodical and liked to entice teams out and then suddenly inject pace and use decoy runners and hit their natural point scorers in the target areas. They liked to take frees quickly. If they were prevented from doing that, they bombarded the referee. Tyrone were brilliant at creating the mentality of victimhood. They needed that latitude to get the ball on the move quickly.

Although they attacked directly, they liked to have a guy left and right hugging the sidelines so that wee out-ball was there as an escape clause. Most of their scores came from within twenty-five metres of the goal, so they worked the percentages. The approach was smart and systematic. Kick-outs never really had an impact on them because they were happy to concede possession as long as the guy was under pressure once he hit the ground with the ball. Sledging was a big part of their game. You had to be mentally tough to withstand that. They were bad for it and were liable to say anything. Some of it was personal. Some of it was just telling you how useless you were. Anything that would frustrate and anger you was material for them. If you showed vulnerability, then you were half beaten. So when you take a team into Healy Park, you are very aware of what awaits you.

On the way up to Omagh, we focused on not allowing Tyrone to be Tyrone – that was of absolute importance. We had spoken about it all week at training and we were clear about what we had to do. And yet for the first twenty minutes of the game, that is precisely what happened. Tyrone just moved through the gears and looked so comfortable and smooth. They assumed control without a second thought. This was their place, their kingdom. They looked as if they were scarcely aware that our boys were on the field with them. We were 0-4 to 0-1 down after twenty minutes. If they had got a goal at this stage and really got a grip on us, there is no telling how bad things could have become.

And then the boys began to make small, important things happen. For the first five or six minutes, it was almost imperceptible – just an occasional hand disrupting the ball or marking a few inches tighter. But you could gradually see them beginning to squeeze Tyrone and then they began to assert themselves. Michael landed a breathtaking point. Leo McLoone reached a personal plateau in that match, attaching himself to Sean Cavanagh and forcing a turnover that led to a goal for us. He just powered away from one of the best players of his generation and played Anthony Thompson through on goal. Brick Molloy followed up on the rebound and just like that we had a goal. It was a very swift switch in momentum and it was a revelatory moment for us because it confirmed to us what we had sensed at training: that when we did things correctly, we could be dangerous. We had seven of the previous U-21 team on the field that night – Daniel McLaughlin, Kevin Mulhern, Michael, Mark, Leo, Brick Molloy, and Conor Classon came in as a substitute. Michael Hegarty and Frank McGlynn also came in from the bench, so the fusion of the new boys and the senior generation was beginning to work for us. After the goal, we began to play the game on Donegal's terms. You could sense a shift in the local crowd – gratified in the opening twenty minutes, then a gradual quietening. You could then hear a few Donegal voices scattered around in the night and they grew bolder as the evening wore on.

Tyrone didn't like what was happening. At one stage, Paddy McGrath went in to tackle Ryan McMenamin and the pair of them became entangled on the ground. As McMenamin broke free, he kicked back and caught Paddy in the midriff. Straight away, myself and Rory tore down the sideline, screaming at the referee. We were practically snarling, to be honest. Mickey Harte was standing on the other side of Tony Donnelly and he didn't turn his head but I just caught him glancing at us out of the corner of the eye. Our intensity registered with him. He could feel our hunger. He was aware of us. With about ten minutes to go, Tyrone started launching big high balls into our square. We had spoken about this. We told the defenders that even though it will feel like the beginning of the real barrage, it is the surest sign that they are out of ideas. That is their acknowledgement that they can't break us down as they would like. The match finished 0-06 to 1-10. We had silenced Healy Park and that was very sweet. We had learned a few things as well. We had played three up front and launched the ball into them as often as we could. I knew I wanted to play a strong, aggressive running game in the summer so we needed to keep Tyrone guessing. We also needed to see if we could hurt them with those long, direct passes. And the Tyrone defenders were so comfortable. They dealt with those all night.

After the boys had showered, we were sitting on the bus waiting for the stragglers. The Tyrone players walked out of their door past the front of our bus. Rory and myself were sitting on the front seats with Pat and Maxi across from us. You could hear the laughter from down the back of the bus and we were all really content. It was a warm feeling. They had noticed us. It was a start.

As it happened, I was in Strabane on the Monday afternoon. Peter Canavan had asked me if I would do a psychological session with his PE class. We met in the O'Neill's factory in Strabane and I had just arrived when an O'Neill's executive marched up to Peter and said, 'What happened on Saturday night, Peter?' He was mystified and indignant. 'How could they beat us?' I felt a wee bit awkward, like I was intruding on a private conversation, so I just began looking around the room. Peter got embarrassed and nodded to me and said, 'You'd need to ask this man here.' The moment passed but it illuminated for me where we were in the minds of Tyrone football people. And it was understandable – they were going for three Ulster championships in a row. But it was astounding too. Those moments deepen your resolve.

Football framed the pattern of our winter and our spring. A typical Friday night in our house would see Yvonne sitting on the couch reading a book and me on the phone, either to Rory or the players. People have often complained to me that I'm impossible to get on the phone. That's usually because I am stuck on the phone. Those conversations could take hours and they could go anywhere. They were really important because people are out of the training environment and they are safe at home and they can relax when they are chatting. A fair few of our league games were on Saturdays, and then on Sunday we either trained or did a recovery session.

Eight days after we beat Tyrone, Kildare came to town. It was a Sunday game and on Saturday afternoon, I got a phone call to say that they were training in O'Donnell Park. I couldn't get over it. Why did we have to be so courteous in Donegal? It was the old Donegal mentality: be nice, offend nobody, accommodate people. I was on the phone with Rory and he told me that when we played Fermanagh in the championship in 2001, the Fermanagh county secretary phoned up the Donegal county board asking if Rory and Raymie Gallagher could get into MacCumhaill Park on Friday night to practise their frees. And they were allowed in! This was a decade later and the mentality had not changed a jot. I was agitated.

There is limited parking in O'Donnell Park so we decided to meet at the Mount Errigal Hotel at noon on Sunday and get the team bus over. Just as we were coming up to the Polestar roundabout, the Kildare bus flies past us with a Garda escort. Sirens and the works. This was just after twelve o'clock on a Sunday. Half the town was at Mass and the other half was hungover. There wasn't a sinner about. You literally couldn't see a person anywhere. We went past the new Dunnes Stores and it was like a scene in *28 Days Later*.

So we were behind the Kildare cavalcade and, of course, the boys loved it.

— Ah, Jesus, boys, we'll never get through the crowd.

— We'll be mobbed.

It was funny. But it was also a sign that Kildare were here to take care of business. This was a Kieran McGeeney team. They would not quit. And they should have been in the All-Ireland final the previous September. They were desperately unlucky not to be. They were bridesmaids to an All-Ireland. We were just another team.

League games can be gruelling. Again, we found ourselves playing into a stiff, stubborn winter breeze and absolutely ferocious Kildare tackling. It quickly became one of those games of resolve: hard and fast-paced and error-strewn because both teams were clearly ravenous for a win – for reasons that went beyond a mere league fixture. Emmet Bolton was detailed to mark Karl and he fronted him from the outset, pushing him back and blocking his road. What McGeeney was doing was attacking the very heart of our game plan, cutting out our running game. Neil McGee was shown a yellow card for three quick fouls, so he needed to become more refined. The teams committed 36 fouls in 36 minutes in the first half. So the match became a game of will – the first side to blink loses. We fired eleven wides in that first half, but the desire never dipped and what I noticed was that the distinction between the older lads and the younger crew was beginning to blur. They were becoming a team. The messages we were giving them had started to register.

We felt that they had bought into our message. For instance, one of the big themes we had during those weeks was about hanging a teammate out to dry. Early in the game, we were whistled for over-carrying the ball four or five times because the support wasn't there for the player with the ball. That might seem like a small thing, but for me, it was central to everything. You had to support your teammate. The system required everyone doing the same thing and thinking the same thing all the time. That was the critical aspect. All the time! So leaving a guy isolated just wasn't acceptable. That was a lesson we learned that day. But in general, they were starting to use the information. If we said go long, the ball went long. The instructions were being taken literally. It was 0-04 to 0-03 to Kildare with 48 minutes gone and after that we hit five points to their one. The last score was a magisterial point by Michael in the 68th minute and he waved his hand to the crowd, something he seldom does. It was an acknowledgement that we had claimed the game.

In the hotel before the game, we had promised the boys that Kildare would not quit until the final whistle. Sure enough, they produced 1-1 in the last two minutes and the game finished in a draw. But it had been a good outing and a really substantial test. At one point, Leo McLoone carried the ball along the sideline. He was on form again that afternoon, just flowing, and almost effortless in his style. He was halted with a high tackle and Pat Shovelin, who had wandered up into the Kildare area, started on to the referee. 'Jesus, they're going to kill him! High tackle, high tackle!' Pat is incredibly strong physically and not the tallest of people. I saw him having words with Kieran McGeeney and then he shot past me with the shoulders hunched. Pat told me about the exchange later.

After he shouted at the referee, Kieran McGeeney called over to him: 'What would you know about it, short arse?'

Pat shouted back, 'Aye, you're a big man, aren't ya?' Then Pat told me, 'Next thing, McGeeney came out of the dug-out and stood over me. And I realised that he was a big man.'

We got no end of value out of it. For weeks afterwards, no matter what Pat said about anything, the stock reply he got was: 'Sure what would you know about it, short arse?'

Pat was with me from day one as goalkeeping coach. His loyalty is boundless and he is very funny. He has this laugh that can make a room laugh. That was important to us.

After that, the season began to speed up. We had our first overnight trip for the Meath game. It's funny: players really like to get away from work and the house for a while because being among themselves is a kind of escape. They don't talk about football or the game ahead. I will say one thing for the Donegal boys: they love a cup of tea. The bus could hardly pass a filling station without someone shouting to stop for a wee cup. Karl or Michael or Colm would usually organise a kitty for some kind of lottery for longer trips. And there'd usually be a card school down the back of the bus. When we travelled on Saturdays for Sunday games, it sometimes felt like being on a sixth class school tour. We always planned to arrive at our hotel for half four. There would always be tea and scones with fresh cream and jam waiting for them. We used to push to the brink at training night after night so it was nice to be able to offer a small courtesy like that. We would have a session in the swimming pool at half five, just stretching and high-knees. There was always a bit of horseplay and you'd be terrified one of them would slip on the tiles. It's like being a parent with them sometimes. The odd boy might hide in the sauna but it was dinner at seven, maybe watch a film and then video analysis at nine o'clock. It was lights out after *Match of the Day*. No card schools or sitting up yapping half the night.

On Sunday, we got the bus over to Mass and had a pre-match meal at about 10.45. Another team meeting was scheduled from 11.20 until noon. We would be at the ground at 12.30 for a two o'clock throw-in. So that became their schedule. The away trips were great because it gave the boys a chance to get to know one another on a personal level. We tried to make it fun. If it was someone's birthday we always marked that. We were like a family. Before we played Meath, we spoke again about hanging each other out to dry. Leo had been hammered in the Kildare match and Paddy McGrath had almost been knocked out cold because he had no support. It was an honest conversation and some of the boys manned up and admitted that they had allowed it to happen and that it wouldn't happen again.

And they were absolutely true to their word. That day gave us shivers of pride on the sideline because the boys were going into things with a heightened level of intensity and they were on song. They were in synchronicity. At one stage, Neil McGee came out and claimed a ball and absolutely buckled one of the Meath lads as he drove out. But the crucial thing was that he kept carrying the ball, attacking the space, and finally played Mark McHugh who found Colm McFadden. It was a statement of intent by Neil because he didn't have the finesse of Frank on the ball, but he had the ability to absolutely boss his sector. He had the potential to become an All-Star full back and he began exploring that here.

Meath play a good traditional brand of football and like to let the ball into the full forward line. We played with six half forwards closing down the area where they liked to deliver the ball from, so they couldn't release it the way they wanted to. At one stage, they were passing about, trying to find a gap, and the voice of a Meath supporter, 'Give her a kick! Give her a kick!' carried on the breeze, even as Ryan Bradley came in on the blind side and shouldered the Meath guy on the ball. And then this exasperated roar: 'Kick the fucken ball, would ya!' And you kind of step out of the game and laugh when something like that happens. Those are great moments. It was absolutely classic Ireland. We won by 0-16 to 0-09. On the way home, we stopped in the Fiddler's in Carrickmacross, which is owned by Seamus McEnaney, the Meath manager at the time. We had our meal and dessert and we had decided that regardless of the result, the boys could have a few pints. I could see a few of them gathering at the bar but no sign of any pints coming. Ten minutes later, Michael came along and said that they had decided not to bother. It was unusual of them and I had actually wanted them to have a few drinks. But this was the so-called party team. A few of them headed down the street in Carrickmacross to get an ice cream before we hit the road again.

Six nights later, we were in Celtic Park playing Derry. John Brennan, their manager, was old school and he had this uncanny record of winning a championship in his first year with every team he managed – including an All-Ireland club title with Lavey. You only had to look at him to see his managerial style and know that he would introduce a serious mental toughness to the Derry dressing room. But we had our best performance that night, scoring 2-18 to 2-12. A newspaper headline referred to us as 'dazzling'. It had been a while since any Donegal team had been spoken of in such flattering terms. We ate in a church in Derry and the local people were very taken by what they had seen. And a big Donegal support had travelled. People were beginning to take a little bit of notice.

When we played Antrim in Ballyshannon, we carried the confidence from the evening in Derry with us. The pitch there is on a height and can be tricky for visiting teams. We were all familiar with it and we controlled the game. So we were unbeaten going into the last game against Laois.

It was a conundrum. As long as we didn't lose by more than

four points, we would be promoted. And if Laois won, they would go up to division one with us. The other team in contention was Tyrone. And I knew which county I would prefer to have for company in division one. It wasn't out of malice or pettiness: I just didn't want to play Tyrone in the league if we were going to play them in the Ulster championship. Their management is so smart and every game they play is like an education for them. In Ulster, it is all about learning. That is why the McKenna Cup is basically all smoke and mirrors. You could win a game in January and the other manager would walk away with a full notebook on you. We were always conscious of that. If we were playing a league match that was being televised, we always tweaked our game plan. If we weren't playing one of the top teams, we rolled out what we were planning for the summer. So against Laois, we subconsciously relaxed. We allowed ourselves to talk about the possibility of being promoted even if we lost the match. It was dangerous and it had an impact on our performance. The intensity wasn't there. Laois beat us. As it happened, other results went our way but it could have been a bitterly expensive lesson for us.

We got to play Laois in Croke Park in the league final. Neil McGee was injured, so Kevin Cassidy stepped in at full back – and still managed to score a point. The team was starting to take shape. By now, Rory and I were finding it hard to believe that Frank McGlynn hadn't been in our thinking when we sat down to talk about the team in the first few weeks. After just a month of training, we found ourselves standing back each evening in constant surprise at his quality and skill level. Frank is one of those players who are slow to warm to a season. He doesn't really hit his stride until March or April. I'm not sure why that is. Colm McFadden is the same. They are both schoolteachers and they room together and are very similar.

They were known as 'the auld married couple'. But you would see this shift in both of them over the space of a fortnight. All of a sudden, Frank was sharp as a tack and really skating around the place. He has some great innate qualities. He is fantastic at injecting pace into attacks at the right time and is a skilful man-marker and you are never really concerned about a forward getting the better of him. Some players are locked into a position. Neil McGee is a full back. Paddy McGrath is a corner back. But we could parachute Frank into any situation and he would respond to it. We were chatting one day about building attacks at pace and Colm and Michael agreed that they loved to see Frank coming forward with the ball because they knew that when they moved, he would read it instantly and always put the ball into the area they wanted. There was never a need to shout or point: this perfect, sympathetic delivery fell in front of them so they could take it without having to check or break stride.

And Frank was gas. I tried to create a culture of openness at training and encouraged the players to question things. It stands to reason to me that players have a really in-depth knowledge of what is happening on the field – more so than those of us on the sideline. And Frank always had questions. He would come back looking for clarifications, have a think about what you told him and then return with an opinion of his own. He spoke a lot at meetings. He is a task-oriented person. And Frank was one of the senior players who was questioned after that Armagh defeat. I don't know how deeply that affected him, but I do know that in everyday life, he is a very soft and wholesome person.

You know that straightaway when you are in his company. And at training, he was a torture because he referees every single game as he plays it. We always had little victories for the winners in these seven-minute games we held. The losing team would do seventy press ups; the winners got to enjoy watching them. That drove Frank cracked because of his competitiveness. So he would be sparking away during games, especially if his team was losing. I would have the whistle and it would be: 'That ball was wide. How was that a point? What about that foul on Tony, there, Jim? Oh, so you're allowed eight steps in Gaelic football now? That's brilliant. Didn't know that.' He might miss the odd night of training because of parent–teacher meetings and when he came back Neil McGee would be waving the finger at him. 'Now, Frank, you shut your mouth tonight. You weren't here the last night and there wasn't a word.' So it was good to see a player like Frank out in Croke Park and thriving.

You could see the difference in the others too. At one point, Colm came from two metres behind his man to win a ball that Rory Kavanagh had sent out towards the Nally Stand. All the dawn sessions with Adam Speer were beginning to pay off. He just powered out and overtook his man and, in that second, all of a sudden I felt excited about the summer ahead. Colm was one of those I had put a lot of effort into. We got a penalty in the second half and as Michael stepped up to take it, I had that queasy, butterflies feeling. That evening in Breffni Park; the ball rocketing against the bar and the chance to be All-Ireland champions evaporating and the devastation afterwards flashed through my mind. I wasn't sure how Michael would take it if this didn't go in because he thinks so deeply about the game. There might have been a residue. Some people jump on any perceived weakness and a miss would have been a perfect platform to do that, to decide he hadn't the bottle for penalties. He nailed it and what I was really pleased about was that he struck it high again. He had no fear of the crossbar.

That was that. We won the league final by 2-11 to 0-16. It was

24 May. We had a cup to show for our spring torrents of hard work. Some of the older boys had won Donegal's only league title in 2007, so I wasn't sure how much winning a division two title meant to them. But it did matter a hell of a lot to me. It was the first trophy Michael lifted at senior level. It was my first title as a senior manager. It was demonstrable testimony to the work, the unbelievable work, the boys had put in.

———

I left secondary school at the age of sixteen. Charles's death had happened just on the cusp of my starting there and I found myself drifting through the years, losing sight of whatever the point of it was supposed to be and falling behind and losing confidence term after term. I didn't in those years have the wherewithal as a person to make the adjustments that might have helped me to apply myself. Not that I believed there was anything to apply either. French … Maths … English … Science … the classes merged into one long class and I found myself daydreaming through the subjects, hour after hour. I just didn't think I was able for it and I wasn't sure why we were being given all this information or what we were supposed to do with it. Some of the others in my class were thriving and they approached exams with purpose. They seemed to have some bigger plan in mind. I didn't have the drive or energy for that and I became more and more isolated within the school system. So I quit. I quit in 1989 with absolutely no clue of what I was going to do.

I learned in the weeks afterwards that the main option was to do nothing. Work was scarce. After a few aimless and very boring weeks in the house, I got a job on the freezer boats in

Killybegs. The pay was good: £4.20 an hour. I had no car then, so we would thumb a lift over in the mornings. There was always someone who would give you a lift handy enough, but those mornings were cold. It would be black out and icy when you left the house and because you often worked until nine o'clock at night, it would be dark again when you came home. The hours were long. At six in the evening you would sit down with a snack box and a can of coke. We were in charge of grading fish or sometimes boxing them. I got to learn a lot about fish in a very short period of time. I also learned that you had to keep your wits about you and your eyes open at all times or you'd get one of those fish landing smack into your face right quick. It is just as unpleasant as it sounds but that was the form. Every so often, a fish would fly when some boy wasn't looking or was daydreaming on the job. It makes this really satisfying slapping sound. As long as you weren't the recipient, it was a lark.

It felt like a huge leap, from the classroom to the fish factory, like being suddenly transported into another world. It was a world of men. But it was fun precisely because the work was monotonous. Boys had to make their own bit of craic to get through the day. There was this one boy known as the Yodeller for reasons that became painfully obvious soon enough. He would just yodel his way through an entire shift. His voice would be ringing in your ear by the time you got home.

The freezer boats were tough places to work, but filled with good people. The work was sporadic, but when you got a decent run of weeks, you could make a few quid. You had lifers there and a lot of guys who spanned the football divide, guys from Ardara, Killybegs, Glen, Dunkineely, Kilcar. It was a fairly complex set of arch rivalries and football hatreds enclosed in one room working together for the good of Donegal fishing. I worked just to earn enough money to get by. I didn't really care beyond that because the football field was still where the most meaningful part of my life took place.

―――

15 May was burnt onto our retinas. Our game against Antrim was the first of the All-Ireland championship. As the day loomed the boys were beginning to feel the pressure. There was an unspoken realisation amongst us that this was the day upon which we would be judged. The memories of what had happened in Crossmaglen were still floating in the background. We had spent the weekend after the league final in Castlebar, on the pitch for nine on Saturday morning for a long and very intense session. We had a sit-down in the afternoon and went to a bowling alley that evening. It was the usual: lights out after *Match of the Day*. Sunday morning involved another very hard early session and we felt spent and satisfied going up the road. Still, the thought of this game was gnawing at us. Four years without a victory in Ulster and the possibility of another defeat in Ballybofey brought a lot of private pressures. My fear was that we were thinking about the occasion more than the game.

The Antrim manager Liam Bradley gave a newspaper interview in which he voiced concerns about our game style. He used the old Pat Spillane phrase, 'puke football'. I wasn't happy about it because it provoked a lot of comment about us, which was his plan. Liam had seen enough of us and was smart enough to know what was coming. So he was trying to almost dare us into playing an open game. The most annoying thing was that word was coming to us from Belfast that Liam was coaching a very defensive game plan. It didn't sit well with me. It was another example of people thinking they had a God-given right to say whatever they liked about Donegal.

The morning of the match was dismal, more like a February day. We got to the Villa Rose Hotel early and had laminated posters hung around the room when the boys arrived. It had a low ceiling and it was warm in there, and we had all these key references of the previous Ulster championship matches in which the boys had played. That we hadn't won a match in four years was the obstacle that we were trying to get around. There was no need to voice it. We were all just impatient to change it. So we spoke about details. We discussed who the boys would pick up. Karl would take Michael McCann at centre half but if Kevin Niblock moved out, then Neil McGee was to stay with him. Frank McGlynn was to shadow Thomas McCann. We had four or five defensive permutations. Antrim were a natural running team so, ideally, we would stop them at source. The other thing was that they ran with a lot of confidence and we had to squeeze that out of them.

When we walked away from the huddle just before the parade and the throw-in, there was a tingle down the back of my neck. During the last notes of the anthem, there is always a huge voltage of anticipation and noise from the crowd. It announces that the moment has arrived. This is it. Getting over the line was all we wanted. But when the anthem was played now, I found myself looking instinctively towards the terrace at the town end of the ground where Mark always used to stand. I could always spot him standing there when I was on the field because he was so tall. It would be thirteen years that summer since he had been killed in a car crash. Anytime I was in Ballybofey, my eyes would sooner or later be drawn to his spot. His absence always took a lot out of me but I was so immersed in this match that the moment caught me off guard. It was like a jolt. My heart sank. And for a few seconds, just before the ball was thrown in, I felt very uncomfortable and out of focus. Nobody around me noticed it but I was kind of tutoring myself, telling myself to get my mind back on the match. You focus on the ball and your eyes follow it and after that, you are just locked in.

None of us would have described it as a perfect hour of football, but we were delighted. We won 1-10 to 0-07, with Mark McHugh scoring a goal in the last minute. We had been solid. After the minor game, we had named Patrick McBrearty on the senior squad and he made his debut that afternoon. The interesting thing was that Donegal got a free just seconds after Patrick ran onto the field and straight away he was up around Michael and Colm volunteering to take it. I loved that. He was seventeen years old and he was saying to them that he was here on merit and that this was his stage. By the time we got home, I felt good. I flicked on *The Sunday Game* and watched the highlights and then the analysis of our performance. I knew that Ryan Bradley had been given the man of the match award and I was thrilled for him. So I couldn't believe just how cutting Pat Spillane was about him. He said that the quality had been so poor that there was no man of the match.

It was a really disparaging dismissal of Ryan. Winning that award meant a lot to him. It meant a lot to his family. For years, I had watched Ryan Bradley from afar. He scored a goal against Glenties in the county minor final that is still vivid in my mind because of his technical skill. Ryan is perfectly two-footed when it comes to kicking. He is an athlete and he has power. But he was in and out of Donegal teams and I saw him playing for a kind of B selection against our U-21 team. The ability was there, but he wasn't in the condition he needed to be. He needed to drop two stone. It was the same project as Rory Kavanagh except in reverse. So in addition to doing the training and gym work,

Ryan ran the roads seven days a week. He went out running when every muscle in his body was screaming for rest. Usually he put up around eight or ten kilometres in the morning so he could burn fat. And he went from fifteen and a half stone to thirteen stone six. But it was more than that. He turned down an offer to go to America so that he could play with Donegal. He had no job at the time, so he had very little money. And he had very little of a social life because of the way we were training. The pundits knew nothing about that. At that time, we had accomplished very little as a football team and any recognition counted. That man of the match award mattered. So I sat watching that television show and I was thinking: Fuck you. I spoke with Ryan on the phone every single day. Just to tell him to keep it up. Ryan knew that if he got his act together, he was in the team. I used to tell him that this was the easiest thing he would ever do in his life. You can't coach what Ryan Bradley has. So all he had to do was run hard, every day, until his body was where it needed to be. When you are talking with someone every day and sharing their triumphs and their concerns, you do become emotionally attached and very defensive of them. In early summer, when the sessions were gruelling beyond belief, I got up and ran ten kilometres every day. After seven I was wrecked, but the final three kilometres to home gave me a small taste of what the boys were putting in night after night. It helped me to connect with them when there was a little bit of pain. I used to blank out over the last twenty minutes and my mind would open up and I used to dive into games. That is when most of the tactical stuff was done in my mind. I'd burst into the house drowned in sweat and, as usual, not be able to find a pen and paper quickly enough. And at training, I could point to Ryan as a paragon of what we were trying to be. The boys were destroyed after a session so the thought of getting up and running ten kilometres at seven the next morning was too much for anyone to stomach. Except for Ryan.

If the RTÉ judgement was that the match was so poor that it didn't deserve a man of the match accolade, fine. Go with that. But then why show Ryan receiving the trophy on national television? And they mock that? If they felt there was no man of the match, then why did they present it to him? It was the same answer. People could say whatever they liked about Donegal football. I decided there and then that if we beat Cavan, I was going to address it. If we beat Cavan, I was going to sort it out.

———

The bus is like a cocoon. We are cut off from the world. It is well after eleven on Saturday evening and we own the road. There is very little traffic and the bus is quiet. We have beaten Cavan and scored 2-14 but the entire day has been annoying and stressful. Uppermost in my mind is that Michael had been sent off with a straight red card and as it stands he will miss our next game, the Ulster semi-final against Tyrone. Everyone is reeling from that thought. None of us saw what he was supposed to have done but Michael is down the back in his seat and he looks worried. He is the team leader but he is also just a young man frightened that he might be denied a chance to play in the biggest game of his life.

It had been a tricky day. Any Cavan team I have ever encountered possesses a reserve of confidence which must echo back to the period when they were the best football county in Ireland. That air never deserts them. They carry themselves with authority, particularly at home. Their lack of fear becomes a sort of unspoken challenge for visiting teams to absorb and we sensed that as soon as we arrived. The day was complicated by the fact that we were going to Breffni Park. It was the first time we had been back there since the U-21 All-Ireland. Nobody particularly wanted to see those dressing rooms again.

Val Andrews was their manager. When I was a student in Tralee, Val was coaching there and he had been very good to me. On the very first evening I arrived, I felt completely uncertain of what the whole college business was supposed to be about and Val and his wife took me out to dinner. It meant a lot to me. He was my manager then. I listened to his plans with absolute trust. So it felt a bit weird to be here in a different time, a different life almost, as an opposition manager to him.

That week, we had been presented with our first significant obstacle by the county board. Our plan was to meet for breakfast in the Abbey Hotel, board the bus and then have a pre-match meal at the Radisson in Cavan. Michael McMenamin phoned me to say that the bill would be cleared for either breakfast or the pre-match meal but not both. The Gweedore and Creeslough boys were getting in the car at seven in the morning to get to Donegal Town. By rights, they should have been put up in the hotel the night before. Now they were expected to take care of their breakfast. This attitude of cutting corners drove me around the twist. I just told Michael to tell them that it was fine; the players would pay for their own breakfast in the Abbey. I knew there was no way they would allow people to see that. He came back an hour later to say that the board would pay for both meals. But it wasn't a victory. It was draining.

When we arrived at the Radisson, the function room we had booked was laid out with a blanket for each of the players. They stretched and lay down and we darkened the lights and walked among them going through the key points of the game plan.

We wanted to press Cavan's defenders early. Our half backs were to hold back from going for the ball on our kick-outs, but our half forwards would come in beside them and support them. When we won possession, the ball would be delivered early unless it clearly wasn't on. Colm and Michael would hold shape inside. Patrick was to be used for outlet ball because he was sharp and fast. Karl would pick up Seanie Johnston. Tony Thompson would follow Michael Lyng. Kevin Rafferty would go man to man on David Gibney, who would be the focus of their kick-outs. Mark McHugh would sweep. Seventy per cent of their attacks were diagonal inside balls to Seanie Johnston, so the sweeper had to play about twenty metres left of centre and read that ball. Cavan would be vulnerable if we hit them at pace.

After we were clear on everything, the boys rested for forty-five minutes. We ate, went through the key points again and made our way to the park. There is a warm-up area behind Breffni and when we arrived, Cavan had cordoned off a small area for us. There was so much sand on the surface it was like a desert. We had no space to conduct any meaningful warm-up session and they knew it. From the second we got off our bus we got this attitude: Youse are in Cavan now. It was all set up to try to unsettle us. Cavan were out there, dominating the warm-up area and going through their drills and stretches.

We got into a huddle. We went through our stretches and when we counted down from ten, every Donegal player shouted out the numbers as loudly as they could. It was just counter-aggression. It was us basically saying: Fuck you. You think you are going to control the terms here. We are here. We are waiting for you. When we walked back to the dressing room, we walked very tightly together. There must have been about fifty of us. There is power in numbers.

When the ball was thrown in, we took control of the game. Patrick scored his first senior goal. After Michael's dismissal on fifteen minutes, we were in a state of shock, but the boys just stuck to the plan. Shortly after the final whistle, a knock came on the dressing room door. They were looking for me to do a television interview with RTÉ. My immediate thought was to refuse. But I was still seething about what had been said about Ryan on *The Sunday Game*. I wanted to set the record straight. 'There was a lot made of the Antrim game and we would be very disappointed with a lot of the comments after the Antrim game. I think Donegal at the minute with the media is a thing that you can poke fun at. You can eulogise about Kerry and maybe talk about Dublin, the perennial, I suppose, chokers and then Donegal – poke fun at them. And ... that's not us. We have a job to do and we are going to continue to do that job.'

I was angry about it all over again when I was finished. A part of me always will be. There had been one incident on the field that really got under my skin also. Colm Anthony had become entangled with a Cavan player, who had taken him by the collar and spat at him. That was really bothering me because we allowed it to happen. None of his teammates had stepped in. Did they not see it? Did we allow one of their players to disrespect us? Did we allow that to happen? Are we too nice? Would they have spat on a Tyrone player? And if they had, would the other Tyrone guys have stood back? I knew the answer to that. Was it okay to spit on us because we were Donegal?

All these questions are just firing through my mind as the bus moves through the small towns of Fermanagh, the shop fronts darkened and the pubs lit up. Tyrone are waiting for us, as always. We couldn't play without Michael. We needed to see the video of what had happened. Tyrone. Mickey Harte.

Tyrone. *What happened on Saturday night, Peter?* That's not us. *Donegal are not on our radar any more.*

It is close to midnight and none of us are talking very much.

———

Rory and myself had just taken our seats in Clones when we saw Mickey Harte and Tony Donnelly walking along the aisle towards us. We were there for the same reason: to watch Armagh and Derry playing in the Ulster semi-final. In seven days' time, our teams would be out on that field. We became instinctively alert as they approached us because it might have been an awkward situation. But Tony just grinned and made a show of checking the seat numbers and said, 'I think youse are sitting in our seats, boys.' It broke the ice and Mickey was laughing hard, which I had never seen him do before. Really, what Tony was saying was: You are the young up-and-comers and we know you want our seat.

The four of us laughed but nothing else was said. It was a nice moment. They moved on and took their seats. Their wives were there with them and the four of them shared a flask of tea and sandwiches at half time. It was a real traditional Irish day out and it was the first time that I had seen Mickey Harte in a different light from the forensic figure on the sideline. We all became GAA supporters for the afternoon because the performance of Eoin Bradley, the Derry forward, was just so compelling that it overshadowed the general themes of the game. He seemed to be able to do anything he pleased. He finished with 1-5 and gave one of the best individual displays I had ever seen in an Ulster championship match. People often misuse the word 'phenomenal', but it accurately described Bradley that day.

I was still smarting over the travel arrangements for the Cavan match. So I phoned a patron of Donegal football who lives in London and simply asked him if he could pay for a hotel for the squad. He said 'Fine'. We were booked into the Slieve Russell and on the Saturday evening we had the last of our meetings about Tyrone there.

Our players needed to know everything about Tyrone in order to demystify the players and to make them manageable in their minds. We broke down their patterns of play and showed the boys how they did what they did: carrying the ball through the McMahon brothers and Philip Jordan and Sean Cavanagh; short kick-outs; an average of thirty-one attacks per match. We studied how they faced the play, how they set up for kick-outs, how their running game worked and where they tended to score from. Ninety per cent of their shots were taken in and around twenty-five metres from goal. They were brilliant at sweeping and turning any unintelligent ball played in by opposing teams, running back at serious pace. They put a big effort into trying to turn the ball over during the first phase or wave of defensive pressure. At training we had worked hard on avoiding the first tackle and keeping the ball away from contact. I had noticed that if Tyrone didn't succeed in turning the ball over during that initial gust of energy, their level of intensity dropped. That was where we needed to be sharp and to protect the ball. In theory, if we beat the initial line of Tyrone cover, we should have more time on the ball. It was critical that we stopped them taking quick kick-outs and sideline balls and frees, and that we prevented them from building their attacks. Our plan was to stop them at source and prevent overlapping runners coming at pace. We had to pressure their precise pass to the inside forwards, hold our defensive shape and force them to shoot from where they didn't want to. We had to stick to the task and ignore the taunts. We agreed that our stock reply would be 'Not today'. Anything that Ryan McMenamin, for instance, might say, our boys would reply, 'Not today, Ryan', 'We are beating ye today.' If we stayed with them for fifty minutes, the match would become fractious. We had to be prepared for that. And I had noticed that they appeared to tire in recent games after fifty minutes. But just to get to that stage, we had to absorb whatever came at us during the first twenty minutes. We had to prepare for a torrent.

Sunday 26 June rises like so many Clones Sundays: breathless and overcast. In the dressing room we are waiting, in our gear, the boys fiddling with their boots, pacing the floor, waiting to get out there. A knock comes at the door. The hurling match between Donegal and Tyrone has gone to extra time, so the football game would be put back. 'For fifteen minutes or so.' Just like that. The room seemed to shrink. We are stuck there. Why couldn't they just schedule the first game without interrupting the senior game? Both teams had been preparing all year for this game. Now we are stuck in a cramped dressing room that suddenly seems stifling. We can hear the supporters outside the window. We can hear the thrum of voices overhead. There isn't enough room for all the players and staff to sit; some of us have to stand. We ask a steward to come in and open the windows, which are narrow and high and secured with metal holdings. We watch the official come in and struggle with the windows. It is like being back in national school when the teacher uses those long steel contraptions to twist the windows open. It is claustrophobic at this point and there isn't any worthwhile breeze, but it is a relief just to see the bit of clear sky through the windows. I run through the game plan again and my voice carries. The windows open onto the main thoroughfare behind the Gerry Arthur Stand where people gather at the kiosk for chocolates and drinks and a chat. Some Tyrone fans hear my voice and start shouting in at us. Then a plastic bottle comes flying through the window and bounces across the floor. We all look at it. The windows are closed again and it is baking inside and everyone just wants to be on the field.

When we are eventually called, our warm-up time is halved, so it feels as though we went straight from wondering when we would get to leave that infernal dressing room to the ball being thrown in.

And we are not there. It was as if we are spellbound by those white jerseys and the names and the pure authority with which Tyrone carry their game to us. We look lethargic and unconvincing in our tackling. Nobody is doing what we had vowed we would do. Time and time again I send Rory running on during breaks in play asking the boys what was going on. 'Why aren't you going for that ball?' 'Why aren't you holding shape?' 'What the fuck is going on?' Rory reports back and we try to figure what is happening. It is the old familiar nightmare. Tyrone had come onto that field with their feathers in bloom. They were like peacocks and they were letting us know: winning this is our God. Given. Right. And it was as if we believed that. We bowed down.

After twenty minutes of play Tyrone are leading by 0-4 to 0-1. Their play is bright and intelligent and full of invention. They pop over another point and shortly after that Sean Cavanagh bolts past me with the ball and something in his expression makes me feel that he has designs on a goal. And I am conscious of this chant sounding from the Hill where the Tyrone supporters have gathered.

Easy! Easy! Easy!

We are being shamed here. We are being mortified. Tyrone are looking to finish us early. If a goal goes in now, we could go down in flames, on some score like 2-20 to 0-9. This could make Crossmaglen look like a decent performance. These thoughts shoot through your mind in a nanosecond and carry with them a feeling of dread. What are the boys thinking? They know now that nobody is going to give us anything. They know that they aren't going to simply get an Ulster medal because they are in some way due one. It is not as if Tyrone are going to say: Look, boys, we see you've put in a big effort this year and have been killing yourselves at training. Listen, we have five Ulster titles and everyone deserves a turn, in fairness. This one is yours! That's fantasy stuff. They know this. They know they are going to have to claw and pull and prise a victory out of Tyrone. I scan the field looking for any sign that they are willing to do this. No goal comes of Cavanagh's possession but we know we are only just still alive.

Out of nothing, Kevin Cassidy lands a brave, ambitious point from way out on the right wing. It may well be the most important score he ever contributed to Donegal football. We need it so, so badly. Then we get a free and somehow we are back in the dressing room at 0-06 to 0-04 down. The scoreboard looks fine but it disguises a multitude of problems. We are blessed. Now the dressing room feels cool and welcoming, a place of refuge.

We gather around and I am livid about those first twenty minutes, livid at the boys and livid for them. We went through each of our promises. Will to win? It wasn't there. Hunger? Decision-making? Courage to get up the field? Support for the man on the ball? Hanging each other out to dry? Competing at midfield? Smart ball? What the fuck is happening? Can I trust you? I need answers! At the minute we have a loser's attitude. Our body language is shocking. Our work rate is shocking. Acceptance of being dominated? Totally. In awe of the opposition? Without a doubt. Lacking courage? Yes. Under a compliment to Tyrone? Yes. Turning our back on our game plan? Yes.

It is a silent dressing room. The message is cold and severe, but we are facing a simple choice. We repeat the mistakes of the past and become a mirror image of all those previous Donegal teams who just melted, or we realise that our game plan is our ticket back into contention. We have to play and think our way through this, ball by ball, play by play.

You can't accurately measure psychological pressure, but the burden on those boys going out for the second half is incredibly heavy. It is down to them. There is a raw feel about the day. It is like seeing someone go under a wave and there is that split second when you wonder if they are going to surface. They find their rhythm and begin to back one another. And they find their composure. Michael and Karl break through the middle and Colm finishes a goal from close range, feinting left and finishing with his right. It is 1-06 to 0-9 when we make the move which finishes the game, snuffing out a Tyrone attack and then breaking hard out of defence. Paddy comes deep to collect the ball and he directs a long high hand pass towards Michael. Two Tyrone defenders read it perfectly and if any player besides Michael had been in their vicinity it would have been safely clear. But he shoulders the ball loose and then manages to hit Dermot Molloy on the turn. Brick is straight through on goal and he strikes low. He goes for broke and wheels away in delight. I feel relief more than elation.

Even after the whistle goes I can't escape the feeling that Tyrone had let us off the hook during that first twenty minutes. Tyrone finish the match with fourteen men. Kevin Hughes had already been booked when he clattered into Michael Hegarty and straight away, our boys are all over him, pointing and making it easier for the referee to come to his conclusion. It was an old

Tyrone tactic and we gave them a jab of their own medicine. So there are all these little mind games in the mix. Their players seemed to be in a little bit of shock by the end. It must have been an odd sensation for them, to shake hands with us as losers.

I don't come across Mickey Harte until I'm leaving the dressing room. He happens to be coming down the corridor. We shake hands, but the exchange is brief. He doesn't lose very often. He says very little and looks at me as if I had severely disappointed him. All that night, I just kept thinking, 'We're in an Ulster final.'

Against Derry.

Just like 1998.

———

On some evenings going down the road, the bus would be priceless fun. Some nights, the boys would sing; other times they were just into devilment. Every so often, this question would come from down the back of the bus, a theme we never tired of discussing: 'Who's the fucking hardest McGee?' It was just a way of getting the two boys going. You'd hear Eamon shouting from somewhere: 'You think I can't beat you, Neil?' Then the brother would appear at the top of the bus looking for the microphone.

— Gimme that mic quick. Seen bigger men on fucking wedding cakes.

— C'mon, so, and try it.

They would just be taking a hand at each other. The pair of them are as tight as anything. Still, there would be an occasional night when Neil would land at training alone. 'That boy ... I couldn't have him in the car. Doing me head in.' Two nights later, they would be right as rain. They are very different people. Eamon is a bit of a free spirit. We sometimes used music at training and the boys took turns hooking up their iPods to the loudspeakers. Eamon's selection was always out there: garbage pop followed by real dark stuff. One night we stood in the huddle drenched in sweat and listening to the end of an Eamon McGee shuffle play. 'Boys, we've joined a lot of dots about Eamon here tonight,' I said. The boys were cracking up but Eamon just stood there with absolutely no expression on his face.

It was something else to come across the McGees on a football field. I had the pleasure a few times while playing for Glenties. Eamon was the conversationalist. 'You haven't touched a fucking ball, McGuinness. There's a boy warming up now. Look it. You're as well off.' This would be in your ear constantly. And then every so often Neil would drift into your vicinity and say very little, which was worse. He would just breathe down your neck. When Neil started playing he wasn't the most subtle footballer, but he was so dedicated to the game. He wanted success more fiercely than anyone realised. Both the McGee brothers did. Few people saw that. Sometimes I would get a lift to matches with Neil and in the boot of his car you always saw loads of training gear and weights. He worked very hard on his conditioning.

The boxer Amir Khan was in Manchester Piccadilly station one afternoon when I was waiting for a train. I had followed his progress at the Athens Olympics and saw this Great Britain bag. He had this entourage of people with him. I wandered over to say hello and just to tell him that I admired what he had done. He was so polite and humble and we ended up chatting on the platform for about ten minutes. In fact, he ended up quizzing me about sports psychology. Then his train was called on the loudspeaker and he had to leave in a hurry, but as we shook hands I placed my other hand on his shoulder. It felt like sheet iron. I actually said 'Jesus Christ!' when I took hold of him. His entourage was in stitches. Down the years I had seen a few boys playing county ball who liked to keep themselves in good shape, but Khan was like a different physical specimen. Neil McGee is the only other person I have ever encountered who is built like that. It is as if they are made of something other than flesh. It is partly just genetics, but he also spent more hours than anyone knows in the gym and lifts weights very cleverly.

Neil has this very droll way of talking, but he is one switched-on boy. And I have rarely come across a competitor like him. I can see him during those training games, tongue out and eyes bulging and absolutely wild to win the ball. He really loathed giving anything to Michael Murphy or Patrick McBrearty. Any joy they got at training he took personally. Neil plays on the edge but through his training he has developed a very disciplined mindset. There is a wild animal in there, so he is always just on the right side of the edge. That is what makes him such a brilliant defender. I have no doubt his presence has scared a lot of guys on the field. He is an intimidating figure. And then he has immense pace for a full back. To see him at full tilt is a sight. He works so hard at carrying the ball at pace. Once he sets on a line, he is very hard to stop. So often in league games I would watch him, thinking: Who is going to get the better of this guy? Why shouldn't he be an All-Star? We started to ask him that question. We started to plant that seed. When I looked Neil in the eye and told him what I needed, that was it. And at the very first meeting in Downings, Neil spoke and he spoke well. He talked about cutting corners. The other boys would often say that there is a madness to Gweedore. There is an edge about the place. So when you come out of there to play ball, you are a man. And there was an element of madness to our training all year. Training was extreme. The games were very aggressive. Nobody was waiting on the whistle. We were asking more of them than they had ever been asked in their lives. That was oxygen to Neil. He thrived in that environment. He is a guy who thinks about football a lot and studies other teams and players. People underestimate him in that regard. He is a winner.

And then off the field, he is a very quiet, laid-back type of fella. A few of the boys like to smoke a fag after a big match. Colm, Rory Kavanagh, Martin McElhinney and Ryan would usually have a smoke or two at the side of the bus or on the side of the road on the way home. They aren't smokers: it's just a method of blowing off steam. Neil liked a smoke. You would see him in the dressing room and he sits in a way that is kind of dainty for such a big man, the legs folded and his arms perched on them. He would be mild mannered and very humorous but you would rarely hear him actually laughing. He has this low kind of grumble when he hears something funny. It's like a growl. It's as if he's saying: Aye, you've tickled me there ... but it's not worth a full laugh.

The thing about the two McGees is that they are two big teddy bears behind the façade. They're just two big soft boys and they care a lot about things. They care about their family. They care about playing for Donegal. And they are good lads. When we had public sessions and families would come along, they were always fantastic with the children. I noticed that Eamon had this really soft, natural way of dealing with children and I told him he would be a perfect primary school teacher.

You couldn't say a bad word about the McGee brothers. And they are the kind of guys you just want on your team.

———

In all the towns and villages across the county, the bunting is hung and the flags are out. It is festive and celebratory, even though we are all highly conscious that we have won nothing yet. Still, it is nice. It gives you a warm feeling. You go through Ardara or Donegal Town or Dunfanaghy and you realise that the boys have created this sense of the whole county in this thing together: the sense of being from here. It's like a wee present for people.

Nobody would have thought of an Ulster final as possible last summer. When the players arrived at training now, they carried themselves differently. They knew that they had been true to the commitment they made that day in Downings. They had the work done and had been honest and had nothing to hide from. It was really powerful to see them.

The Donegal county board had organised a round of club championships the weekend after we beat Tyrone. That reduced our preparation to the Thursday night, Saturday, Sunday and Wednesday before the final.

When you spend so much time in a county squad, you see the players becoming this fiercely tight unit. They have one another's back, always. But once they return to their club, they are immediately – and rightly – wedded to local concerns and, if anything, the friendship they develop at county level brings out a sharper competitive edge when they meet in club games. I had gone along to watch Glenties play Glenswilly. A huge brawl broke out at the end of the match. It was impossible to tell who was involved. I was at home when I got a phone call to say that Leo McLoone's cheekbone had been fractured by a punch. He would miss the final. At this time, winning an Ulster title would have marked the fulfilment of the wilder ambitions any of the boys entertained. They had all been primary school children when Donegal last won a title – except for Paddy, who hadn't been born. Now they had a chance to make a little bit of history that mattered in our part of the world and Leo McLoone would miss out. I felt sickened for him and so disappointed. When I called to visit him, he was inconsolable.

Derry had suffered equally bad luck. Neil McGee sent a text to say that Eoin Bradley had torn his cruciate ligament at training. Even as I heard about it I pictured him as he was that day against Armagh, merciless and untouchable. It is a funny sensation when you hear that the opposition have lost a key player. Part of you sympathises. Then you try and work out how their squad will perceive the news and how our team will react when they hear about it. After that you try to imagine how the game itself will be affected by his absence. I figured fairly quickly that it was a big blow for them and a lift for us, but I knew it wasn't going to deflate Derry because John Brennan wouldn't allow it to.

In an interview with the *Irish News*, John referred to our tactics. He was very defiant. He said we'd see who came out on top in twelve days' time. My belief is that managers should not address other managers through the media. But John was speaking to our players as well. He made it clear that Derry were coming to take us down. That gave us a chance to visualise and articulate their intent. How would it feel to be there watching Derry players jumping up and down after defeating us? After leaving us bereft? The boys faced a stark choice now and we held it before them at training.

— They get the cup or you get the cup.

— They get the medal or you get the medal.

A big crowd gathered at the Abbey Hotel to see us off on Saturday afternoon. The afternoon was fresh and summery and it was a nice feeling to be getting on the bus, but it was balanced with the collective obligation we felt to see this through now and be back in this same place with the Anglo Celt Cup on Sunday night. At the team meeting that evening we spoke about seeing it through. There was a lot of tension and anticipation in the room. That night, I didn't think about all of the Ulster final losses I had been involved in. I was thinking only about tomorrow. I'm not sure how well anyone slept on Saturday night. But we felt ready. It was just a matter of the hours passing.

Driving into Clones on the bus is always one of the special moments for any team in an Ulster final. The streets in the town are narrow and deep and they are always thronged. The scene never changes and that is what makes it wonderful. The hours before throw-in are just a party for both counties. Supporters wave when they see the bus, and you get the odd shout, and cars sound their horns. It has the feeling of organised chaos. It is a nice prelude to what comes next. But then the bus is through the crowd and you go up that hill past St Tiernach's church and from the windows of the bus you can actually see over the wall of the park. Clones: that field. We have been here before on these days. The one thing we have spoken about is that Ulster final days only turn out good if you win them. Some of the boys know this. The younger boys don't. I know this. 1993. 1998. 2002. 2004. 2006. 2007. Donegal people know this. When you lose those finals, all the promise just leaves the day and you are thrust into a void. You feel somehow deceived. You are just managing the hours when you lose. What started out as one of the best days of your life reveals itself as one of the worst.

A crowd gathers as soon as our bus pulls up outside the gates. People are on a high. It is an emotional day. Supporters can lose themselves a wee bit. The boys are always courteous and always have time for a word. But today they keep their eyes fixed on the ground and they walk quickly through the blue gates and keep moving until they are all in the dressing room. The pace of the day quickens. When we are alone, I hold up these photographs of other Ulster final days, other Ulster final captains. Kieran McKeever of Derry is there. Kieran McGeeney of Armagh is there. I hold up a photograph of Henry Downey and my eyes fall on Ryan Bradley.

— Who's that, Ryan?

— Who the fuck's that?

And Ryan's eyes are blank and I start to do the maths: Downey was captain in 1993. Ryan would have been ... eight years old. That's how long ago it was. 'That's Henry Downey,' I tell him.

I told them what I felt. I was sick of watching other captains walking up those yellow steps and smiling out at the crowd and lifting trophies at our expense. I was sick to the heart of Donegal players with hands on their hips watching them. I was sick of other teams leaving this town with that cup on the dashboard of the bus to go back to their counties with everything while Donegal went back to emptiness. Because that is what you are left with when you don't win these days. You are left with hollowness that you can never quite fill.

It was time. It was time we did that. It was 17 July 2011. Clones was sold out.

———

In the last minute, time begins to do strange things. We are on the sideline, studying the referee. We are close but we all know this feeling, of being tantalisingly near, and then other Ulster final days are flashing through your mind. This time, nothing bad is going to happen. You have heard the sound of a final whistle what seems like a million times in your life but you can't fully believe that you are going to hear this one, today, now, soon.

Any second now.

Seconds earlier, Colm had hit a point, curling off Michael on the loop in front of the McGrane Stand and instantly shooting with his left, striking the ball so high in the sky that it seemed to hang there in the blue for an eternity. Everyone knew the score was good, so you could just admire the quality of the strike. It left us 1-11 to 0-08 ahead and it was only then that you allowed yourself to believe. And then you hear that whistle and it is as if you are being thrashed about in a wave. You are hugging Rory and Pat and Maxi and it seems as if there are dozens and then hundreds of people around and you just go with it. Everyone is jubilant and completely carefree. It is the strangest thing. It is like being at a massive wedding or something where you haven't seen people for ages and everyone is in the form of their lives. You bump into Big Neil Gallagher and you both hug, but he seems to be whirling one way and you going the other. You come across Ryan and then you're funnelled in another direction and just catch sight of Colm, but he's laughing and talking with someone and suddenly you aren't sure where on the field you are.

The match has been finished for no more than a minute, but already we are all moving quickly away; we are escaping from those nineteen years. And that is what you can feel moving through all those Donegal people on the pitch; their joy and their relief. You end up celebrating with anyone at all, with whoever crosses your path, and you get to be a Donegal supporter. And then you turn around and there is your brother Frank and neither of you can believe it. You both take a second to make

sure you are not seeing things. And then you are laughing and
hugging. Frank says: 'I'm so proud of you.' Daffy O'Donnell is
there too, one of your oldest friends from Glenties. It is perfect.

You are away across the field now and you want to get over
to the stand to see Michael lift the cup, so you are fighting your
way through and people do a double-take when they recognise
you and their reaction is comical. But there is such emotion all
about you. Tears. Men and women from all over the county,
whose faces you have known for years. Faces of people who
have shown up on all the bad days and on the grim league
days. Donegal lifers, league and championship. And they are
in tears. Still, it is the faces of the players you really want to see.
And it is worth it. Not too many words are said. There is no
need. The boys are in a state of disbelief. They are dazed with
happiness. A tug comes on your sleeve because you are needed
for television, for radio, for the newspapers. You stall them until
you hear Michael's speech and then you answer the questions.
You try and make sense of how you are feeling. And to your
delight, Yvonne is waiting in the tunnel with Toni-Marie, Mark
Anthony and Jimmy. You only get a few moments together but
it is then that it begins to seem real.

It is about forty minutes later when you make it back to the
dressing room with Michael. The two of you walk in holding
the Anglo Celt and a huge roar goes up. The boys are showered
and polished and they are soaring. It is heading for six o'clock
by the time you all walk across the pitch to the old dressing
rooms, where Jimmy McGlynn has food waiting. The stadium
is empty and there it is ... the quietness and those empty stands
and all the sweet wrappers and bottles on the terrace. That
moment with Mark in Croke Park comes back to you.

You are starving but you can't eat. You try to eat chicken curry
but there is too much adrenalin flowing. You try some sherry

trifle and that works. One of the boys says, 'Jesus Christ, can we not get a different dessert?' 'Almost everything is negotiable, boys,' you tell them.

We gather for a team photograph on the pitch. The place is ours now. No Armagh. No Tyrone. No Derry. Not today. It forces us to be still for a moment and it is a private, important moment because these hours can so easily slip by. Outside the ground, there are still a few stragglers knocking around the car park and they can't believe it when the gates open and the entire squad come strolling out. Our bus moves down the hill where the last of the supporters are still outside the Creighton, squeezing every last bit from the day. Clones feels serene. It feels magical to be leaving that town happy, to be leaving Clones as Ulster champions.

At Derrygonnelly we stop at the off-licence and buy a few slabs of beer. This is a new sensation: drinking to celebrate achievement and not to forget, not to feel less crushed. The bus is just noise, voices over voices and all happy. Every so often, you shout: 'Boys! Boys!' and when they stop to listen, you shout: 'We have her! We have her!' Then it kicks off again.

None of them pay much heed when the bus stops on the side of the road. The road is quiet. The engine rumbles in neutral. You get out at the wee headstone that marks the spot where Mark was killed in a road crash in the summer of 1998, just a few weeks after we lost another Ulster final, also against Derry. Pat Shovelin is beside you and JD McGrenra is there. This moment has been in your mind for a long, long time. We put the cup down and say our prayers and you tie the ribbons from it around the headstone. So many thoughts then, and back on the bus you are in your own private world and it takes you a few minutes to realise that the boys have gone very quiet. Rory has explained to them what is going on.

The boys are talking in quieter tones. The last thing you want to do is dampen it for them. You want them to know that it is okay. So you turn and shout, 'Any man for a song?' and the party kicks off again. And you sit there for half an hour and you aren't really thinking about the Ulster final that Donegal have just won but about that one in 1998 and about Mark and about those days. And you are wishing the Giant could be here now to enjoy this. No better man to enjoy this. 'We've done it, Mark,' you tell him.

You tell him that a few times.

We've done it.

We've done it.

And the bus moves towards Donegal. It is not quite dark and every so often you pass the big drinking buses, stopped on the side of the road with a line of boys facing into the bushes, smokes pulsing in the twilight. Buses from Fanad, Gweedore, Bundoran, all moving in this chaotic cavalcade towards the Diamond.

Pettigo is the first stop and it is bedlam. Somehow they have found time to construct a stage. When the emcee introduces the team, there is such raw emotion in his voice that we get the shivers. The street is packed. Some of the boys nip into the pubs for a proper pint. There is this wonderful feeling of goodwill about the night. We want to stay. We want to get to Donegal Town. That journey from Pettigo towards the Diamond is like being a child at Christmas. We are excited and a bit nervous. Some of the boys are on to you to sing a song, so you take the microphone when we're about five minutes outside the town and sing 'Destination Donegal'. The Diamond is full of people, full in a way that it hasn't been for decades.

Once we leave the bus, it is going to be madness. Karl Lacey has arranged for a room to be set aside for players and family. It is agreed that, no matter what, everyone meets there at one in the morning. The door of the bus opens and July air rushes in along with this huge cheer. You step out.

———

The DJ stopped playing at four. He started up again at five. I remember sitting on the step of the dance floor beside Yvonne chatting with Neil McGee. It was about six o'clock in the morning and it would be bright soon, but nobody seemed to care. Neil turned to Yvonne. 'You're a fine-looking doll.'

I said, 'You watch your mouth, McGee.' We were all laughing. I thought it was good because it meant there was no barrier, no player–manager divide. It was just Neil throwing a wee grenade into the conversation, which he likes to do. It was his way of saying to me: Even you are not out of bounds. It must have been a quarter to eight by the time people started to call it a night.

When we got up a few hours later, the Monday party was in full swing. A fair few boys had made it to the front of the hotel and were draped around the bar. Most of the squad were down in the Reveller. The Monday newspapers were scattered across the tables. The juke box was on full volume. The Ulster final was being replayed on silent. Half of our bucks were out dancing. It felt like walking into a bar at midnight on a Saturday night. Eventually we got a bus to Letterkenny and went into the Clanree. Yvonne came along and collected myself and Colm in the early evening. A fair few boys headed home, but it turned out that a good number took a detour by way of the Burtonport Festival and finished the night there. They deserved it. Myself and Colm were drowsy with tiredness and happiness and alcohol on the way home. My mind kept turning to that final point he kicked, the ball just billowing in the sky and falling in a way that was almost leisurely. It was when I was watching that ball that I knew we were going to be Ulster champions. That was an unbelievable moment in my life. A lot of things got sorted out for me during those few seconds watching that football falling from the sky, like the thousands of footballs I had watched falling from the sky in Glenties. A lot of pain that I had held for many years evaporated.

'I'll never forget that point,' I told him.

Colm just grinned. He didn't say a word.

———

Two days after the match, Billy Boyle arrived at the door with a present. He handed me a three-foot cut of red Wavin pipe.

———

On Thursday evening the boys reported for training in Ballybofey and we put them through the most severe session they had ever experienced in their lives. I demanded more than we ever had before, left shorter recovery intervals and kept urging them to test themselves; to push themselves beyond what they thought was their limit. It was really important. Almost all the boys felt that winning an Ulster medal was the very most they could achieve as footballers. Their season was complete. So that session was a way of communicating that nothing was over yet. It is human nature, after you achieve something, to coast for a little while. That is probably what they expected when they arrived. They were in high form. They were jaunty and good-humoured. By the time they left, they were thinking about nothing except a shower and sleep. At the end, we ran ten 200-metre sprints flat out with absolutely no slacking off. Nobody was talking at this stage: it was just breathing and the sound of galloping.

A lot can change in a small space of time. We had created a new space for ourselves. In their minds, many of them felt that they had reached the end point of their sporting lives. So we had to move them on from that mindset. By the end of that session, the Ulster championship was dead in their minds. All they were thinking about was getting through the next run. A lot of men were pushed to the very brink that evening, getting sick and reaching the point of distress. They pushed one another on. It turned out that Michael pulled his hamstring at some point. He said nothing until Saturday morning. 'Just a bit tight,' he said, insisting he was perfect. But by the time we headed to stay in Ashbourne on Friday night, we weren't certain if he would be able to play. On the way up, a journalist phoned to say that a Kildare selector had contacted his newspaper to make comments about Donegal's cynical fouling. The Kildare view was that if the game was properly refereed, they would have a chance. Our discipline had been exemplary throughout the championship: not conceding frees was crucial to our game plan. I felt it was another attempt to try and portray Donegal in a certain light and promised myself to address it after the match.

On Saturday, Michael failed a fitness test and by the time our bus reached Croke Park, Frank phoned me to say that the rumour was all over Dublin. Clearly, somebody on our bus had texted someone else and the next thing the news was everywhere – including the Kildare dressing room. It just drove me mad. We went through the pretence that Michael would play, right up to the throw-in. He walked around in the pre-match parade and then David Walsh slipped into the team. But Kildare knew fine well he wouldn't start.

It was strange: an All-Ireland quarter-final on a Saturday evening at five o'clock. The central truth about Kildare was the same as it was when we played them in Letterkenny. They were a Kieran McGeeney team. They would not quit. We couldn't let them build from deep. We had to stop their overlapping runners coming from deep. We had to meet them at the halfway line and squeeze the middle third of the pitch. We had to tackle with everything we had. We had to use our bodies. We had to pressure their long kicks. We had to be willing to dive at their boots because they would be free to shoot at will and from speculative distances. They were programmed to do that. We had to defend like animals.

Rare stuff can flash through your mind in the minutes before games. I was really dismayed that Kildare had gone to the newspapers the day before the match. I felt it was bad form and didn't think it was typical of Kieran. We had come across each other on the pitch on many occasions and maybe on the odd night out in Belfast. But the funny thing about the county scene is that you can know a guy by reputation for over a decade without ever having had many conversations with him.

As the teams warmed up on the field, Kieran was standing on the sideline and fragments of a long-forgotten league game between our counties came to mind. It took place in Davitt Park, Lurgan, on 16 November 1997. I remember the date because it was my birthday. Donegal won on the very peculiar scoreline of 3-01 to 0-12. The day was as bleak as anyone had ever played football in, the sky dark and the pitch oil-black with mud. John Hanratty broke his leg in an accident that ended his county career. There was a sense of uneasiness about the afternoon when John was carried off. The atmosphere created a cloud all of its own and the players responded to it. Everyone was tense and the hits became wilder. Winning that match was more important to us and Armagh were vexed because they had seen one of their guys badly hurt. It became very toxic. JJ Doherty ended up rowing with a fella and I got caught up in the tail end of it and as I turned to leave, one of the Armagh boys absolutely flattened me with a punch. A full-on twenty-six-man skirmish broke out and it ended up taking place in the goal mouth. I was marking McGeeney at midfield that day. For some reason, the two teams had to share a shower room that evening. It wasn't a good idea. Damien Diver ambled into a room full of unhappy Armagh men in the midst of performing their ablutions. Damien is one of those guys who is instantly happy-go-lucky after a final whistle and he was cheerful as anything when he spotted Kieran. Words were exchanged and voices were raised and the next thing you had twenty naked men squaring up to each other and trying to act with a bit of bravado. It was all, as one of our boys remarked after order had been restored, 'a bit fucking weird'. But it was part and parcel of the county scene at that time. I had nothing but a long drive to Tralee to look forward to that night. Outside, Mark, Frank, Noreen and Mum were waiting for me in the car park. There was hardly a sinner left at this stage. I threw my bag in the boot and they started singing 'Happy Birthday'. I made a fuss about being embarrassed. But secretly, I was delighted.

That memory came and left in a few seconds and then I was back in Croke Park, lost in the moment. We started nervously, gifting Kildare two early scores through sloppy fouling. Kildare looked sleek and strong and it was clear from early on that both teams were ready to expose themselves to whatever the nature of the game demanded. It wasn't a brilliant first half but, as a contest, it was deepening all the time. We were whistled for our third foul in the twelfth minute, which was a damaging sign for us. We sent Michael into the match earlier than planned, but Kildare were on the front foot for the first half. Mark McHugh chased down a ball and conjured up a hugely significant point just before half time.

I think that was the night Donegal people fully fell for this team. This was the night that they understood: No matter what, this is a team we can be proud of. The match just kept twisting in directions that surprised us all. Kildare had a goal disallowed and then Michael landed one of those huge booming points of his that actually take your breath away. There was nothing fancy about the game. But both sides were just slugging away and nobody was flinching. Eamon McGee had been on the bench all summer but he was terrific here after being called in at short notice. Tony Thompson kept winning these gruelling battles for possession and it became evident that Karl was in a zone all of his own, playing aggressive and smart and moving all around the field as if in a kind of trance where he could do no wrong. It was hard to keep my eyes off him because we knew that we were watching him play his best ever game for Donegal. He was sublime.

Both teams were just probing for a way to win, stress testing for weaknesses. It was seven points each when I called Christy Toye down. We had decided to take Colm off, which was a gamble because it would leave us without a left-footed free-taker. Plus, Christy hadn't played for Donegal for two years because of a cursed run of injuries and health problems. We sent him on in midfield and because we already had two midfielders there, we hoped he wouldn't be picked up for a few minutes. He was standing beside me and all I said to him was, 'Christy, go on, get ahead of the ball and stick it in the back of the fucking net.' You say these things in hope rather than expectation. Christy just nodded in that way of his. And within twenty seconds, he had done just that. Only Christy Toye would have the coolness to step into a quarter-final after two years away and instantly score a goal. I had played with him for years and even though it was unbelievable to see it happening, it wasn't entirely surprising. And the move contained reflections of a goal he had scored seven years earlier against Armagh in the All-Ireland semi-final. Everything about the moment was pure Christy. He has this strange imperturbable streak in him. He doesn't over-think things: he is just a very cool customer and plays life as he sees it. You give him the nod and he just trots in and before people know it he produces this electrifying goal. It was surreal to see.

Kildare didn't blink. As the tenor of the game rose, so they responded. Darryl Flynn was playing out of his skin and John Doyle punished two more poor fouls and then James Kavanagh took a ball out near the Cusack Stand and he leaned back and sent this shot fizzing over our crossbar. He punched the air. By the time Kildare scored the point that brought it into extra time, the noise from their crowd would stop you in your tracks. It was guttural, just filled with absolute passion.

While all this was happening, the natural light faded from the sky and the floodlights came on. I'm not sure why, but that transition made the occasion very special for everyone present. We were all aware that something transcendent was happening out on that field and the changing light cast it as a once-in-a-lifetime kind of evening. In extra time, Alan Smith scored a point that made it six in a row for Kildare. We were playing fine but just not finding a way to score. Then Karl replied for us and both teams were locked into it again, just playing with complete lack of inhibition and complete honesty and drawing in everybody there with their collective effort. Most times,

Croke Park can seem empty with forty thousand people in it. But that night, it seemed full.

During the second period of extra time, the evening became about pure will. At some point, for Kieran McGeeney and myself, the coaching was finished and all the work had been done and it was purely over to the players and we were all just watching. That is the magical part. That is when you feel the exhilaration of being part of something that you might never get to see again for the rest of your life.

So I watch along with everyone else. Kevin Cassidy steps up and fires an ambitious shot, even though Christy was open inside him. I bite my lip in annoyance. Time is almost up. Kildare are a point ahead, 0-14 to 1-10, and they are in possession of the ball, carrying it into our half, but their attack breaks down. Everyone wants on the ball. Nobody is frightened of making a mistake. We attack again and when the ball spills loose and away from three white shirts, Christy reacts first and collects it and just strokes it over on his left foot. There is a huge roar. On normal evenings both teams would mentally settle for a draw. But nothing feels ordinary about this night. David Coldrick, the referee, has called for two minutes of added time and he has every intention of playing them. Kildare attack again and launch a long ball towards our square. Neil McGee gets a hand to the ball and it glances off his fist at an oblique angle and is safely gathered up by Neil Gallagher. Kevin Cassidy takes possession of the ball and he carries it forward with intent. Christy angles a long, diagonal ball for Michael to chase down and he eclipses two Kildare men and manages, at full speed and inches from the sideline, to get the ball into his hand and turn out of trouble. Somehow he has the strength and agility to keep the ball in play and everyone is truly riveted now. Kildare have regrouped and all avenues are closed and the boys are keeping possession, keeping composure under immense pressure, but it is high risk. Christy is almost stripped but manages to get his foot to the ball and chips it back to Rory Kavanagh, who turns to find Cass, who has stepped back just beyond the 45. Everyone in the stadium is trying to figure who he will pass to, but even before he gets possession Cass has been eyeing up the posts, getting his bearings. He's standing not far from Rory and myself and we know what is on his mind. You would see him do that at training from time to time, hanging back in space and letting fly. But this was the last minute of a drawn match in extra time of an All-Ireland quarter-final. And he had just fired a wide two minutes earlier. None of that fazed him. He is stepping into the shot even as he receives the pass. Everyone can tell that the strike is sweet, but Cass knows immediately that the ball is going over the bar. He turns his back on it before the ball has finished its journey. We hear the delirium behind us among the Donegal section in the crowd. It is a Saturday night in summer in Dublin and it all feels dreamlike. Then the whistle goes.

Maybe that's the moment I would return to in my sporting life, given the choice. There was nothing like the pure euphoria after that final whistle. It wasn't because we had won a quarter-final. It was because the boys had come through a really magnificent test of character. They had answered the questions that had hung over them all of their adult lives: all the dismissive comments about not having the heart or the pride; that they didn't deserve to wear the Donegal jersey. I felt limitlessly proud of them all. Karl Lacey, in the seconds after that match, could hardly walk off the field, his legs wobbly underneath him and his lungs burning for air. Kevin Moran said later that he was in an advanced state of exhaustion. And this noise was raining down on us. We have played in front of bigger crowds but nothing compared to the emotion coming from the Donegal people. They were lost in this, for a few minutes anyway. Nothing existed outside this moment and it belonged to everyone. The boys were overjoyed. I said to Cass, 'You're fucking lucky that one went over,' and he just laughed.

The Kildare sections of the ground were absolutely still. On the field, their players were shattered. They had been unlucky and they deserved something from the match. I felt for them, but I was still smarting about what the Kildare management had said about us in the newspapers and so I spoke about it during the television interviews afterwards.

We stopped for food in the Skylon Hotel. Brian McEniff sat down with us. Our dining room was private but the foyer and bar were swarming with people. It was the same when our bus turned on to Dorset Street at Quinn's corner. Donegal shirts everywhere, ready to take the city. They cheered when they saw it was our bus. It is a funny thing when you are at the epicentre of a team whose county has begun to embrace it. We would hear afterwards about how brilliant that Saturday night was in all the towns and villages across the county. Great stories about impromptu parties and lock-ins, but most of all about how it just put everyone in a good mood and allowed people to put all the wee problems and worries of life to one side. While all that was happening, we were sitting in a bus rushing through Ulster and it was dark outside. We got a carry-out and we drank and sang the whole way down, but we were on our own. The boys were anxious to get to a disco in Letterkenny but it was well after two in the morning when we pulled into the Mount Errigal. The coatroom was already empty. The anthems had already been played. We just about got a drink in the hotel bar. I got a taxi home to Creeslough and the adrenaline was still shooting through me as I chatted with the driver about the match.

They had come so far. You don't often get perfect days, but this had been one. I knew that as I turned the key in the front door. As soon as I got inside I felt exhausted and delighted to see Yvonne and the kids – and to fall asleep thinking that today had been a good day.

———

And it brings me here, to Croke Park again, on the very last Sunday in August, where the world is not happy with us.

What we had wanted to do was force the Dublin players to think their way through us rather than merely play through us. We weren't convinced that they could do that. So how we ran the ball would have a huge bearing on the game. Dublin had looked ominous in their game against Wexford, but small things stood out. There were times when they struggled with Wexford's defensive shape and whenever Wexford dared to run at them with belief, they asked big questions. So we formulated our ideas and decided that at heart Dublin were a cautious and defensive team. The back six would always stay at home. We went to Redcastle for a weekend and everything was hashed out. It was then that we floated the idea of bringing every single player into our half of the field to try to lure them out. We knew it would cause outrage. But we decided that we didn't care what anyone thought. If we could switch from defence to attack with swiftness and precision, we could hurt them.

Dublin made it plain that they were confident. The manner in which they had beaten Tyrone made them feel as if they had put the Ulster hex to bed. The players came out and talked about how demanding their internal A versus B games were and stressed how tough it was to make the first fifteen. The message was clear. We put out a few feelers and discovered that they didn't rate our midfield. They feared Karl Lacey. They were eager for goals because they felt that goals scored in Croke Park can crush the morale of visiting teams.

On the Sunday morning of the game, we gathered in a huddle. I told the squad that I was putting my phone in a bag for the day and hoped everyone else would do the same. I didn't want a repeat of what happened prior to the Kildare game. Not on this of all days. Then we went through our game plan. We decided to cede Dublin the kick-out because of Stephen Cluxton's quality: we didn't want a situation where he outfoxed us with pure quality and got us turned, resulting in the goal Dublin wanted. We felt that they were a team that was programmed to do certain things. And as the game wore on, they stayed loyal to their form, their defenders refusing to go past the 65 and kicking long balls to where their forwards were making timed, aggressive runs. We were perfect in every facet of our game except that once we got the ball, we were cautious in how we attacked. Karl had been taken out of it with a late tackle and couldn't continue in the second half.

We were almost clicking, but not quite. Just after half time, Colm had taken a long ball and as he fell into his striking crouch, we knew it would be a goal. That would leave us 1-04 to 0-02 ahead. But it flashed over the crossbar instead of under. Dublin were still there.

We became mired on six points. The match was very cagey and Dublin showed real mental resilience to just stay with it. They began creeping back into it on the scoreboard and the local crowd found its voice. The terms had changed. Now it was just about surviving this game. Diarmuid Connolly was sent off and our boys fell into a siege, trying to preserve what they had. But six points were never going to win a championship match. In the last ten minutes, it slipped away from us. We stood there and watched it. We believed we could win it until the final whistle. But it was just a step too far for us.

When it was over, I felt nothing except the familiar hollow pain that comes with losing a championship match. We had almost forgotten what that was like. Pat Gilroy, the Dublin manager, came over and we shook hands. I was still trying to figure how we had been beaten and why we didn't take advantage of the situation we were presented with. It had almost been the perfect hijack.

Almost.

––––

Letters fell on the mat in Creeslough all through the winter. Once the season ended, I maintained my practice of not reading newspapers or listening to the sports bulletins. And it is quiet in our part of Donegal in the autumn. It is easy to lose yourself in school runs and walks. I was vaguely aware that there was a degree of unease and even hostility about the way we had presented ourselves against Dublin. Some people felt it had made an abomination of the game and weren't shy about saying it. Family and friends who are close to you try to deflect all that from you, so what I heard was a Chinese whispers version. But I had heard what was said on *The Sunday Game* simply because I actually sat down to watch the recording a few days after the match. Figuring out why we had lost that match would preoccupy me for the rest of the winter. What some former footballers thought about it didn't matter to me. We hadn't committed any sins. We hadn't broken any rules – our disciplinary record was exemplary. We hadn't sent our players out to hurt an opposition player. All we had done was come up with a plan to try and put our county in an All-Ireland final. I had repeatedly said over the summer that if the rules were changed, we would go and coach those rules.

I'm not sure if our boys were concerned about the portrayal of Donegal as being somehow 'bad' for football, because we never spoke about it. The season had catapulted the team into a different realm. Donegal represented something significant now and that was all they cared about. But they were certainly aware of how they were being spoken of nationally. There was a perception emerging of me as an austere and controlling figure and of the team as almost socialist in its beliefs; that we were purely functional and joyless. Nothing could have been further from the truth. I felt certain that the senior players in particular had never enjoyed a football season more. In November, myself and Yvonne headed down to Wicklow as I had been invited to take part in a conference organised by the St Patrick's GAA club. I was on stage with Henry Shefflin and Darran O'Sullivan, with Mícheál Ó Muircheartaigh moderating in an open forum. At one stage, when I was talking about our approach to the season, Mícheál said, 'You know, Jim, there is a way to win an All-Ireland.' It was said gently, but it was a reproach.

I said: 'Well, we are here, Mícheál, in Wicklow and they haven't found a way to win an All-Ireland. We in Donegal haven't found a way to win an Ulster championship in nineteen years and have only won the All-Ireland once ever. Henry and Darran are sitting here and I don't know how many All-Irelands they have between them. And we are trying to close the gap on them.'

And the audience responded to that. It made sense to Wicklow people. Most counties feel oppressed in terms of their GAA triumphs, including Donegal. Everything we had done in the past year was designed to try to change that. The only thing

I cared about that winter was that we hadn't made it to the All-Ireland final. The rest of it, the outside stuff, was just noise.

Next year.

2012.

That was what mattered.

———

In the summer when I was very young I would go to bed around seven and I'd be lying there listening to the older ones playing outside. Occasionally I'd be able to hear and follow Charles's voice as he moved across the green and wish I could be out there with him.

I would have followed him anyway. Because I looked up to him and admired him and loved him so much, I would have wanted to be a footballer if he had lived too. Any time that I think about Charles now, I don't think about him negatively. I just feel very sad. But I also feel so privileged that he was there for me for the first thirteen years of my life. Even at a young age, he taught me so much about how to try and live life. Pure. That is the word I most associate with him. He brought so much love and sincerity and fun into our family. Up until the day we lost him, he could not have lived his life any better. I consider it a gift to have had him as long as we did. As I grew up I could see even more clearly that he was exceptional in the way he engaged with people and in the way he carried himself. His fire was burning very brightly. I suspect the imprint that he has left on his friends runs very deeply with them.

There were nights in those early summers when I'd fall asleep on the couch before I'd even made it up to bed. And I'd wake up and Charles would be carrying me up the stairs. I would look up and see his face. I can still feel his arms under my arms and around my neck and under my knees. I can still feel that. And any night now that I carry our own children up to bed, I remember that feeling.

2012

One game left. One more game in a summer teeming with beautiful games.

This day will be no different to any other.

But this day will be different to all others.

All-Ireland final day.

All-Ireland final day and Donegal are there.

We are there.

Tír Chonaill.

Sam's for the Hills.

20 September 1992.

Donegal will play.

23 September 2012.

The boys will play for their All-Ireland medals tomorrow.

That idea fills our sky.

That thought fills our dreams.

Stay meticulous, Jim. Focus. Stay the same as all summer. Think about the next job, night after night, Sunday after Sunday. No dreaming. No distractions. But how? Tomorrow is All-Ireland final day. This day holds its own power and it pulls on the mind.

Early Saturday morning now and out in the utility room, fussing over the bag, checking everything for the tenth time. Fidgety and excited. What time is it? Jesus, time to get on the road. The boys will be waiting. Footsteps coming. Toni-Marie. Holding something, and a very serious look on her. A wee plastic golf ball in her hand from the toy room.

— What's that, darling?

— That's for you, for luck, Daddy.

Takes the breath from you. Not for the first time either. Too young to fully understand, but sensing the importance of whatever is going on and she wants to help. You. Steady. Steady yourself, boy. Mark Anthony and Jimmy appear and observe this. They want in on the act and tear off to find more lucky charms. Two more plastic golf balls go in the bag.

Out of the door and into the car and the short drive to Glenties to the house. They are all waiting. From the hallway comes the feeling. It never goes. Mum and Dad and Frank and Noreen and you. This is when Charles and Mark are missed the most. This is the thing about loss. The bigger the occasion, the more you miss them. Mark was here in 1992, on All-Ireland weekend, here in this hallway and saying good luck to you on the Saturday morning then too. The tingles and the solemnity of that day. It is so clear. It can't be twenty years ago. Backwards and forwards between both days. It is the same journey, after all. It is the same day.

Up to the graveyard for ten minutes. It is so quiet and nobody is around. Sure the whole town is headed for Dublin. Sit down in the usual place, reach out the right hand onto the grave. Just for that connection. Close eyes. Prayers. Silence. It is good. It is always good. The warm feeling comes, as if they know. And it is fine to leave then.

The boys gathered outside Leo's, same as every game we ever played. It was decided very casually to get a bus over to Donegal Town – Anthony, Leo, Brick, Marty Boyle. The kit man Joseph McCloskey. Paddy McGrath has come over from Ardara. The seventh Glenties man, we call him, because he won't wear that. There is a reason for the bus. No cars to worry about if we win ... if there is a celebration and that. If there is a tour of the county. Nobody says that aloud, of course. Nobody talks at all about what will happen after the game because nobody has the faintest idea.

Into Leo's. He is there, waiting, making himself busy. Hiding the nerves, so he is. The man who started you in football.

Did ye ever march behind the band in Ballybofey boys? Not a one of yez! Come back to me when yez have!

Leo's son will play in an All-Ireland senior football final tomorrow. So much to say in these few moments, so nothing is said. A few quick hugs.

— Good luck to yez now.

— Sure do your best, now.

— That's all anyone can do.

The van is waiting. Just as a van waited on 4 July 1991. Parked in the exact same spot. Heading for Boston for the summer that day. Independence Day over there. First time going to America. Out to play football with Donegal-Boston. Along with Stephen McKelvey and John Gildea and Gerry Doherty. All of us feeling important. Like big shots. Say goodbye to Charles at the graveyard and then get the bag out of the van to get into McGeehan's bus across the road. Mum in the back seat, her eyes filled with tears. It'll be grand, Mum. Climb halfway into the van to give her a hug, half not wanting to go at all. Heavy heart the whole way to Dublin. The unforgettable strangeness of that day. Starting in Glenties and standing at a barbecue in Boston that afternoon. The sky endless blue. A syrupy smell in the air and the heat hitting you as soon as the doors slide back at the airport. Meat sizzling on the grill. Shorts. Sunglasses. Actual summer. She had asked you to ring home. Leaving the barbecue and walking down the street with immaculate gardens and bunting. Haven't a clue where anything is. A wee shop – 7/11. Asking for ten dollars in quarters. Emptying these into the AT&T phone box. Standing there and the heat baking. Quarter after quarter. The phone ringing. Close to midnight at home. Mum comes on. Once she hears you are okay, she is okay. Go and enjoy it now. Have a great summer. At ease once you put the phone down. That comes flying back now.

On to the bus and it is hard to shake this. Pulled between two times. Nostalgia, is it? Not like you, Jim. Almost lonely leaving the town. Listen to the boys. Listen to their voices. Hear their energy and let them take you back. The squad will be waiting in Donegal Town. They will need you to be here and now.

The boys are in deadly form. They are laughing. They are relaxed. They are thinking: We are going to win this. That's good. That's what they want to be thinking. Look at them. Tony Thompson. Smiley, from when he was ten years old. Young Leo. In a flash they can be children before you, and look at them now. Men. Away to play the biggest game of their lives.

Why is all of this so important? A day from decades ago and a story I was told after Na Rossa had beaten Killybegs in a league match. Everyone is delighted because it is a huge thing. Killybegs was a giant of a club and Na Rossa shouldn't be able to live with them. But they have played out of their skins on this day and the pints are flowing. The mood is jubilant. The Killybegs boys are big enough to make an appearance. Barry McGowan from Killybegs is in the corner, taking the scene in in that reserved way of his, same as on the pitch for Donegal. At some point, there is a bit of a row, the usual shouting and jostling. One of the Na Rossa players is overcome with the passion of the moment. He jumps on a table, raising his fist in the air, and makes his vow.

— I'd diiiiie for Leitir!

Howling out the words.

He means it, too, at that minute. Barry McGowan waits for the lull after the huge cheer and his timing is perfect.

— You'd be the quare fucken eejit, then.

Thought of it still makes you laugh. But the moment stayed. It was important. People can get lost in their team and their place. That is what the whole thing is about. 'I'd die for Leitir.' Our boys felt that way about Donegal. All winter long that has been our message and our vow.

Our season has gone by in a flash. Was there a turning point? Was it that day in Kerry?

Another bus journey. A Sunday night in February gone, all the way from Killarney to Donegal Town and the motorway up towards Galway empty and straight. Six long hours of driving and a big defeat to think about. Kerry 2-16 Donegal 1-08. Twice as good, they were. The boys stunned after it. Hardly a word spoken until we were through Limerick. They had all these notions about Kerry. Our boys were Kerry admirers – of the tradition, of the green and gold hoops, of the skills, of the beautiful ball players, of the names: Maurice Fitz, Gooch, Moynihan, Darragh. Our boys believed in the romance of Kerry. They grew up watching Kerry win. Sharing the same field as them? Life was wonderful.

And Kerry send out a message when they get us on the field. They had watched us last year. Last thing Kerry wanted was a new set of Ulster upstarts. They hit us hard and then harder, and they hit us fairly. Oh, the skills and the passing and the casual accuracy are there too, but what is shocking our boys is just how hard Kerry are hitting them. Leo, clotheslined right in front of us. Our boys cowed. Too respectful. And once Kerry have a run on us, they bring out the silk. Weaving twenty-five passes as the Donegal boys chase shadows. They kick a point and a huge roar of satisfaction goes up. Standing there on the sideline with blood boiling, but there is nothing to do. Kerry aren't doing anything wrong. Just tougher and better and showing our boys that. Making fools of us. Jack O'Connor over to shake hands. Grimace of sympathy. Hard luck, boy. Their players over to shake hands. Very sporting. Understanding.

— Ah, ye just didn't get into it.

Nodding. Saying: 'Thanks, well done.'

Thinking: 'Fuck you.'

Livid.

The boys troop to the dressing room, heads bowed. Beaten. The radio men and journalists waiting on the field and they ask their questions. Answer on automatic but you want to be in that dressing room. To find out how bad the damage is. Fitzgerald Stadium is empty in no time. It is a beautiful ground, a proper football ground, with the old hospital building high above and the mountains in the distance. But it is hateful at this moment. Empty. Judgemental. A Kerry player talking with reporters down the pitch. It's Paul Galvin: you'd know the cut of him even in winter light. As it happens, the two of you are walking towards the tunnel at the same time. Sharing Fitzgerald Stadium for those few seconds. Paul Galvin is about ten or fifteen metres in front. Does not turn back. Does not look or acknowledge that anyone else is there. He starts shouting as if to himself.

— C'mon, Ker-ry!

— C'mon, Ker-ry!

As if to say: You are in Kerry now, boy. And you know what you'll do? Go into that dressing room. Pack your bags. Get your players. Get on that bus. And fuck off.

As if to say: That's youse told.

Staring hard at the back of his head, at the head of black curls just before he disappears. Promising: Next time we meet you, we'll be fucking ready.

Silence in the dressing room. Shocked, they are, to a man.

Huddle up.

— What the fuck happened?

No answer from anyone because we all know the truth and nobody wants to voice it: I was in awe. I respected them too much. I was subservient.

— How the fuck do you expect to win an All-Ireland against

these boys if you respect them so much that you can't play football against them?

On the bus. Dark quiet. A half-hearted game of cards around Ennis.

Sitting beside each of the players now, going around the seats one by one. Not saying much at all now, but wanting their opinion. Just listening. Like confession. They're getting to grips with the day. Getting beaten like that had nothing to do with skill or with tactics. It was just about awe. Kerry. Five All-Ireland medals. Overawed. Demoralised. Honoured just to be there.

And fuck that.

Fuck that.

Somewhere through Mayo. A memory of Colm's shot in last year's All-Ireland semi-final against Dublin. Had he scored, had that shot gone under the bar, we would have won. We would have met Kerry in the final. And thanking God now that we lost that match against Dublin. Because if we met Kerry in that final, we would have been massacred by them. Because we would have carried that same respect onto the field. Dazzled by those green and gold hoops and by ourselves marching with them behind the band. Marching with Kerry! They would have murdered us. We might never have recovered. Thank God we lost. The boys can recover from this one. This one is okay.

That day in Kerry was one of the disguised days: a bad day from which good things come. All winter on the training field trying to figure out who we were and who we could become. Ignoring the newspapers and the radio. Those words. Those stupid words. Austere. Messiah. Control freak. Gruelling. Robotic. Minds were made up about Donegal. Fine. The boys didn't care. They were becoming tighter, even after Cass.

That was another day. Meeting in the Clanree, in the usual place. Sitting beside Rory, Cass opposite us. Did we shake hands?

Can't remember. Still in disbelief more than anger. Opening the *Donegal News* and reading as Kevin laid out everything, everything that we did in black and white. An extract from a book that you knew nothing about. Accounts of our training. Of what was said in private about other managers. Of our team meetings. Tactics. Game plans. Performance goals. All of this laid out in newsprint, and more of it in a book, and you are speechless. That phrase, not believing your eyes? This is what that is. Thinking: This must be some kind of fucking joke. Kevin wouldn't do this. More than anything you want to know why.

Kevin is a senior player. A former teammate. Big and powerful, he can win ball in the air, he can play halfback or midfield, he can take a score. A bit of a warrior. Always played with an edge. That was why you asked him out of retirement, explaining the vision down the phone, talking about winning Ulster. Give it one more season, Kevin. He was thirty-one; it wouldn't be forever. Kevin was in, but he and his wife, Sarah, had just had twins and he needed some time. No problem. Delighted to have him. Settled in straight away. And he was brilliant all year. He had his Ulster medal.

So why this? Looking for some explanation. Maybe he thought 2011 would be his last season, so what harm? Then realising that maybe Donegal could win an All-Ireland. Maybe he should stay another year. But he sits before me and doesn't say anything like that. There is no remorse. Maybe it is just stubbornness. Talking for over an hour without really getting anywhere. Reading from passages in the extract and just asking him: Do you not feel that was over the line there? Why give this information to other teams and managers? Why rile them? Why expose everything we have worked to create? Kevin acknowledging that he was over the line. But still no remorse. Feeling there is nothing to work with as every minute passes.

Saying again and again that this compromises everything we had been about all year. This broke the trust within the group. There is no acknowledgement from Kevin and then Rory, sensing a decision and looking across at you, saying, 'Hold on, are you sure?' Rory wants this resolved. There is a line between keeping your core values and holding on to your best players. No other way to go.

— You're leaving me with no choice, Kevin.

A horrible moment, very heavy and very grave. Nothing to do with personality. It would have been the same if it had been any other player. But Cass is a big player. Who wants to lose a player like that? This is November. There is nothing happening. This will catch fire. Axing a senior player; a former teammate; an All-Star. For giving interviews for a book. It still broke what we held sacred. What Kevin has done has compromised the group, not an individual. If you don't act on it now, you compromise yourself. Kevin is a smart man. He understands this. He isn't backing down. Your mind is made up for you. He is gone. Nothing more to say. Three of us walking to our cars in the hotel car park. That's it.

In the newspapers and on the radio over the following days, more words: Dark. Uncompromising. Vindictive. Cold. A Leader of Sheep.

Let them talk. Let them write. Bigger things to worry about.

Up late night after night that winter. The house asleep. Rain beating against the window panes. The sky black. Leaning over a notepad. Trying to figure out a puzzle. What had happened against Dublin? Hadn't I coached them? Hadn't I given them the game plan? Couldn't they see that it was there for them if they had just run at Dublin? Maybe they didn't believe they could win against the big teams. Thinking about this night after night and getting nowhere. Almost quitting on it, accepting it

as just one of those days. But then one night just sitting there
and there it was, shining and in full sight. You had coached
them generalisations. Hadn't shown them how. You had told
them to attack at speed but you hadn't shown them how. You
hadn't given the boys enough direction. You told them what to
do but not how to do it. No detailed instructions.

This is what we needed. We needed to break it all down and
coach principles. Sketching away on the notepad now, evening
after evening. Scenarios. Where we wanted to turn the ball
over and what happened when we did. Who went. Who stayed.
When we looked to go long. We wanted to attack like an arrow,
direct and at speed.

So at training, in winter, working on this arrow idea, night
after night. Three-man runner drills, from the 21 to the 21 over
and over. Repetition. Again. Again. The ground hard, the sky
freezing. Seems like the whole county is indoors. Except for us.
Team talks all the time, between drills and after training. On the
phone to Rory for hours. On the phone to Michael for hours.
Repeating our core values until they become automatic. Savage
discipline. Savage attitude. Need to commit. Solo the ball at
pace. Nobody left out to dry. Don't take the ball into contact.
I *know* you can score versus I *think* you can score. Every single
ball counts. Chase down lost causes always. Die for the jersey.
Half backs are aerobic animals. Midfielders able to do it both
ways. We don't back down – ever. Prepare to be hurt. Prepare
to be tired. Those are the enemy. They stand in the way of our
success. We do all of the above every day.

Away from the training ground, the boys have lives and jobs
and families and worries. They are ordinary people. On training
nights, they become different people. Month by month, they
are changing. Becoming stronger, faster. Bodies are no longer
in shock. They are getting used to working through exhaustion.

The standards aren't slipping, the mistakes aren't there. It is exciting to watch and it is exhilarating for them. They are taking themselves to places they didn't know existed as footballers. They are discovering a new threshold. They are banking all of this work on the field and in the gym and they are feeling strong. And when the day comes they will be able to look someone in the eye and think: I am going to take you down today.

We are Ulster champions. The Ulster championship had been won from the preliminary round just once in sixty-seven years. Never back to back. That is our task. Win Ulster. Again. Keep the Anglo Celt. Move on. Win the All-Ireland. These are records to go for. The boys are in a good place. But are they? Are we?

Are we really there? Do we really believe we are good enough? Do we believe we are destined to win this? Maybe deep down they are happy that they won an Ulster medal, that it is enough. They have earned respect. Did they really believe they had the right to play, to truly play, the establishment?

— *C'mon, Ker-ry!*

An evening in May now. Bayern Munich and Chelsea playing the Champions League final and the whole squad watching it on television in the golf clubhouse at the Slieve Russell. Trainers off, relaxed. Tomorrow we will play Cavan. The boys are confident. A pool has been organised around the football final – first goal scorer, winning goal scorer, all that stuff. The fun is good. They are happy. And they deserve these moments. They have worked so hard. The match goes to penalties. All eyes riveted to the screen. Didier Drogba hits the winning penalty for Chelsea. Half of our boys delighted, others disgusted. Off with the television then. Time for the team talk. We all move into the meeting room nearby and they are in high spirits. Promising it will be a quick meeting tonight. They settle down and you just say it out.

— I'm not happy, boys. I'm not happy with where we are at.

They are a bit taken aback by this. And it's understandable because they have given everything they have been asked all season. They have drained their bodies night after night. Every ounce. Too exhausted for sleep. No complaints. And this is what they hear at the end of it.

— I want to ask you a question and I want you to answer it very honestly. Put your hand up if every single morning you wake up, the first thing you think about is winning an All-Ireland medal.

A few seconds' delay and then two hands go up. Just two. Dermot Molloy. Michael Murphy. The boys honest. Nobody just sticking their hand up for the pretence of it.

— That makes perfect sense to me. That's answered the question that's been rattling around in my head for the last number of months. I don't know who Katie Taylor is, boys, and I've never met Katie Taylor, but I do know this: She's going to win the Olympic gold medal, and the reason she's going to win the Olympic gold medal is she's absolutely locked on, every second of every hour of every day, she's thinking of winning a gold medal at the Olympics. And that's the reason she's going to be fucking Olympic champion.

— How do we expect to be All-Ireland champions if we're not locked on? If you don't believe one hundred per cent, if you don't see that finishing line, if you don't fucking drive towards that finishing line, if every single thought process you have does not lead you to that point, how the fuck are we going to win the All-Ireland? It's not going to happen. If we want to, we need every single player locked on. You need to ask yourself these questions: Have you locked on? What's involved? How much are you going to give? How much are you going to sacrifice? How hard are you going to drive? How fucking hard are you going to hold on when time goes away from you in a tight Ulster Championship match? These are the questions, and when you're locked on you've got the answers to those questions. But if you're not locked on you're going to let it slip at the key moment and it's going to be another year where we don't fulfil our dreams. And I want to fulfil our dreams. I want us to fulfil our dreams. So we need to get fucking locked on.

All the fun gone now. It is delicate. There is no lightness in the room now. Instead a heavy, horrible silence. Taking a medal from your inside pocket and holding it before them. An All-Ireland senior football medal.

— How many of youse think about this every day? How many of youse dream about this every day? Because you have to if you want to make it a reality. What the fuck gives Dublin the God-given right to have that medal? What gives Kerry the God-given right to have that medal? What gives Tyrone the right? Why can *you* not have that medal?

Holding it up in the room before them and all eyes looking back, all eyes spellbound. The boys at the back leaning forward. Silence in the room. They are studying that medal. Trying to get a better look. And it hits you. These boys have never laid eyes on one before. This is as close as they have come to touching one. And as close as they will. For now. Back in the pocket. No handing it round. No touching it. If they want that medal, they have to go and get their own. Find out for themselves. The medal disappears. Nobody speaking. Everyone sombre. The Champions League final forgotten.

— That medal's there for you, if you want it. But if you're not going to give everything in your body, everything in your mind, everything in your fucking soul, every single day, in the quest to get that medal, you're not going to get it. It ain't going to happen. You need to commit to getting the thing, and making the thing happen. If you do that, you'll get there. You'll get there. The same as all the other teams who get there. They're not magical players from magical counties. They're fucking football players who want something bad. And that's the next thing. You have to realise that there are other teams out there that want it bad, really, really bad. And if they want it bad, you have to go to a level above that. You have to say you want your hands on that medal. Fuck you. Fuck you – this is my medal. I'm going to fight harder for this medal than you could ever imagine. I'm going to dig deeper than you're prepared to dig. I'm going to go for a dirty ball, a hard ball, I don't care. Whatever it takes, that's what I'm going to do to win the All-Ireland. That's the way you need to start moving, and that's the way you need to start thinking. And if we do that we'll be successful. And if we don't, that's the fucking sword we'll perish on. Because we have the footballers, we have the fitness, we have the power, we have the strength, and we have the game plan, and when we implement our own game plan to the letter of the law nobody can beat us. We can't be beaten. That's a fucking unbelievable thing to be able to say to any group of players, boys. When you deliver at one hundred per cent you cannot be beaten.

20 May: Donegal 1-16 Cavan 1-10
16 June: Donegal 2-13 Derry 0-09

Something shifting. Like they are on a new course. Clear in their minds about where they want to go. Coming onto the training field with this collective energy. Thrilling to be close to it. They had become different. All summer long, fuelled by this adrenaline rush that they are getting from being around one another, from training together, from playing football together and making each other better. All of us feeling as if we are gliding from one training session to the next, from one game to the next. That word synchronicity. Slippery, but this is surely what it means. Everyone highly concentrated and focused all the time, feeling part of something special and moving in unison. Knowing we are part of something very special and not having to talk about it because it is present as a feeling; a surge of energy that rushes from the bottom of your stomach and up through you. Tingles.

Pushing as hard as they can on the pitch on warm nights and walking off knowing they can give nothing more. But daring themselves then to go that bit further. Coming back two nights later and asking them if they can't go that bit further. Faster. Harder. Feeling as if nothing else in the world exists when they are in the middle of demanding more and more from themselves. In between games.

Our summer broken down into those key dates: Cavan. Derry. Then Tyrone. Then Down. Weeks between the games fly by. On the outside, talk of how punishing, how hard, how merciless the Donegal training sessions are. Knowing that the opposite is true. Watching the boys eating up sprints and ball drills and seeing the light in their eyes. Seeing how pure and liberating it is for them to be performing and moving like this. Almost ... addicted to it. The only word. No escaping it when they land into the car park every night. They are craving more of it.

Around the county, people are feeling that energy. It moves from the pitch and into the stands on match days. Flags in the towns. A good atmosphere. You can feel it, but stay clear of it. Making the same journey all summer. Driving from training to home and back again. Very little else. In the office most nights, thinking about where we are at, talking with the players on the phone, watching videos, making notes. Not wanting to sleep much. Sometimes two in the morning when you stop.

Sometimes waking up in the middle of the night and your mind buzzing until everything is written down and then you can sleep again. Planning. Running things through, over and over. Going quiet on Saturday afternoons, walking with Yvonne and the children and promising yourself to not think about football for a while. But then some little thought or problem ... you drift. Yvonne saying only: Are you okay? Is everything all right? And having to pull yourself out of that thought and back to where you are: on a gorgeous summer's day, with your family. It is hardest on family. Your obsession becomes theirs.

Tyrone are coming. Always Tyrone. Tyrone on 30 June. Gunning for us. Fixating on us. Mickey Harte has never lost to the same team twice. They would bring everything they had. They were coming for us. This is what we tell the boys at training. Hearing on the grapevine about what they were doing in Healy Park. Moving at phenomenal pace, trying to get up the field in less than ten seconds. Mickey had spoken about beating Donegal by matching our style of play. They would throw everything at us. And that's how it feels when the match starts: a deluge of intensity hitting our players. And our boys resisting it. Anthony Thompson using his body like a shield to somehow absorb a Tyrone man who just wanted to run through him. The two teams pounding at each other, tackle for tackle, point for point. And the Donegal boys becoming stronger in the second half. The points seldom and of high quality. A proper football game. Two teams just playing. An impossible save by Paul Durcan at the end. Stretched across the ground.

30 June: Donegal 0-12 Tyrone 0-10

It is tight. No time to dwell. The team is getting stronger. Growing. And by the evening of 3 July, a new obsession to fill our thoughts. The Ulster final. Back-to-back. Down. Down and James McCartan. Still looking as he did when he was the footballer you looked up to; when James McCartan was the last word in class; when he carried the ball in that low, guarded way, tormenting defenders with that jinking low centre of gravity. A true Down footballer. Full of skill and full of devilment. Cocky. A glimmer from some Railway Cup game around 1990 or 1991. McCartan scoring this outrageous point where he had gone for a ball near the end line, didn't get it and then running behind the goals and reappearing on the other side, taking a pass and kicking a score. Was that even allowed? Nobody had even seen anything like that before. McCartan didn't care. Mayhem all around him. Wee James jogging away, cool as a breeze. So accomplished so young. Played minor and senior the same day. Carried himself with this extraordinary confidence.

James McCartan was football royalty in your mind.

Ulster football royalty.

Sitting in dressing rooms for Railway Cup games in the mid-1990s, McCartan looked and behaved as if he was born to do this. You never had that feeling because the McGuinness family was not a football family. Dad had no real interest in the game. And that helped because it meant that there was no pressure either. He took an interest in us. He would always ask how it was going and he would listen in on the radio when we were playing, even if he mightn't have fully followed it. The odd time he would drive us and stay. An image from a championship match in Glencolmcille, a tar-melter of a day: spotting Dad down behind the goals during the warm-ups and being delighted that he was sticking around to watch the match. Keeping an eye during any breaks in play and there he was on the bank, stretched out and enjoying the heat of the afternoon. Mild interest was the height of it. If he wanted me to succeed in football, it was only because he knew how much

I wanted to. But never once a word of chastisement. He let me grow. No sense of being destined to play county football. So to sit in a dressing room with James McCartan at the age of twenty-three or twenty-four and with boys like Peter Canavan or Mickey Linden was very special.

A moment too from the 1991 All-Ireland football final: Mickey Linden through on goal with just John O'Leary, the Dublin goalkeeper, to beat. The world knows he is going to score it. What an electrifying feeling that must be: to bag a goal in an All-Ireland. But Mickey feints as if to strike and then flicks a lateral pass for James McCartan to roll into an empty goal. So gloriously unselfish. A lesson that you never forget. If you ever coach a team, that is one value you would hope to pass on. Watching that All-Ireland in a schoolhouse in Brighton. Brighton in Boston, which you thought might become home. Now in a dressing room with these players. Part of you can't believe it. That they are accepting you. Peter Canavan standing beside you one day before a Railway Cup match. Looks up at your long hair and the beard and says, loud enough for everyone to hear, 'I hope the commentators don't get the two of us mixed up today.' Just a small thing but Peter made it easier for you to feel welcome and as if you belonged. A wee moment like that can stay with you through your whole career. Anthony Molloy, too, during the first days of training with Donegal:

— You're here on merit. You're here because you're a good player. Enjoy training, enjoy being here and give it your best.

Never forgot that. Never will.

So to look down the sideline on Ulster final day and see James there as manager is nice. Football is funny like that. Faces and names from the past can just reappear. Moving through the days and lives intersecting every so often. The Donegal support so loud during the parade. This fierceness now in the way the Donegal people support the team. The boys sense it. A closeness developing between team and supporters week after week. Could see the pride in people's faces and when they spoke you could see that this team mattered to them. Maybe it was because we beat Tyrone twice. Or because of what was being said about Donegal. The Donegal people made all the words and all the voices less than zero. Every day about putting pride into Donegal football. Now the people of the county reflecting that back on us.

Down are crafty. Down have a team full of ball players. So many notes taken on them. The boys have heard chapter and verse. Have heard about Down's very short, sharp kick-outs in their league games. Technically illegal because the goalkeeper didn't restart from the right spot. He would just roll it anywhere and restart while the referee was running back out into the middle of the field. Also, when their forwards were fouled and drew frees, they were brilliant at stealing an extra few yards. So simple and so smart. Down would try to hit us on the counter-attack. So not taking the ball into contact and being smart with it was going to be important. Putting massive pressure on their delivery from the middle of the field would be critical. Stopping Danny Hughes and Mark Poland dropping deep to retrieve ball and supply quality ball was vital too. Down liked to mark their men in front of the angle of the ball so they could knock it away for a sweeper to collect. They were good at this so our approach play had to be smart.

Fifteen minutes in and we are ignoring all that. Down score four points and look assured. Scanning the field. No sign of the boys putting our game plan in motion. Down are doing a good job of frustrating us. Or it may be the occasion or going for the back-to-back titles. Clones is packed and colourful. The boys aren't playing badly, but we aren't flowing either. We'd worked on going long and early on our kick-outs to see if we might steal a goal. Sending our midfielders from the centre out to take possession maybe six or seven metres from the sideline, turning sharply and looking for the early diagonal ball to see if we could create a goal chance. And then it happens: Paul hits Ryan Bradley with a perfect kick-out, Ryan is fouled, gets up and directs a quick free into Leo, who solos in and puts it into the net.

A few nights later, watching the video back, one of the boys notice that after the goal Rory and myself are just standing there, expressionless. The supporters behind are jumping up and down, delighted, going mad. One of the boys says, 'Yez aren't too happy with the goal.' Saying back, 'We were happy with the goal all right. We just weren't wild about what went on before that.'

Leo's goal gives them a release and a way back into the game. The boys thinking: We created that on the training ground. We made that happen. That was not about chance. That was about practice. And the boys click after that. In Ballybofey we had talked about running the ball at Down. They had half backs who liked to attack to a degree that was dangerous. So if we attacked that line – and their midfielders – we were attacking guys who were really half forwards in their approach. They were players, not stoppers. So we should run at them aggressively and with intent and ask questions. Colm, Michael and Patrick would stay inside. So if we had runners pouring through, the cracks had to show. Frank McGlynn comes through in the second half on the overlap and leaves us two goals clear. Strange in the last ten minutes. Comfortably winning the Ulster final and keeping the Anglo Celt for the first time in our history. The final whistle brings a different happiness. Calmer. We are delighted, but this day no longer feels like our summer is complete.

22 July: Donegal 2-18 Down 0-13

All of this – the season – bouncing around as the bus moves towards Donegal Town. For an All-Ireland final. How often have you been on this road? With Frank? With Dad? With the family? Hundreds of people waiting in the Diamond, in the foyer of the Abbey Hotel and on the footpath. Just to see the team off. People driving from around the county just to be there to applaud the team on to the bus. It is a magnificent thing, that. Nothing has changed from 1992. The very same that time. The suits were different. The haircuts were different. That is all.

Kerry in the quarter-final. Rory and you doing a whistle-stop tour of the country to take in three qualifier games. Racing back to hear the quarter-final draw in the car. You had seen Down, Kildare and Laois win their games. Kerry the only winning county you haven't seen. Laughing when they are called out. Excited by the thought of it. Talking about scenarios and match-ups the whole way home.

Not much sleep the night before that. Up until half past two thinking about this and awake until four. Getting bright outside. Killarney and that journey. Need to be positive about this match. That will be the message to the boys.

This is the match we want, boys. This is exactly the team we want. This is our chance to knock out a big county and move on.

Training on Sunday morning in MacCumhaill Park. For some reason the old dressing rooms have been opened for us. Where you trained when you started playing with Donegal. Haven't seen them for years, but the room smells the same and looks the same. Navy blue linoleum squares on the floor.

Brown benches. Pegs. A 1970s dressing room. The boys in there waiting when you arrive. And as soon as you open the door a vision: Brian McEniff standing on the left-hand corner bench with that lemon-coloured sweater on him. Calling out the team on some summer's Thursday night twenty years ago.

Him brown as a berry from the sun.

Blue eyes looking out at us.

— Gary in goal. Martin, Matt, Noel ...

For a split second you are back there, starting out, and you have that old apprehension. The butterflies. Who's in? Who made it? But now it is your turn to call the team out.

For Donegal supporters, the game is a world apart from what it is for us. Playing Kerry is an occasion for them. It is something to get lost in. Something no Donegal team has ever done. Romantic. For us it is a task. It is a series of small, essential tasks. Strip down the myth. Execute a game plan. Watching all the tapes of Kerry available. The ultimate possession team. Moving that football carefully, smoothly out of defence. Always looking for the honey pot, always looking for the pass in that patch of green inside the opposition 45 and twenty metres in from the sideline on both sides. A dink pass or a hand pass: never too much weight or speed on the ball. Inviting. And then always one or two men charging through to support the man winning the ball. Over and over again. We have to make this a physical test. They have six or seven boys over thirty years old. We are in the shape of our lives. The shape of our lives. Kick-out strategies to suck the Kerry midfield in so Papa can launch the ball beyond them. Green, amber, red. Get out in front. Set the tone.

Almost the perfect start. Kerry win the throw-in, but from their delivery, Eamon drives out in front of Kieran Donaghy, gets a hand on the ball. Frank collects and flicks the ball to

Patrick. Karl Lacey absolutely sprints flat out to be there in support. Everything we are looking for is there to be seen in the first ten seconds.

Two timeless gems we take from that game when we study the tape afterwards. Watching Colm Cooper for Kerry's first point as he peels away from Neil McGee and then gets the ball on the loop. Neil just delays a split second in his reaction and then spreads himself as Cooper kicks and he is just a fingertip away from getting the block in. Running those few frames of film and talking for maybe twenty-five minutes about all of us being ready and staying sharp. Later in the match, another Kerry point from Anthony Maher where Neil Gallagher comes out with his hands up. Not reacting fast enough or pressing the kick with aggression. That was hope-you-miss kind of defence. That was not for us.

So little to fault in our play for the first hour. Our six defenders have been winning their battles, our attacks are confident and direct. We are in control. The Kerry half forwards non-existent. Then a Kerry kick-out. We are sluggish at closing it down. Ball comes up the left, recycled to the right, Kerry find the space, get across, a hand pass and Donaghy fists a goal. Two more kick-outs won and they get a point. Patrick Curtin misses a chance to level the game.

On the sideline. How is this happening? Are we going to fucking lose this game? Not really believing that was possible. But we had ground to a halt out there. The boys are reeling. In disbelief after Donaghy's goal because this is the first goal we have let in all summer. In their minds, we don't concede goals. And then two quick excellent points and all of a sudden this was the Kerry that the country has feared for decades. Moving like they knew what the outcome would be now, Kerry moving with purpose and with energy.

Thirty-six All-Irelands. This is why.

Just a point ahead. Papa teeing up his kick-out. Signalling a play. 'Derry.' An anchor, an old reliable, something we could turn to. Two half forwards dropping back as the two half-backs bolt forward. Big Neil goes to fetch the ball. Rory Kavanagh grabs it as it breaks and he pirouettes out of trouble. Karl steaming through on his right, all alone. Karl gets the ball and there are options ahead of him, but we all know what Karl is thinking, that he has the courage and he is going to go for it. Steadying for the shot. One of those angled, floating little points of his. That is enough. That gets us home.

5 August: Donegal 1-12 Kerry 1-10.

Should never have been so tight. The Kerry boys very classy afterwards, wishing us well and no animosity. Used to these days. Not knowing what to think. A bit subdued. Bothered that we had nearly blown it. Bothered that our last ten minutes diminished the shine of the previous hour. Taking a little while to absorb that we had won, that we were moving on, that it was a semi-final.

Together on the bus back to Donegal that evening. Texts coming in from across the county. Everybody partying. The boys on iPads and phones trying to stream the Olympics. Usain Bolt is running the hundred metres final in London. That passes the journey. Drinking tins and watching the build-up. Then watching this tall Jamaican streak away from the fastest men on the planet. Our bus rattles through the darkening countryside. Whole world watching this race. Olympic stadium dazzling on the tiny screens. The boys shaking their heads at Bolt. That's serious, hey. Would he take Christy, do yez think? Be tight. Christy'd be quicker over the first ten anyways.

Big night for Jamaica. Big night for Donegal. Karl sits down

A rare photo of all of us together, celebrating my sister's first communion in Granny's house. *L-R*: Granny; Mum with me on her knee; Noreen; Dad with Mark on his knee; Charles; my cousin Seán Wilson; and my brother Frank.

With Mum and Dad and a pocketful of pound notes on the day of my first holy communion, June 1979.

The kitchen in Glenties; the craic in full flight. Mark (*l*), Charles (*c*) and me (*r*).

Myself and Charles sitting with Mum in the café in Glenties. The curls had yet to kick in for either of us.

Myself and Mark, school photo, September 1982.

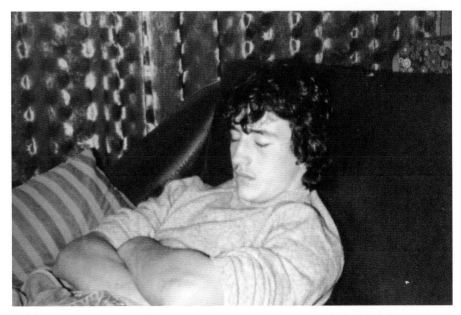

Charles asleep in Michael Quinn's house at the end of another long day.

With my brother Mark, the Giant, June 1988. I'm wary of a stray fist.

Myself, our neighbour Michael Furey and Mark at the Mary from Dungloe Festival.

Christmas 1992, the night we received our All-Ireland medals.

Taking Sam into Glenties for the first time. My club mate Michael Gallagher (*l*) and Brian McEniff (*c*) standing alongside me.

Outside our café in Glenties, *c.*1996. *L-R*: Mark, me, young Leo, old Leo, Dr Cooke and Mum.

With my friend and mentor Columba McDyer at our club dinner dance. Mum is on my right, Columba's wife Peggy on my left.

The first Glenties team to win the senior championship, in 2005, before the county final with St Eunan's.

With the game level, an injury-time goal from Brick Molloy sees us past Tyrone and into the 2011 Ulster final. This was the moment we started to believe. (© *Oliver McVeigh/*SPORTSFILE)

Ulster final day 2011. After so many disappointments, this had to be our day. The focus of the players is reflected on their faces. (© *Brendan Moran/*SPORTSFILE)

The final whistle in Clones sounds; 19 years of pain washed away and with it a chance meeting with my brother, Frank, in the crowd. (© *INPHO/Morgan Treacy*)

Celebrating with Brian McEniff, 19 years on from Donegal's last Ulster Championship success – under his management. (© *INPHO/ Morgan Treacy*)

Seconds before throw-in, in the middle of a deluge, All-Ireland semi-final day 2011. Dublin wait while we put the finishing touches to a game plan we believe will take us to the All-Ireland final. (© *Dáire Brennan/*SPORTSFILE)

Paddy McGrath throws himself into the line of fire, with Eamon, Neil and David Walsh in close proximity as usual. (© *Paul Mohan/*SPORTSFILE)

One of the moments that makes the sacrifice worthwhile. Celebrating with Yvonne and the kids in the tunnel in Clones after winning back-to-back Ulster Championships, July 2012. (© *Donna McBride/Donegal News*)

The moment I knew we had it. Frank McGlynn wheels away after scoring the crucial goal against Down, Ulster Championship final, July 2012. (© *Donna McBride/Donegal News*)

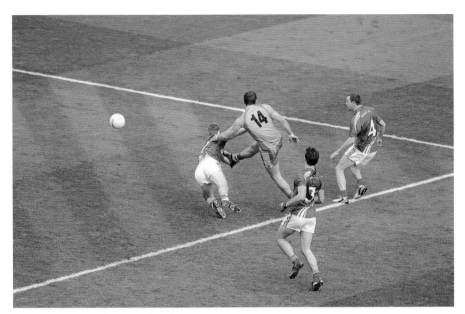

Breakthrough. Michael scores an unbelievable goal to fire us into the lead, All-Ireland final day 2012. It was incredible to see hours and hours of repetition come to fruition in the first few moments of the game. (*© Dáire Brennan/SPORTSFILE*)

Colm scores to put us seven clear of Mayo in the 2012 All-Ireland final. I had two thoughts: we hadn't lost a game from more than two points ahead all year, and today was not the day to start. (*© Dáire Brennan/SPORTSFILE*)

Sharing a private but powerful moment with Big Neil Gallagher seconds after the final whistle against Mayo in 2012.
(© INPHO/*Morgan Treacy*)

A moment I'll always cherish. Toni-Marie, Mark Anthony and Jimmy in my arms. In the stands, a Donegal man prepares to lift the Sam Maguire for the first time in 20 years. In the background, a loyal friend, JD McGrenra, looks on. (© *David Maher*/SPORTSFILE)

We have her!
(© *David Maher*/
SPORTSFILE)

'It's all in the Wavin pipe!' With Billy Boyle the day we brought Sam back to Creeslough, September 2012.

On the sideline with Rory, facing into another Ulster Championship. Ballybofey, 26 May 2013. (© INPHO/James Crombie)

6 September 2013: The arrival of Bonnie and Aoibh, a special moment for us all. L-R: Yvonne, Toni-Marie, Bonnie, Mark Anthony, Jimmy, myself and Aoibh.

Our reign as Ulster champions comes to an end in 2013. Michael looks on as Monaghan players celebrate at the final whistle in Clones. A fortnight later our season would get worse. (© INPHO/Presseye/William Cherry)

All-Ireland semi-final day 2014, with my new back-room team. *L-R*: Damien Diver, Donal Reid, Pat Shovelin, me, Paul McGonigle and Dr Charlie McManus. Conspicuous by his absence is team selector John Duffy. (© INPHO/Morgan Treacy)

With my family after the dust had settled in Brewster Park having won the Ulster Championship with the U-21s. My first taste of success as an inter-county manager.

Joy. Bringing the Anglo-Celt home to Glenties the morning after the Ulster final in 2014.

The squad was about more than just the players. Behind every one of them there was a family just as dedicated to Donegal football. Here's my mother, Yvonne and me with the McBrearty family after our Ulster Championship win in 2014.

Mark Anthony keeps a close eye on proceedings at a Donegal open training session, September 2014. (© *INPHO/Cathal Noonan*)

The pain of defeat. Donegal versus Kerry,
All-Ireland final, 21 September 2014.
(© *INPHO/Donall Farmer*)

beside you at one point and says, 'I never thought we were going to lose.' Just quiet. No bravado in it. Just saying it. A memory from years ago. Might have been Karl's debut, shortly before you finished up. On the road to Kerry for a league game and Karl is innocent enough to leave his phone unattended. Christy and some of the boys grab it. Christy sends Brian McEniff a text from Karl's phone. Brian up the front of the bus, back managing the team because nobody else wants us. Christy writes: 'Brian im ready. if you give me a chance this weekend then im ready to take it.' Half time. The game not going well. Brian turning to Karl who had in fact done his hamstring. 'You told me you wanted your chance. This is it. Go take it now.' Bewilderment all over Karl's face. Christy burying his face in his jersey. Always mischief then. Always fun. That never disappeared. A wild crew for taking a hand at one another. Taking a hand at you. This habit you have of saying, 'Right, that's good. That's good' – every now and again one of them will repeat it back and you can hear the guffaws. They need that. They need fun.

The All-Ireland semi-final. Donegal a serious proposition now. A far cry from the first game of the year. Laois in the league in Letterkenny. The match live on TG4. There is an element of curiosity about us after the Dublin game. Even if they consider us an abomination. A request comes out to the back pitch where we are warming up. 'Would you mind doing an interview?' It is fifteen minutes to throw-in.

— It would need to be quick, boys.

— Two minutes, Jim.

— Right so. No bother.

Walking across the pitch in O'Donnell Park, making chat, not paying much heed. Just steps away from the camera and the interviewer when you see that they have Kevin Cassidy standing there. Cass does some media stuff for TG4. But you can't believe this. Tap Cass on the back. How's it going, Kevin? Hiya Jim. Answering the questions. About the game at first. And then about Kevin. Is it definitely over for Kevin? Is there no way back? The camera right in on my face. Have you right where they want you. Don't need this. Walk away. Fuck them. No: Retain your dignity. Go through with it. Answer the questions. This is going to look cringeworthy. Sitting at home watching the RTÉ news with Yvonne that night. And there it is. They have moved a pre-match interview to the sports section of the main evening news. Not only that, when they did the interview the camera was right there. But now there is footage from above so they could get Kevin and you both in the frame. They had used Kevin. Used both of us. Feeling sick to the stomach watching it. The whole thing set up and distorted and designed to make you uncomfortable. Because they didn't think we were a serious team. Donegal were just a flash in the pan. It was unforgivable. It was just underhanded. Because we were nobody.

We looked that way, too, playing Laois. First game of the year. Cobwebs and creaks, all that. But still. Electing to go man-to-man all over the pitch. Just to see. The boys didn't believe in it. They didn't want it. Too much of a shift in such a short space of time. Standing on the sideline on a damp spring day watching a disaster unfold. All at sea. Down 2-08 to 0-4 at home! Scramble a few goals at the end but it was a lesson. A good lesson. Afterwards the boys are more wedded to the game plan than ever. It doesn't matter what anybody says now. This is the way for us. This is our approach. Vowing that day not to do another interview for TG4. Several phone calls made in the months afterwards. A letter written. Absolute garbage of an excuse. They knew what they did. They knew they did it because Donegal was a nothing team. But now we have beaten

Kerry in an All-Ireland quarter-final. People are beginning to see us in a new light. What if Donegal aren't pretending?

What if they believe they can win it all?

That is what we believe.

Into the special time in Donegal now. All through the county. The county pulsing. The summer blooming and flags everywhere and everyone, everyone behind the boys now. Everyone seeing that they are a special crew. That they are going for this. That they know no fear now. That they could have no more respect for the jersey. Living everything we promised in Downings like a motto.

Them people are waiting for a team for a long, long time. They are waiting for a team to be proud of and we are going to be that fucking team.

The people getting that. Eyes lighting up when they see the boys. Back slaps. People getting a lift just from being close to them. This is their team as much as it is the players' team. This is the point. This is the thing of it. A song, everywhere, overnight. Some boy from Kilcar called Rory Gallagher out in Ibiza or somewhere on a beach with a guitar. 'Jimmy's Winning Matches'. It's catchy. It's too catchy. One of those songs that, once heard ... Do you like it? Doesn't matter: you are going to be hearing a lot of it. Huge interest in Cork now. Donegal people confident in a way that is foreign to us. Hearing this word, 'revolution'. Staying away from all that. Driving from the house to training and back again. Very weird to see your face on gables, on T-shirts. In a beret. Like seeing somebody else.

The boys in full flight at training now. Completely uninhibited in the way they express themselves, hungry to improve, to push themselves. Moments looking at them when they were slick and confident and delivering at phenomenal pace. Refereeing a game and allowing yourself to step outside it for a couple of seconds, just to soak it all up and take in the scene and the feeling of everyone trying to achieve something that is seldom achieved in life. These nights are precious. These nights will only go on for a very short time in all of our lives. This is what playing for an All-Ireland is actually like. Summer evenings at training; the stadium empty and the players soaring. Very humbling to be in the midst of that honesty of effort and that attitude. To be so close to that energy. Their confidence climbing. Everybody thinking about the next game, the next goal, working towards it.

The stakes very high now. Cork. An All-Ireland semi-final. No easy path. Them or us. Cork are going to want this bad. At least this game is all about football. No history between us and Cork. This is just a game of football against an exceptionally good team. They cruised through Kildare with thirteen points to spare the day we beat Kerry. All-Ireland champions in 2010 and favourites to win it this year. One shot. A moment in our life that would not come around again. Studying every DVD late at night, taking notes, reading newspaper interviews looking for anything. Thinking about Cork and finally whittling it down to a checklist of what we felt they liked to do.

Cork liked to stretch the football wide early in their attack. That left room for runners coming through. When they attacked down the wing, they liked to kick the ball into the same corner, which was unusual. Most teams liked to kick across to the other corner. A traditional team, getting long high ball into the square early on and testing full backs. Excellent at getting ahead of the ball. Rarely went down the middle on their kick-outs – even though they had huge men scattered all over the field. Highly accurate on free kicks. No sweeper. They would allow us room to play inside. We could play Patrick, Michael and Colm up front.

A nugget of gold, then, in a newspaper interview with one of the Cork players. He mentions that Cork would need their running game against Donegal, with fellas coming off the shoulder and breaking tackles and not giving away silly possession. He said that that should create scoring chances. Something about the way he said it made you feel it was true: that this is what's coming down the track. Cork wanted to keep the ball, maybe try to draw us out, recycle it and then run at us with power. Mark McHugh as sweeper was mentioned as well. They wouldn't kick stupid ball deep. The last thing that was mentioned was that Conor Counihan was encouraging them to have a go at training if they were through on goal. Not to be afraid to miss. So they'll shoot on sight. And we need to make sure that we are ready for that. We need to be sharp and tight all day. Everything in the article was what we had been planning for. Makes us feel as if there will be no surprises in Croke Park.

The day is hot. And both teams just go at it from the off. The Cork boys moving the ball so well and looking really well coached, and they rack up a few scores that make you shiver a wee bit. So much quality in their play. Going to have our hands full today. There's a difference between knowing what they're going to do and preventing them doing it. So difficult to contain their movement. Knocking over excellent points with ease and our boys responding. Like the old heavyweight fights: big honest hits and very open. Nine points each or nine–eight at half time. Not sure. Didn't matter. Saying in the dressing room, 'Cork couldn't have played any better, boys. There's only so many times that people can be repelled, you know.' Starting to get a grip on that towards the end of the first half. Just stick to the game plan to keep asking the questions. Offensively we are there. Defensively we need more. Need to be able to squeeze them more intensively.

'Thirty-five minutes. Thirty-five minutes away from the All-Ireland final. We are thirty-five minutes away from the All-Ireland Senior Football Championship Final. How many teams have been there only to find that is as close as they ever came? How painful must that be? How long does a player think about that disappointment? Forever? So do the right thing, boys. Face the challenge down. Be true to yourselves.'

Running ourselves into the ground. We tackle. We chase them. We are relentless. Rory Kavanagh comes off with exhaustion. Boys going down all over the pitch cramping. Frank McGlynn the same. Hardly able to talk when it is over. Then the same as in the Kerry game. A few seconds of distraction and everything changes. Donegal boys keeping the ball for the sake of it. Playing it around. Something that we never do, just keeping the fucking ball, flicking it around and toying with the other team. Trying to demoralise them. Trying to be clever.

On the sideline watching. That is not the fucking way to go. Keep the ball, keep it sharp, keep it moving. Wait for the option. When the opening comes, attack the space and look to score. Now our supporters are joining in. Cheering every pass. The players will respond to that. Human nature. We are vulnerable. We could get caught. And now it is happening. David Walsh carries the ball into traffic. It is not David's fault. It is the team's fault. Cork have it. They look for the long early ball. Just like they promised they would. And we are out of position. A long ball towards Colm O'Neill. Goal. The game uncertain again. A jittery minute or two until the whistle goes.

26 August: Donegal 0-16 Cork 1-11

Just like Kerry, the last few minutes means it takes a while to sink in. The end alive with danger and it should never have been. We'd have struggled to live with ourselves if we had blown this game. Had played so well. Defensive play of the highest order. Moved the ball just the way they have moved it in Ballybofey night after night: cleanly and with urgency and intelligence.

Hugging the boys and smiling, but inside is relief for a few seconds. And then, slowly, elation. The All-Ireland final next. Keep saying that to yourself the whole way down the road. We are in the All-Ireland final. Everyone in high spirits by the time we get to the Harcourt Hotel. Balmy evening. Street crawling with supporters in Donegal shirts of all vintage. Still a few 1992 tops about the place. Mingling with players now. All of us in this brilliant, unexpected place. The players living their dreams. On the bus and beers and the usual debate: Letterkenny or Donegal Town? They decide to head for the Abbey.

After midnight by the time the bus pulls into the Diamond and the place is in full swing. All the pubs busy and traditional bands on in many. Skip into one of the bars off the Diamond for a quiet one or two and a chat and then on to the Abbey to the nightclub. Tried to go out as a team on celebration nights. Hadn't eaten after the game at all and so leave the disco at around three in the morning and wander off to the chip shop. The street as busy as the disco. Night still warm. Look in the door of the takeaway. Neil McGee and David Walsh and Leo and Brick Molloy among the crowd, chatting away, waiting for their quarter-pounders and chips. Standing back and looking at them through the window of the takeaway for a few seconds. Remembering what they had been at a few hours earlier in Croke Park. And now in the crowd in the early hours. With their snack boxes and Cokes. All of them laughing. Perfect.

How many of these big championship nights have you lived through? Might never have happened. A cold day up the Rock in Ballyshannon. Christmas 1991. Home for the holidays on a crowded flight from Boston. Just for two weeks. Thinking of staying in Boston. Giving it a go. Nothing at home. Working with a construction firm there and getting on well. The winter sparkling cold. Going along to see the Bruins play ice hockey, the Celtics play basketball. Not long back home when someone phones to leave a message about a Donegal trial. A challenge game. In the dressing room then with players you look up to. Joyce. Anthony. Martin Gavigan. Friendly enough, but not paying much heed. Used to seeing young fellas come and go. Marked by Donal Reid in this game and getting a few touches. Finish up scoring 1-3 and walking off the field delighted to have scored a goal against Gary Walsh. Thinking: This is nearly enough. If this is as close as I get to Donegal, it's not so bad. Getting showered and heading down towards the gate in Father Tierney Park. McEniff standing there with a sheepskin coat on him. Thanks for that, Brian. His right arm reaching out to halt me.

— Did you enjoy that?

— Yeah. It was great.

— Well, what do you think?

Not sure what to say. Not sure what he means.

— Would you be interested in joining the panel?

Heart pounding. Everything changing right there on the spot. Boston melting. Vanishing. Return ticket in the bin.

— That would be ... thanks very much, Brian.

Walking to the car dizzy. Trying to absorb it. Adrenaline coursing through me on the road over to Glenties. Can't wait to tell my family. Jim McGuinness. On the Donegal senior football panel. Can't believe it.

That was the start. In for training in January with Mark Crossan. Brian Tuohy, the All-Ireland U-21 captain in 1987, was leaving. A class player. Starting at the bottom. A debut game against Tipperary. Playing even though you were ill. Doing nothing much wrong but nothing much right either. The first lesson you learn. Don't play unless you are right. Barry McGowan, the best out-and-out ball player on the team, stood out that way. Unless he was absolutely perfect, he didn't play. The senior boys so welcoming. Rooming with Martin Gavigan for league games. Telling me I belonged here. You are part of it now.

Not knowing then how blessed I was to be here, in this year. No sign that this year would turn out to be magical. Beaten in the quarter-final of the league by Dublin. Charlie Redmond giving his city smile and telling Noel Hegarty: 'It's not over 'til the fat lady sings.' Scraping past Cavan after a replay in the championship.

Then a showdown in the dressing room after a win over Fermanagh. Martin McHugh standing up and saying that training wasn't hard enough. That we needed to be fitter. Into Ballybofey on Tuesday night and Anthony Harkin, our trainer, giving us what was asked for. Two hours of punishment. Four hundreds. One hundred-metre agility runs. Fifty-metre sprints. Over and over. An instant, massive uplift in training. Running us until men were dropping. That set the tone. All summer. Nineteen years old. Feeling like you belonged but feeling like a kid too. Watching a group of men trying to get over the line and win their All-Ireland before it was too late. Up close to brilliant players. Martin McHugh. Martin Gavigan, a phenomenal athlete. Joyce McMullan playing a modern-day half forward role before it was even invented. This attitude coming out in them. Cussedness. Toughness. Beating Derry in the Ulster final with fourteen men. John Cunningham, our captain that day, sent off for nothing. Ulster champions anyhow. A siege of beer up in Killybegs. Starting out with the seniors but joining the minor boys who had lost their final. Declan Boyle and Odhrán McBride and that gang. Closer in age

to them anyhow. Training so sharp. The sessions heightened by
Anthony Harkin week after week. Everybody skating over the
grass. Everybody enjoying the feeling of their fitness increasing
by the week. Michael Jack O'Donnell, the *Donegal Democrat*
photographer, there on the sideline for all the training sessions.
Michael would give you a lift back to Glenties. So tired that
you would be out cold in the front seat by the time he was
in Fintown. Shattered. Beating Mayo in a terrible All-Ireland
semi-final. But beating them. Into an All-Ireland final.

Madness in the county. Margo brings a song out. Into Magees
to get fitted for suits. The dressing room musty now with tension
and apprehension. Everybody wanting to play. An A versus B game
in Donegal town on the Saturday. All the boys sitting in the car
park with their car doors open listening to the radio commentary
of Michael Carruth boxing for gold at the Barcelona Olympics.
Nobody saying a word, and then this proud, inspired mood in
the dressing room. An Irishman had won gold. Eight days out
from the All-Ireland. McEniff just letting the boys go at it in the
game. Fists flying. McEniff keeping the whistle quiet. Joyce and
Donal Reid, good friends, boxing one another. Brian Murray
trying to separate them. A few minutes later, Brian Murray and
Anthony Molloy squaring up in the middle of the field. Two boys
who'd been the Donegal midfield for a decade. Fists closed and
staring each other down and swinging at each other. Violence
in the air. A wee while later and John Joe Doherty comes across
to cut out a ball that Declan Bonner is going for. Both of them
completely committed to winning the ball. Neither is going to
yield an inch. JJ catches Declan full on. Nails him. Declan is out
cold on the grass. Watching then as JJ just looks at Declan lying
there. He doesn't go to check on him but walks straight back
over to his corner back position, puts his hands on his hips and
stares straight ahead up the pitch. As if to say: This is my fucking

patch. I'm waiting for the next ball. Thing is, JJ wasn't in the team then. He was a substitute. When Martin Shovlin had to give up his place on the morning of the All-Ireland, McEniff gave JJ the nod. In your mind the reason McEniff chose him was because of that moment. JJ saying: I don't give a fuck. I am ready. And JJ was tight. A strong man and a good footballer. Manus Boyle in for Tommy Ryan when the team for the final is named. Tommy had lit up Ulster for us. Carried us. Faded against Mayo. And just this sense that Manus would get the call. So tough on Tommy. Manus would not be fazed by it. Manus was Manus. Would score 0-9. Would get man of the match. Would shrug. Would laugh. They were raw boys, all of them. Aching for an All-Ireland medal.

McEniff bringing us to the dog racing at Shelbourne on the Saturday night and then instructing the bus driver to go down O'Connell Street on the way home. Wanting us to see the lights and the flags and the Donegal people on the streets. Wanting them to see our bus. Eleven o'clock at night and the city on the tear. Chaos once they copped it was the Donegal bus. The boys bouncing in the door of the hotel. Pure McEniff. Showing us what it meant. Look at your people, boys. Shrewd. Persuasion. Standing at Mass earlier that Saturday evening, in a track suit and a pair of trainers, listening. No, day-dreaming about football. And this thought: I feel so light. Feel as if I am floating off the ground. Ready. And I was a substitute. Playing well but never in the reckoning. Happy to play hard and watch and learn. Knowing the senior boys felt the same, though. Walking on air. And that was the lesson to be taken from 1992. On the weekend of the All-Ireland final, Donegal were ready. We were prepared.

At home late at night. Yvonne had moved us on the day when you went to Croke Park to watch Dublin and Mayo. Moved everything from Creeslough to the new house in Glenties. Here now a few days later. New house scent. Getting the television set up. Looking for the Mayo–Dublin game on the recorder. No sign of it. Not thinking. Saying, 'Ah, Yvonne, did you not tape the game for me?' Yvonne looking at me and saying slowly, 'Oh God, sorry, Jim ... what was I at that day? Oh yeah, I was moving house.' The pair of us laughing. Mayo had beaten – no, destroyed – Dublin for most of the All-Ireland semi-final. Donegal versus Mayo. Nobody saw that coming. Sixty-one years since Mayo's last All-Ireland. A fierce hunger in that county. A need. A big county. A west of Ireland county. An Atlantic coast county. Much like ourselves. Late at night in the office. Slowly writing down a plan to try to beat Mayo.

1   We use the long diagonal ball.
2   The running game – we have to have a defensive shape driving forward.
3   Sweeper to play between the middle and right corner position because a lot of their key players – like Kevin McLoughlin and Aidan O'Shea – are left-footed and will kick across themselves.
4   Double up on Aidan O'Shea's boot because he's their most accurate passer.
5   A fast defensive shape. We hustle to recover our defensive shape. Because any time we had played them, they struggled to break us down once we had that in place. So we couldn't let them transition.
6   Coach kick-outs. Big Neil our go-to man.
7   Recycle the ball at pace and avoid contact in the middle third because that is where all the action happens for them. Once we get through that, the pitch will open up for us.
8   Coach breaking hard on their kick-outs.
9   We want a lot of dink ball in the second half because we will push them back if we execute what we want to do.

10 Our shot-to-score ratio is sixty per cent and we have scored
17.5 points on average. We conceded an average of 12 points
and Mayo's average was fifty-three per cent.

So if we did our job, we should win the game.

Folding the piece of paper up: This would be what we
would go with. Live or die by it. There were goals for us in this
final. Maybe three goals. So we practise those. Mayo will not
change. They are firm in their convictions. They will not play
a sweeper. No matter who marked Michael he would cause
them trouble on the edge of the square. If he got the right
ball. So we practise. We practise for that. Running hard, fast
lines to the edge of the 45 and looking to deliver anywhere
from about seven metres out, where we would get premium
accuracy. Some of the boys better than others. Anthony, Karl,
Daniel, Rory, Dermot, Frank and Leo are hitting the sweet
spot. Practise that one delivery for maybe nine or ten hours
before the final. Worried deep down during those last few
sessions that one of them will roll an ankle or get a crack in
the ribs or something that will prevent them from playing.
Nothing could be crueller. 1992. Coming through the door
of the Burlington on the morning of the final. McEniff and
Martin Shovlin coming the other way. Tears on Martin's face.
Shocked by that because there was none tougher, none more
taciturn. Had his fitness test. Couldn't play. Just a terrible
thing. So thanking God as we all leave the field after the final
training session. Thank God we got through that.

Home always an escape. A distraction. The one place you
don't get asked about Donegal football. Just one question from
Yvonne before the final.

— How do you feel about the game?

Thinking about that.

— I feel good about it. We are in a good place.

A good place. But the wrong place, on All-Ireland final day. Arrive in Croke Park to discover we haven't been given 'our' dressing room. Presumptuous, maybe. Since when did Donegal boys have tenants' rights in Croke Park? Still. The boys had been in the same dressing room ever since the Kildare quarter-final in 2011. Felt like home. And there was a Croke Park man there who was good to us. After the Dublin semi-final, coming in and nodding and saying to us:

— Ye'll be back.

— Hope so, hey. Hope so.

— Ye will. That's for sure.

Always looked after us. Sticking his head around the door. Do you need anything? Any more water? So this is a bit ... disorienting. A wee bit of a stand-off. Why can't we have that room? Sure it's empty. No budging. In we go. The lay-out is the opposite of what we are used to. A mirror image: the showers should be there, not here. A minor thing, but it is different, so you worry a wee bit. A rumble from above. Cheering. Music through the loudspeakers. Boys leafing through the match programmes. Sitting back with headphones on. Slowly getting changed. Lacing boots with extra care. Night before the 1992 All-Ireland a boy came in from Adidas. They supplied the boots for the final that year. He went around and collected everyone's boots and spent a few hours whitening the three stripes with Tipp-Ex so that they would show up on the television. Couldn't believe this. Wide-eyed at it. This was big-time stuff.

Huddle in when the boys are ready. No big speech. No roaring or emotional stuff. Just a simple guideline: Everybody doing the same thing at pace all the time. That is how we will play. With an intense, hard edge. Trust the game plan with our life. Trust our teammates. With our life. Aim for the perfect performance. Do what we need to do.

Michael talking then. Taking up on those points and addressing them clearly and driving home the importance of putting them into action. On the field. In the All-Ireland final. Absolute silence. Boys are absorbing every word he says. Eighty thousand people above us, but this room is locked, sealed. All ours. Hard to believe this guy is only twenty-three. Such presence.

Michael finishes. The boys tear out of the door. All thirty of them. Like a gust of fucking wind. The support staff vanish too. Rory and Maxi are gone. Kevin Moran's gone. All want to see the team running onto the field. By yourself. In an empty dressing room. On All-Ireland final day. Thirty-five minutes to throw-in. The room so quiet. Clothes on pegs. Bottles of water abandoned. Quiet. Peaceful almost. Deep breath now. This is it, so. Time to leave. A series of wee corridors before you get to the main tunnel. Narrow corridors; painted, lights overhead. Nobody about at all. Strange for those few seconds. Could just head through an exit door and walk away. Like a dream. Thousands of people to be heard but none to be seen. Turning then and there is the mouth of the tunnel and the sky above and the grass perfect. Immaculate. Heart pounding now. Begin to jog. Like you are a player. Old habits. Fix the strap of your watch on your wrist as you move. A distraction. Look up and there, just feet away, is the Sam Maguire sitting on a plinth directly in front of you.

All by itself.

Breathe in sharply.

The reason we are all here, but you don't expect to see it. See him. Heart takes a jump. Reminds you of that moment when the children were born. Knowing for nine months that you have a baby coming but not understanding that until the moment she or he is there with you both.

The cup is gleaming.

Sunlight bouncing off it.

It looks fabulous.

Must have caught the boys off-guard too when they ran out. Nobody told us it would be there. The beauty of the GAA. Find out the small details for yourself.

The warm-up routine. A huddle. A last huddle. Repeat the message. Look into their eyes. 3.26 p.m. No turning back. A long way from Dunfanaghy now. Then leaving the boys to themselves on the field. In their circle. Always like that moment when it is just the players and they are really tight. We are walking for the sideline but they are on the field. They are independent. Starting to play for their All-Ireland medals at that moment. Ceremony. Red carpet. President Higgins waving. An eye on the watch. Not long now. Mayo boys look cool. Confident. Anything we have forgotten? Anything not covered? Green and yellow all over the stadium. How did we get so many tickets?

The parade. Nothing to be doing just now. Waiting. Proud. Excited. Impatient. 'Amhrán na bhFiann'. Mark would love this day. Charles would love this day. Referee bends down to pick up the ball. A massive pent-up collective roar as soon as he touches it. From Mayo and Donegal people. From all along the western seaboard and from Boston and Chicago and New York. All desperate for this. All certain: This is our day.

Whose day? Read the boys' thoughts in the first few passages of play. Look at what they are looking for. Three times the boys look for the long ball in the very first minute. Makes you happy. Switched on. Thinking about it. Looking for it. Still. Not expecting what comes next. Not so soon. Two minutes in. Kav driving forward with the ball towards centre field. Ryan cutting across him, but Karl is moving out along the wing on the Cusack Stand side. Rory plays him. Looking out of the corner of my eye.

Michael down in front of goal, Colm drifting wide and Patrick pulling out, so Michael is alone. Back on the training field at Johnstown House now. Set-up is exactly right. Karl has Séamus O'Shea in front of him and goes to power past him on the outside but then jinks inside. He is clear. This is on. This is fucking on. This is down to the quality of the kick now. Michael signalling. Karl looking and then dipping his head to pull the trigger. As soon as the ball leaves his foot, as soon as it is travelling, the work is done. How many of these has Michael converted in the past fortnight? Hundreds. He claims the ball. Powers inside. The shot ferocious. Unstoppable. Goal. Three minutes later another attack. Leo on the burst and a long hand pass into Patrick's path. Patrick curling a shot which falls off the post. Colm watching it, reading the line of the ball and moving across and scooping it in one movement and then rolling it into the net. Two goals in five minutes. Then Karl attacking again and Michael and Colm working this reverse hand pass move. Their thing. Worked it on the training pitch and came to you with it one night. Check it out. Could work. Practised it night after night and Colm is through again. David Clarke saves.

A ridiculous start. You don't even dream of a start like that. And this evil little thought then: If we lose this final from this position, it will be the biggest disaster ever. Banish that. Don't let that in. Mayo settle after that. Our boys in control but slowly becoming careless, moving away from what we had spoken about. Just three points up at the break. Into the dressing room. Angry with them for the first time all summer. Actually angry.

— Do not fuck it up today. Of all days.

Hard and down on them and once you open that door and invite that in, it can be difficult to return to where you want. But. An All-Ireland final. There is no second chance. Stick to the game plan. See it through.

Fifty minutes gone in the match and still only three points up. Those goals skewed our approach a bit. Some of the boys thinking: Jesus, let's just get it into Michael and he will do the rest. Kicking from too far out. Our passes hopeful, inaccurate. Three points and it is Russian roulette. A break and a goal and Mayo would have the momentum. Time keeps moving. Big Neil comes through and Frank slips him a pass and he taps it over. Five up. That should be enough. Photographers beginning to gather near where we are standing. This line comes to you from the 1992 All-Ireland video. Must have seen and heard it a thousand times that winter, at home and in the bars. The end of the game and the stewards are gathering near McEniff. The commentator saying: 'Like the undertakers coming into the wake house.' Hear that in your mind now. Time is nearly up. Richie Feeney not far from us, firing a point for Mayo under no real pressure. But not long now. It is going to happen. A new sound coming down from the stands. An anxious, restless kind of murmur. Everyone realising the day is done. It has been settled. Both sets of supporters preparing to win, preparing to lose. Just a few seconds left. Impatient now just to hear it.

The final whistle.

23 September: Donegal 2-11 Mayo 0-13

Everything quiet. Like a mute button on the world. Faces: eyes wide and saying things but not hearing the words or sounds. Running onto the field. Everyone moving about in slow motion. Cameras flashing. Is this happening? Have we done it? Slowly making sense of things. The two McGee boys down the pitch together. Embracing. They have their moments, those two, but they made their way to each other anyhow. Finding each of the boys and hugging them. Moving through the field. Heart thumping. Slowly realising. This is real. Incredible happiness welling up inside now. Yvonne and the kids seated down a bit from the Donegal bench. Jogging down to see them. Hugging Yvonne and all of a sudden this face appears over your shoulder.

Gogie. A friend from Philadelphia. Haven't laid eyes on him since the 1999 championship. Had tracked you running down to Yvonne and made his way down the steps.

— Je-sus, where did you come out of?

Laughing. Rushed plans to catch up later. A minute with Yvonne and then being pulled elsewhere. Michael going up the steps. Michael Murphy. All-Ireland winning captain. This is happening. Stay on the pitch. No interest in going near the cup. This is for the players. Waiting then for the moment until Michael gets to raise the Sam Maguire.

Twenty years after Anthony.

Sam's for the Hills.

Second Donegal man ever.

So proud of Michael. Thinking about that evening of the U-21 final in Cavan. That penalty crashing against the crossbar. That heartache. Had that experience made him a better player? You know how much that had hurt him.

The supporters stay off the pitch. 1992 was bedlam. It was a crush. Happy, but a crush. Now the players own the field. They have the cup and they get to do their lap of honour. Jimmy in my arms. We stand back, the pair of us, about forty metres as the boys trot around the field. What a sight. The boys framed by the crowd and the sun coming across the pitch and streamers scattered across the field and the light is dreamy, doesn't seem real. Like a painting come to life.

Jesus, it's some pitch.

Can't get back to the dressing room. Takes forever to leave the pitch and then escorted through to do television and radio interviews. How does it feel? How does it feel? Feels fantastic.

Into the auditorium for the newspapers. Sitting there at a table in this little theatre, the seating staggered above you. Faces looking down. Someone says that the journalist who wrote the book with the Kevin Cassidy stuff is in the room. Feel uncomfortable. Can't have double standards here. That book had been upsetting. It contained inaccuracies. The whole episode had threatened our entire project. Hypocritical now to just sit here in celebration. Felt wrong. Look about the room. Don't know the man to see. Had never spoken. Leave the room and explain to the GAA press officer. I am not doing any interviews while he is there. Leave it up to them. Hoping they will say: That's grand, away you go. Just want to get to the dressing room. The journalist is asked to leave and does so.

Not a nice moment. Not upset now but heading in that direction. Shouldn't have to deal with this today of all days. But can't be a hypocrite. That whole thing could have destroyed us. A few questions then about that. Explaining yourself until your patience gives out. More questions about the game, about the day. How does it feel? It feels fantastic.

And it does. Heart soaring, even in this room.

The questions end. Leave. Time is your own. Finally. The corridors are empty. The stadium a ghost town now. The dressing room is empty. Again. The boys have been and gone. Shampoo and sprays in the air. Michael is still there, getting ready to leave. You are on your own. Time for a quick shower. The water cold by now. How much water do they go through there on All-Ireland final day? All those meals. All those teas and coffees. Too late to go upstairs to the lounge for a beer. The bus rumbling and most of the boys on board when you get out. The Sam Maguire up the front. Look at that. Daniel O'Donnell waiting outside the bus. Saying he is booked to head to America for a concert on Monday evening. And it is killing him because he doesn't want to miss the homecoming. Wants to be in Donegal. The pair of you laughing. You'll be more than welcome if you can make it. Beers cracked open on the bus. Mood is high. Giddy. Sixth class school tour giddy. All of us so, so proud. We have done this. Bus pulls out of the tunnel and up into the street. Light of evening beginning to fade. Huge crowd outside the hotel on Jones Road. All cheering, fists raised, smiling, pointing phones. Boys peering out of the window. Sam Maguire at the front of the Donegal bus. Best feeling in the world. All you ever wanted for this team. This moment. Kevin, our driver, takes us down O'Connell Street. Slowly. Supporters stopping on the street and others tumbling out of the pubs. As if word is spreading seconds ahead of us. Gathering then to form a guard of honour. And applauding the bus. Many, many people in Mayo colours standing there too. Applauding us. Humbling, that grace. Their good manners. Hope they have their day soon. Hope they have their day. The bus moving over O'Connell Bridge. Away from Croke Park. Tourists in the city. Students outside Trinity College. Guys doing art on the pavement. A life beyond the All-Ireland. Still. Feels like we own the city at this moment. The Burlington decorated in green and yellow. A private room reserved for us. Just for forty minutes or so. Get drinks. The Sam Maguire sitting in the middle of us. Tell the boys what I feel.

— I'm very proud of all of you.

Just ourselves for that little while. Half the county in the foyer of the hotel. Nearly two thousand people for the function. Boys drift off to get themselves suited up. Time speeds up now. So many people to talk to. New shoes too tight, so walk around the room in evening suit and socks. Floating. Find a wee room with Yvonne and a few friends for late drinks. Must be four in the morning. A few hours' sleep at dawn. Light with exhaustion as soon as our heads hit the pillow. Instant, happy, pure sleep.

Breakfast and more press interviews. Outside it is raining steadily. Some of the boys are back at the bar by noon. Others may not have left. Over to Crumlin Children's Hospital with Karl and Michael and Leo. Over and back in the back of a Garda van. The cup sitting there. Strange moment. Staff in the hospital are wonderful. Could spend the day chatting with the kids. A schedule is taking shape. The plan is to leave Dublin at half past one. Everyone mad to get home, but a fair few boys getting settled in the bar too. The rain lashing down. Someone rounds all the boys up. No small feat. Bags on board and onto the bus.

Leaving for Donegal.

Once we hit the suburbs, a huge lull. Mind and body in overdrive for the past fortnight. Quietness for a short time. This is the calm. The calm in 1992 all over again. Went by train then. Train to Sligo and the run of the bar the whole way down. Crowds gathered at every station even though the train was express. Waving flags and standing in wee clusters just to salute the team. A really lovely gesture. A bus then from Mac Diarmada station in Sligo down the road to Bundoran. Brian and Anthony walking the Sam Maguire across the bridge outside Bundoran, across the county boundary. Into Donegal with the Sam Maguire for the first time.

Ever.

A huge crowd for us in Cavan. Another stop. Energy coming back into us all now. Fearing half the boys will just disappear into the night and not make it home at all. Heading on towards Donegal. Party mode now. Beers going and hooking iPods up to the sound system on the bus. This one tune. 'I Follow Rivers'. Someone had it and it kind of became the anthem of our summer. On the bus. Late at night. After winning. A Garda escort as far as the border and then the PSNI are waiting to take over. Out for a quick photograph. Garda and Northern Irish police and the Sam Maguire. All those stories about going North during the Troubles. The hold-ups. The nerves. A far cry. A lot has changed.

Keen now to get there. Counting down the miles to Pettigo. The lights. The faces. The roar. This furnace of a roar. Overwhelming. This is the beginning. Days merging with nights merging with days. The homecoming. A procession. Peeling around the corner now on the way into Donegal Town where the Opel garage used to be. Thousands of people outside Dom Breslin's bar. So many people who couldn't even get up the town. Scary to see so many people in such a small enclosure. Too many people. The bus inching through people. Terrifying for Kevin, the driver. You are concerned at that minute. If anything ...

Yvonne and the family upstairs in one of the rooms in the Abbey overlooking the Diamond. Too chaotic to bring the wee ones out. Probably the best seat in the house anyhow. Inch by inch we move through the people. The rain thumping down and nobody noticing. Out onto the stage. It is crowded. Daniel is here after all. America bit the dust. Speeches and cheers. Warmest feeling you could imagine. 'Destination Donegal'. The night spins off.

Tuesday morning comes and the party does not stop. At eleven in the morning the Abbey bar is at full throttle. Normal life suspended.

The homecoming. One town into the next. Rounding up the boys becomes a miracle of organisation. Not sure who is doing it. It is a mystery but somehow we lose nobody. Some boys get a few hours' sleep. Some get none at all. Moving from one town to the next with whatever few clothes are thrown in bags and sleeping wherever. Hotel rooms. At the bar. Not at all.

Evolve, this clothing company which had sponsored the team, had sent you on a few outfits. As manager. So you wouldn't be looking shambolic on the stage. A pair of jeans, a white shirt, silver jacket and shoes for the Tuesday morning. Feel halfway presentable on the bus. The boys shuffle on. Colm a bit worse for wear. Bleary head as he comes up the steps of the bus and looks at you and does a double take then.

— Je-sus, Jim! You're looking very well.

As if to say: You're cheating here. You're showing us up. Half compliment, half outrage. Bundoran and Ballyshannon packed. On a cavalcade now. St Naul's, Killybegs, Kilcar, Glen, Ardara. Off and on the bus and the boys mad to be in a pub. Any pub. Anywhere. Too late for the planned stop in Glenswilly, so it's called off. Annoyed by that because it is Michael's club; the captain's club. That night is spent in Letterkenny. Fifteen thousand people there alone. A wee room reserved in Voodoo. The boys let off steam and next thing it is eight in the morning. A pattern is established. The boys absolutely hanging in the morning. Trying to get breakfast and find any kind of half-decent clothes. Sleepy on the bus and a few smart comments. A few tins cracked open around noon. Then a bit of music. Then the craic starts up again and a crescendo at about seven in the evening and drunk again. Ready for another big night.

This going on for a full week. Day and night for a week. All about getting home. To their towns. That is their moment. Boys from their local clubs sitting up the front of the bus for that part of the journey. In Creeslough, six players from St Michael's got to walk up the main street of the town with the Sam Maguire. Club only came into existence twenty years before. A sad hour in Termon, Michael Boyle's town, because the club was mourning Andrew Duffy, who had died in a drowning accident in the Grand Canal just after the Cork match. Everybody sombre on the bus leaving there for Dunfanaghy. A wee bit apprehensive about Gweedore, Kevin Cassidy's home club. Just not sure how you might be received. Neil McGee leaving the hotel in Dunfanaghy early in the morning to go into Letterkenny so he could buy a new outfit. Because he knew we were headed to his home. Said so much, that. That pride thing. That respect. Three days on the beer but now coming into his town as an All-Ireland champion. He respected the moment. Wanted to look his best. Neil sits up front on the journey over. Joking about how he had to get away from the pandemonium down the back. That he wanted to be in halfway decent shape. Late afternoon and Mount Errigal in shadow but the sky around it on fire. Angle ourselves and the Sam Maguire and somehow manage to take a wonderful photograph of the cup with Errigal in the background as we pass. The McGee boys' grandmother waiting in a chair outside her house on the main street in Gweedore. Ask someone what age she is. A right age. The two boys bring the cup over to her and bend down and make a fuss. The reception all through the town is extraordinary. So warm. So grateful. Thanks. Thanks for this. Over and over. Walking down the town towards the pitch. Finding an ambulance with a busy crew when we arrive. A woman had broken her ankle in the crowd. In the back of the ambulance with Michael and the cup and this poor woman smiling through her pain for photographs.

The Gweedore GAA club crowded with people. A heavy blanket of people out before us. The club officials welcoming us. Getting up and saying my few words. Neil then. Very direct. Very solemn. Catches you off-guard. Saying thanks to you for everything you have done and a lot of emotion in his voice and turning and looking directly at you as he speaks. One of the toughest men anyone could meet. Choking up a bit listening to Neil. Feeling emotional about it all for the first time since we won it. There are different kinds of applause. Polite. Enthusiastic. But this clapping and cheering is from somewhere else, somewhere deep and going back generations in Gweedore. A powerful noise.

Then Eamon stands up and speaks. People hanging on his every word. What a trip with Eamon. All of it flashing before you as Eamon speaks. Back to the days in autumn 2011 when you got the job and wondering if you would be able to rein Eamon in and get the best out of him. Asking him up to the house. Living in Creeslough at the time. A long chat. Where we could go. What it would entail. A weights programme. Talking him through everything. Shaking hands and feeling happy as Eamon headed off into the evening. The phone rings two weeks later with bad news. Eamon had headed for a pub after he left the house. Went on a tear and ended up in Dungloe on the Friday. The weights programme found on the floor of a bookies. Missed a club game. Gatecrashed a wedding. A fair old go of it by anyone's standards. The phone call came just before our first training session. Like someone had presented you with a first test.

A choice. Old Donegal – New Donegal.

If Eamon shows up after that, then what has changed? If he is dismissed, half the boys could walk with him. On the phone to Eamon. Denies it happened. Fair enough. Check sources and make phone calls. Ring Eamon back. Before you speak, he says: 'Listen, Jim. I fucked up. It won't happen again.' And having to say then, 'It won't, Eamon. It won't happen again because it is over. I told you in the house I couldn't be in this position. I like you a lot as a person. I want you on this team. I wish we were going in a different direction here. And I wish there was a different solution here, but if I don't deal with this then I lose the squad before I even start.' Eamon says, 'I understand.' Anne, his mother, phoning a few days later. Talking for an hour. 'I would love to have him on this team. But how can I justify this? Everything – the talk about trust and loyalty – will sound like a joke.' Anne saying, 'Okay, fair enough.'

That is late October 2010. Another phone call in May. The league over and getting ready for the championship. Anne calls again. Is there any way we could reconsider things?

None of this was to hurt anyone or to punish Eamon. Thinking: If Anne is ringing, then they are talking. And that means Eamon is keen. It means he wants this. We speak on the phone and this time I visit Eamon in his house. Neil is there watching telly. Staying out of it. Anne and Eamon and you talking. Really honestly. Really solemnly. Serious feeling. Knowing that Eamon would do whatever it takes to get back in. We agree a programme, set boundaries. He turns up. Welcomed back. No bones made about it. Just hanging in there with the training because it was heavy, heavy going when he came back. Surviving through pure footballing ability. On the bench. In the substitutes. Earning his time. And living so quiet. Seeing no minutes and then calling him down in the All-Ireland quarter-final against Kildare. And he walks into a game of that magnitude and he is brilliant. He is awesome. On the front foot; brave, confident, dealing with high balls, getting his hand in to break up ball, cleaning his man out. Born for it. A first team player ever since and long through that period in his life. Watching him become what we all knew him to be. Man enough to face up to everything that was wrong in his life and to change it. And to see him up on the stage now. Holding the room. Showing his true colours.

Touring for a full week. Never sure where we will finish the night. Wherever you lay your hat. Seeing the county through this haze of celebration and well past exhaustion. Landing in Glenties on the Wednesday night. Late. Hopelessly late. After two in the morning when we get back in the town. Our turn now to be at the front of the bus and to exit. To lead the cavalcade up through the town. We are put into Leo's Jeep. In 1992 it was Leo's Jeep too, with McEniff and Michael Gallagher. Middle of the night and the whole town is open. On a black dark night. Feels strange. Faces. Some from all your life. Others strangers. Look up towards Ard Gill and Ard Patrick, where Mum and Dad's house is. The lights on in all the houses there. An old woman standing at her front door. Looking out at the excitement and framed by the hall light. In her nightdress. Waving down at us. Thinking: This is brilliant. Thinking: This is wild. But we are keeping this poor woman up.

Up the main street and stopping beside the café, at Dad's childhood house. Aunt Nelly and Zita sitting outside the door. Waiting. Getting out of the Jeep and bringing the cup over to them. Back in the Jeep and not sure what is going on. After the county championships, the homecoming was at the bridge. But around past the barracks now and through the chapel car park and through the pathway onto Chapel Brae. A lorry there and another huge crowd waiting for us. Hadn't pictured it like this on the way down the road. Could picture Donegal Town, but everything else was new. Strange. Far more people than live in Glenties. Realising later that there are All-Ireland tourists; people from other counties who just follow the cup around. Like Mark. Would have loved this. This night was cut out for him. Speeches. Late, very late by the time we get to Leo's. Into a makeshift bar that young Leo had arranged out the back. Sitting around the kitchen there. Yvonne. Leo senior. All the lads from the club that I grew up playing with. Beers delivered into us. Just chatting. Feeling as if the world is slowing down for the first time since Toni-Marie handed you that wee golf ball. Was that only ... Tuesday–Monday–Sunday–Saturday ... four days ago? World seems to have changed since then. Just a few of us sitting around a table in Glenties. Laughing. Nowhere else we would rather be.

A photograph of 1992 in the kitchen of young Leo and his sister Catherine with the Sam Maguire. Leo about four. Sitting there in front of you. An All-Ireland medal winner. The same cup a few feet away from him. Thinking: How fucking incredible is that? Twenty years of life and here we are.

Take the photo down. Getting Leo to hold it and sit in the armchair. Put the Sam Maguire beside him. Someone shouting, 'Where's Sam? Where is he?' The Sam Maguire is a person. No question. More than an object. Magical. Taking a photograph of Leo holding the 1992 photograph and the cup beside him.

Sleeping at home that night. Walking down the road the next morning to Toni-Marie's class in the primary school. Only twelve of them in the room. The wee uniform on her. The road so peaceful.

Thinking: All of this is about place. Who we are. Where we are from. Deep down in us all. Buried sometimes so deep you don't know if you can find it. The boys tapped into that. All feeling the same about Donegal. Proud of the music, the Irish language, the coast. The beauty of it. Knowing we are a big county, a football county. Knowing we need to be showing that.

People need things in life. To give people something powerful and positive and uplifting; that can change things for people. The county team can do that. It belongs to everyone. Players are the representatives. They get the cheers. And the rest. But the team belongs to everyone. Look. That's where I am from. That is my county. Look at that team. Look at how far they are willing to go. For us. For Donegal. No difference between the players and the supporters. No difference between Michael and

Leo and Papa and all those children in the towns and an old man watching on television in Frosses or somewhere in America. It is a connection. Belongs to everyone equally. A week like this just twice ever in Donegal. Sacred to us. Photographs of 1992 still everywhere in all the bars.

Photographs of 2012 now.

All-Ireland champions.

It is just a day. It goes by in a flash. But it stays, too. These are rare days. A chance to step outside of life. Outside of time. To celebrate. To stand back and to look at ourselves.

To say:

This is Donegal.

This is us.

2013

It was four days out from the Ulster final and the heat would not leave the day. I drove home from training in Ballybofey with the windows down and although it must have been half past ten by the time I got to the house, there still wasn't a breath in the evening. Yvonne was in the kitchen. The weans were fast asleep. We were getting a lawn put down so we went outside to look over what the men had done that day. Where we live, the sun sets between the ninth hole of the golf course at Portnoo and Arranmore Island. It kind of bisects them. We were outside one evening in June and Packie Quinn, our neighbour, landed down. He was shouting, 'Ten eighteen! Ten eighteen!' He told us that that was the time the sun sets on Gweebarra Bay on the longest day of the year. It was about twenty to eleven now and the sun had disappeared, but you could still see its reflection on the clouds. Perfect Irish summer days don't come along too often, but when they do there is nowhere on earth you'd rather be. So we were just chatting, the pair of us, and then a scream came across the field. It stilled us. It was a wild, needy sound. And it kept on coming. For all the world it sounded like a baby. I said to Yvonne, 'What the hell *is* that?' But we were both listening and we were freaked. It had to be a baby crying. It was crazy, but that was what it sounded like. We'd heard enough over the last few years to know. So I went to the back of the house, over the fence and through the field and it was growing louder all the time. It was coming from these bushes across the top road and I held my breath as I pulled back the undergrowth.

A kitten.

It was still in infancy and was poorly, very skinny and shivering. We both come from dog, rather than cat, families, but we knew straight away that there was nothing for it but to keep it. So we made a wee bed in the front porch and got it some milk, and it was out like a light. We said nothing the next morning but when the children were at the breakfast table they heard this mewing and just stopped. 'What's that?' They went through the hallway to investigate, pulled the porch door open and saw her. She was jet black. We decided to call her Lucky.

That Sunday, we lost the Ulster final and the title we had held for two years.

A week later we scraped past Laois in a bitter, bitter game.

The next weekend, we were humiliated by Mayo in an All-Ireland quarter-final in Croke Park. It was the longest day of my football life and we were no longer All-Ireland champions.

Somewhere during the haze of that fortnight, I lifted the new arrival up by the nape of the neck and held her close to my face.

— Sure your name's not Unlucky?

———

Things fall apart.

The day after we were beaten by Mayo, I took a flight to Glasgow and went straight into the office at Lennoxtown, Celtic's training ground. I hadn't slept and couldn't really eat, but I didn't feel anything either. The peculiar thing was that nobody in the office really knew what had happened. Some of them had a vague interest in Gaelic football and knew that I was the Donegal manager and that the team had lost. Neil Lennon knew for sure and was good about it and said the right things. He was consoling.

But there is a difference between knowing we had lost the match and understanding what had happened – understanding what we had lost. That was the first time I realised the essential difference between the world of professional football and the

All-Ireland championship. In soccer, across the world, teams win and lose all the time. Celtic play so many games that they don't dwell on the result. But a defeat in the championship can cut you to the quick. It can lodge in your soul. For days. For months. For years. Some defeats cannot be erased because they are not just defeats. They are not merely about being on the wrong side of a scoreline. Big championship days become ingrained in that period of time. If you are close to the team, whether as a player or manager or supporter, a significant defeat can stay associated with that time in your life for evermore. The All-Ireland championship is about rare days. For most counties and their teams, it is about reaching a place that you either seldom or never reach. Losing on big days and not knowing if or when you will get to be there again is a disturbing feeling. It is irreversible and it is anti-magic. One day, we were Ulster and All-Ireland champions. A fortnight later, we were nowhere. We were just out. Out.

For that full week, I checked in for work with Celtic. But I had to force myself out of where my mind was. Every evening I went straight back to the apartment and I spent night after night just staring at the wall and searching for answers. I needed to understand how this had happened to us. I needed to know how everything we had worked so hard to build up had been torn down. Things came back in fragments, as they always do.

A shift takes place when you are All-Ireland champions, no question. Your world shifts on its axis a little bit and routine is knocked sideways. The autumn had been unusual for us. Seven or eight of us were on the All-Star trip to New York in November. It was fun; the usual bar-hopping and bringing the Sam Maguire around and Donegal people showing up everywhere we went. Paul McCormack, a Ballybofey man who ended up joining the

NYPD, took all the Donegal boys to a firing range one afternoon and ran us through the full artillery. None of us had even held a gun before and within minutes we realised that it was just as well. Anthony Thompson was a natural, though. He just pulled on the goggles and even with the pistol he was hitting the target dead on, time after time. Paul was genuinely amazed. He kept shouting: 'This guy's a fucking killer. He's a fucking *killer*.' Anthony is so laid back that he didn't pay any attention to it, but the rest of us were very impressed.

Yvonne made it out for a few days because it was my birthday, and then a few of us were heading up to Boston for a Donegal GAA dinner dance. Gogie, a guy I lived with in Philadelphia when I was playing football there, with whom I had become re-acquainted about six minutes after the All-Ireland final – bridging a thirteen-year gap – decided that it would be fun to travel together. Seamus 'the Bully' Sweeney was going to drive us. So myself, Paul Durcan, Gogie and this elderly gentleman, John Flood, whom we knew only as Auld John, set off from Manhattan that morning in a Jeep. It was meant to take four or five hours and we were in good spirits. We had a few beers going and Paul was sitting in the back with the iPod out, blaring out the music. He was sitting beside Auld John, who was a bit hard of hearing. But Paul was chatting away with him. He was perched in the back of the Jeep, downing a few beers and flicking through his playlist. Paul always liked his tunes. He'd stick on a tune and sit there nodding away and then he'd turn and shout:

— What do you think of that, John?

— Who is it?

— Mumford & Sons.

Auld John would just nod at this.

— Mmmh Mumford.

Gogie had lived in Boston in the late 1980s and had driven this road many times. Seamus was belting along at a fair rate, but we seemed to be driving a fierce long time. The rest of us weren't paying much heed but every half an hour or so Seamus would ask, 'How are we fixed, Gogie?' And Gogie would wave the hand: 'Straight on! Straight on!' Then, as we're rattling along the road, twilight fast approaching, Auld John notices a cop car by the side of the road and shouts: 'Fucking Ver-mont. We're headin' to Canada, boys!' Seamus just turned to Gogie with a single reprimand: 'Ya fucking bollocks, ya'. Gogie shrugged and sighed, 'Don't be blaming me, Sweeney. You're the man driving.'

We made it to the function, just about. Nobody cared if we were late. Nobody cared. That was the mood during those months. Donegal had the Sam Maguire. It was a special time. In New York and Boston, so many people said the same thing: 'I can't believe you are here. I can't believe ye have taken the cup here.' And they meant it. You could tell that it was a really significant thing for them. They would ask if they could get a photograph. We all understood in an abstract way that the team and the All-Ireland was a really symbolic thing for Donegal people living away. But it wasn't until we actually met them that we grasped it properly. Can I get a photo? Of course. Of course you can.

———

We held our first real training sessions of the year in Dubai, where the team was on holiday. We arrived back in Dublin on the eve of our first national league game against Kildare in Croke Park. And we lost the match but we looked good. We were slightly behind in our training pattern but it was nothing we couldn't make up. I felt we were in a good place. Our approach would be the same. We would prepare for every single game as if our lives depended on it.

The big difference was that in the previous year we put every ounce of our souls into trying to possess something that was almost impossible. Now, as All-Ireland champions, we were trying to keep it. And all the other teams wanted to take it from us. It wasn't hard to sense that. If we had any ambition in the league, it was to stay in division one.

On Sunday 3 March we travelled to play Tyrone in Healy Park. From the moment the door of our coach opened, you could feel a hostility about the place. It wasn't nice. It wasn't nice walking into the dressing rooms and finding that there was nowhere for us to do a warm-up. It wasn't nice standing on the sideline when the boys were warming up, the wind sharp against your face and hearing the abuse coming in torrents from the Tyrone crowd, voice after voice. And it wasn't just what they were saying, but the aggression in it, this deep discontent coming in from the Tyrone supporters, as if they didn't understand this: how they could be living in our shadow. They wanted to set the world to rights that afternoon. It set the tone for a very physical, edgy game.

There was a nasty streak about the day. Fifty frees. Thirteen yellow cards. Ross Wherity went on a run just before half time and was pulled down by Ryan McMenamin. Michael took the penalty. It was saved and as Michael stretched to get to the follow-up he kicked Justin McMahon. He was shown a second yellow card and was sent off. I had been getting constant, low-grade abuse all through the game – shut the fuck up, you're always crying – but as Michael walked off, hundreds and hundreds of people rose behind me in the stand to boo him off the field. And I stood there watching this, thinking: This is an All-Ireland winning captain being booed off here. And he hardly did anything wrong.

The antics continued. Neil Gallagher got a second yellow before it was over, so we finished with thirteen men. When I was going into the dressing room, someone told me that Karl Lacey had been spat on. He had been watching the game in the stands because he was injured. Tyrone had won the match, 1-13 to 0-12, but the mood was baleful even after the final whistle. The counties would meet in the championship in May. I got everybody together in the little warm-up area behind our dressing room and stood in the middle of the huddle and told them to remember this, to remember what it felt like to come here as All-Ireland champions and to be treated like dirt, to see our captain and a perfect role model booed off the field, to have the Footballer of the Year spat at in the stands; to remember it every night at training; and to finish them when we get them to Ballybofey in the summer.

I was in full flow when there was a disruption in the circle, so I turned around. Mickey Harte was standing there. I wasn't sure how long he had been there, but he had to walk through our dressing room to reach us so he would have heard something of what I had been saying. He apologised for what had happened to Karl. And as he was leaving, he turned around and said, 'You were great All-Ireland champions.'

Past tense.

When he had left, I repeated it to the boys. 'You *were* great All-Ireland champions.' It was a slip of the tongue but it betrayed Tyrone's line of thought that evening. By beating us in that league game, they felt they had us again. 'You *were* great All-Ireland champions. Think about that, boys.'

So we got changed and scooted over the border. It had been a weird day, the only day, apart from the league game in

Armagh years ago, when I could feel a darkness hanging over a football pitch. It seemed as if nobody was in full control of the emotion swirling about the place; anything might happen. And although we had lost the match, I felt happy because we had all the reason we needed to want to beat Tyrone in the summer. We just needed to get through the league.

Neil McGee dislocated his knee against Mayo in Castlebar. And the atmosphere that day was like nothing we had encountered in a league game before. It was like a signal. This is what we could expect. Everybody wants to take you down.

By the last match we needed to beat Dublin in Ballybofey in order to stay in division one. We had a fair few injuries at this stage and we had some new players in. Eamon Doherty was in at corner back and Ross Wherity, who went on to have a good championship, started. Leo played in the half back line. But Dublin came to Ballybofey to tell us a few truths as well. They backed down from nothing. We were playing very well and then there was a big delay in the game when the referee, Padraig Hughes, was injured after colliding with Philly McMahon. Both teams got into a huddle, but Dublin's Diarmuid Connolly and Paul Mannion came over to our huddle to listen to what the players were saying. They were told to leave fairly brusquely. They wouldn't leave.

With the arrival of the replacement referee in the forty-first minute, everything changed. More decisions went against us. We had been so comfortable in the game and it gradually turned because he seemed to whistle us for everything. We were still a point up during injury time when Dublin's Paul Mannion kicked a point to get a draw. So we were relegated.

Patrick McBrearty had been bitten by a Dublin player in the first half. You could see the bite marks on his shoulder. In the dressing room at the break, we were examining Patrick when

Michael McMenamin, who does the door for us, told us that a couple of people from the Dublin support team were standing outside the door listening to what was being said. So we opened the door and, sure enough, there they were. They refused to leave. We asked them politely at first. Then they were told to fuck off. They refused. So when the boys were going back onto the field, there was this barging match on the way through, just clearing them out. It was ridiculous. Then the Dublin players came out of their changing room at the same time. It was all very stupid and spiteful. When Patrick's case was brought to Croke Park, the GAA authorities wanted him to come up and actually point the finger at the Dublin player involved. He didn't want to do that – Patrick has family in Dublin – and I sympathised with him. Since when does a player have to publicly call out another player? And Patrick ended up in a really compromised position because the GAA authorities laid the blame squarely on him for obstructing them in their investigations. But they had all the facts. The Dublin doctor was brought into our dressing room and was shown the mark and he agreed it was a bite. We had photographs. We had medical confirmation in the hospital that he had been bitten. Everybody knew what had happened. But because Patrick didn't want to travel to Dublin and name his assailant, they refused to deal with it.

———

But the league didn't worry us. The key moment for Donegal in 2013 didn't happen on the football field. Our chances of defending our All-Ireland had been compromised months earlier when our own county board held a fixtures forum in early January and decided to play the club championship during the

Ulster and All-Ireland championship. Through the All-Ireland championship in 2012, I had made two direct pleas to the club delegates asking to have our club games put back. I understand how frustrating it is for club managers and players to have fixtures postponed and called off and you aren't sure when you will be playing again. But I felt that the Donegal team had a chance to do something exceptional and I told the delegates that. I said that I believed Donegal could go back-to-back in Ulster for the first time ever, and go on to win the All-Ireland.

And that's what happened. Our winning the All-Ireland and the celebrations afterwards meant that the club championship was played deep in midwinter, almost like a tournament, with midweek and weekend games scheduled. It wasn't a perfect situation for the clubs. But we did have the Sam Maguire. That vindicated the decision. And that wouldn't have happened without the co-operation of the clubs. When I thought back to that autumn, during the celebrations and the talk about Donegal and the club championship, I began to feel that some of the officials on the county executive became convinced that they were losing their grasp on power. They were beginning to fear that Jim McGuinness was running Donegal football. So they held a meeting sometime in January and just quietly decided to run the club championship through the summer. It was done quietly and efficiently and my opinion was not sought.

I had had a fairly strained relationship with some people on the county board from the very beginning. My face didn't fit. Columba McDyer was the only other Glenties man who had ever managed Donegal and I don't think I ever matched their perception of what a manager should be. I think that there were people on the county board who wanted the team manager to be independent only to a point.

I understood that on the evening I first went for the Donegal job. I hadn't been recruited; neither had I lobbied people in power for the position. I just applied. Brian McIver had stepped down as manager and was up for reappointment. I knew Brian was favourite to be retained. But I wanted to give the most professional presentation I could. So I got a phone call to be in Jackson's Hotel on a certain night. The interview was based on set criteria, with questions on budget and squad size. It felt to me that they were ticking boxes.

After I finished playing with Donegal, I had spent so many Sundays standing on the terrace looking at the team that I felt I could see what we could become. It was always the boys who were questioned when Donegal lost games; their character was doubted, every time. Their hunger. Their honesty. They were regarded as some kind of collective joke. And by inference, the character of everybody in the county was regarded as suspect or unreliable. That never rang true for me. It annoyed me and I simply didn't believe it. And the more I watched them the more I was convinced I could do something. There were problems. Clearly, they weren't fit enough. They weren't properly conditioned. When I watched Donegal play, I would see what the game plan was for the first twenty-five minutes. Over the next twenty-five, it would weaken. And in the final ten minutes the team would bear no resemblance to what they had been at the start. The players were just making it up. There was not enough coaching going on and the message was getting lost in the white heat of games. Nothing was automatic to them. Other teams became more focused in the key moments, whereas our boys became more vulnerable. And that was not their fault. That had nothing do to with character. That was what I said at the first interview. I said that I felt we were operating at about fifty-five per cent of our maximum fitness, fifty per cent of our overall strength, eighty per cent of our technical ability and about thirty per cent of our tactical awareness. I said that our mental strength was about thirty per cent as well. I couldn't comment on nutrition because I wasn't inside the squad. I told them that our analysis was poor. All of this was met with the overwhelming silence that administrative meetings can generate. But the atmosphere wasn't good. This wasn't news that the executive was thrilled to be hearing. It all felt uneasy. The longer I spoke, the more certain I became that I wouldn't be getting the job. I felt that they didn't want me there, that they were seeing me just so it couldn't be said that they didn't. They didn't take me seriously. But they had no choice but to hear what I said.

The position came up again in autumn 2009. Brian had left the post in a way that wasn't well handled. I applied again. I phoned ahead to ask if I could do a presentation with a projector and was told that would be fine. But that day, I just had this weird feeling and I said to Yvonne: 'They are not going to let me do this.' The word around the county was that they had a shortlist of three names and mine wasn't on it. So the last thing they would want was me delivering a highly detailed presentation outlining a four-year plan with the main objective of winning the All-Ireland. Yvonne suggested ringing Jackson's to confirm that they had a projector. The hotel receptionist said that they would have one in the room. But when I walked into the interview room, sure enough, there was no projector. When I enquired about it, Charlie O'Donnell said: 'Naw, go on, fire away there.'

I said that I had clarified with the hotel that there would be a projector there.

— Ah, sure it's only a couple of questions. It's too late now anyhow.

And I knew then. They had their man picked. Again. The interview was meaningless. But anyhow. I would go through with it. I told them I'd brought my own projector – just in case. I told them it was down in the boot of the car.

And nobody spoke. It was as if everyone was thinking the same thing: who the fuck does this boy think he is? Nobody was talking. Charlie walked down with me to the foyer of the hotel, but we weren't chatting. He stayed in the foyer as I walked over to my car. And I was so disappointed and angry. It was all a big joke to them. I was nothing more than a nuisance, delaying them getting home. I called Yvonne to tell her what had happened and I was thinking of just driving home and leaving them there. She didn't pick up; it turned out she was putting Toni-Marie to bed. So I went back in with the projector and headed up to the meeting room. I had resolved to continue. They knew they weren't giving me the job. But they had to sit through this. I could make them do that. They had no choice. So I took my time setting the projector up and hooking it up to the laptop.

— This is unfortunate, isn't it?

Nobody replied.

Then I started talking. I had this 'model of excellence' done up, a sort of overall plan for the county squad and the support system around it. And the lack of interest and engagement was too blatant to ignore. It was disrespectful. As I spoke, one just stared at his pen. Another stared at his shoes. I just thought: Fuck this. Walk. But part of me was enraged, too. For a split second I thought I was going to toss the table in front of them. I had a passion for the Donegal team. I desperately wanted to do something to bring them forward and these people hadn't even the interest to hear about it. It didn't feel to me like they cared. They wanted me out the door so they could ring their

man and tell him that he had the job. But I was going to make
them sit through what I had to say and they resented that. The
atmosphere became heavy with mutual contempt. They asked
me a few questions afterwards. It was just the usual bullshit, the
same old culture of mediocrity. I left.

Driving back to Creeslough I had this deep, bubbling
feeling of resentment. I had had it with county board officials.
I remembered doorstepping the county treasurer outside his
house at the age of eighteen just to get expenses I was owed for
months and months. And I knew of endless instances down the
years when players had felt badly treated, particularly players
who had been influential but were jilted once they got injured.
It was all about power. So I told myself that what had happened
was just true to form. The county chairman phoned me at home
to say that I hadn't got the job. Thanks for applying. That was it.

And it turned out that they made a fiasco of the appointment
and it led to a really awkward situation in which nobody was
sure whether Declan Bonner and Charlie Mulgrew or John Joe
had been appointed. It was a disgraceful way to treat two All-
Ireland winners. I was driving home through Ballyshannon one
afternoon trying to pick up Highland Radio because Declan was
on air with Charlie Collins, giving out yards about the process.
By coincidence, a researcher from Highland rang and asked
me if I would come on. I said, 'Fine'. I was still smarting and
I said what I felt about the way Donegal football was run and
how I was treated. Pat Shovelin told me later that he was down
the town in Letterkenny and he could see people sitting in their
cars, not leaving shops. It was probably really good radio. But it
was disastrous for Donegal football. And I felt horrible for John
Joe during it all because he was a brilliant, passionate player and
he is a decent man. I knew he was there because he wanted to
restore those qualities to the team.

After that I ceased to believe I'd ever manage Donegal. I was convinced that the opportunity had never really been there for me. I followed the team and studied them in an abstract way, idly thinking about what I might do if I were in charge. We played Cork in the 2009 quarter-final and they pulverised us. And I was the same as any other Donegal supporter: I felt sorry for the players and for John Joe. And I was struck by the attitude of the Cork players. They were so consolatory afterwards, as if they hadn't wanted to do that to us but couldn't avoid it. The minor management post came up and I was tempted to apply, but I heard through the grapevine I wouldn't be getting that either. So I just let it go. I was resigned to never getting a chance. Then, out of the blue, Brian McEniff rang me and asked if I was going to go forward for the U-21 job as it was about to become vacant. I told him that there was no way I was applying for another post and that the county executive knew my views and my plans at this stage. Brian said that if I went forward, I would be guaranteed a fair hearing.

And the peculiar thing was that this time, there was no tension and it was all very relaxed. I didn't give a presentation either. I just felt sort of weary of the whole process by now; of going through this charade. So I did the interview. And I think one night later I got a phone call to say I had the job and that was it. Yvonne was sitting beside me on the couch and she was delighted for me but I was more puzzled than anything. I think I doubted that it was true for a few hours. Then I called Michael Murphy and asked him to be captain. That was the beginning.

But that undercurrent of tension I felt when I was around some of the county board officers never went away, even after we won the All-Ireland. We managed to step around each other and keep our communication to a minimum. Every so often we would bump into each other at club games and there would be very little mutual acknowledgement. But as we went into this Ulster championship, they had control of things. The dates had been set for the club championship and we had to adhere to those. I had to adhere to those. If it was a power struggle, this was their way of demonstrating who could wield the most.

And it destroyed us. They destroyed us. Their decision meant that, starting with the Tyrone game on 26 May, the boys would play championship football nine out of the eleven weekends it finally took for us to get knocked out of the All-Ireland. We could feel the energy and dynamism just draining from the squad, week by week. It was the opposite of 2012: instead of growing stronger by the week, we began to fade.

On the day we beat Tyrone, things looked fine on the surface. If there is one moment in that game I will carry with me for as long as I live, it will be the collision between Stephen O'Neill and Neil McGee. To me, all of the history between Tyrone and Donegal could be distilled into that moment and it was where we took control of the dynamic. Stephen had initiated the contact: he had lined Neil up as if to say, right – I'm going to have a good go at this boy now. And he put his foot down and he led with the shoulder and then he kind of just crumbled against McGee in a way that made everybody recoil. And this wasn't just an ordinary footballer. This was Stephen O'Neill. Tyrone's talisman. And Neil just absorbed his best hit and it was as if the energy of it rebounded through Stephen's frame and caused him to buckle. Neil hardly seemed to notice. He drove on with the ball. You could feel the reaction in the stadium. People were shocked. I tracked O'Neill for a few seconds and he had done really well just to try and keep moving, to pretend that he could keep going. But then it was as if the pain took over and he had to stop and hunch over. I felt that he would have given anything in the world just to keep jogging through that pain, but he had to bow to it. Everything changed at that moment.

But it was a small victory. We beat Tyrone 2-10 to 0-10. Mickey was the same as usual afterwards: polite, distant, brief. The following weekend, the boys went off to play in the club championship and when they reported back, nine were carrying new injuries. And not only that, they were bringing the tension of the club games back into the dressing room. We were trying to recreate the same atmosphere as the previous year, based on loyalty and respect for each other. And then they were going out on Saturday evenings and marking each other and taking the skin off each other. Club games are big-hearted and spiteful all at once. Several times we went along and saw some of the boys boxing one another. Three nights later they were back training alongside one another. We could feel ourselves losing control week by week.

We met in the Aura Leisure Centre one Sunday morning before the Ulster final against Monaghan. There had been club championship games on the Saturday evening. Both Glenties and St Michael's had been knocked out, so about a third of our squad were physically and emotionally wrecked from that. There was a bad buzz in the room. We could smell beer off the boys. And I could understand why they had gone out. The club means a lot to them and it takes time to get over a big defeat. So they weren't really where we needed them to be. Their minds were elsewhere and the mood was tense. It was negative and oppressive and it was difficult to shake. It was falling apart in front of us. And it was driving me to distraction. To my mind, there were people on the county board who wanted me to fail, and if that meant that the Donegal team failed in the process, so be it.

The summer became stripped down to a repetitive exercise in frustration. I had taken up a coaching role with Celtic football club in the New Year so I was flying between Glasgow and Donegal during that time. My pattern was to fly over to Glasgow late on Tuesday night after training, fly back to be in Ballybofey on Thursday, over to Glasgow again first thing on Friday morning and back on Friday night. So I would spend every Tuesday morning in Glenties on the telephone getting the latest updates from the physiotherapists and the various doctors. The rate of injuries was accelerating to the point that it became difficult to keep up with them. You jot down who is out and what their prognosis is and how long rehabilitation might take. And you are wondering: Will they be able to play? With each of these conversations, I felt more frustrated and more helpless and more and more angry at the foolishness of what was being imposed on us. Couldn't they understand how hard the boys had worked to become All-Ireland champions? I would sit there feeling really agitated, feeling the stress build up and a kind of tightness in my chest, and then I had to force myself to be composed and to focus on what was really important. It felt like being involved in a stupid, needless battle with our own administrators; the very people who were supposed to be the custodians of Donegal football. The only way to answer them was to keep winning games. And there came a point in the day where you had to divorce yourself from all of that and take out a piece of paper and write down what we wanted to achieve at training that night. Our goals were the same: to soar in our fitness, pace and power; to stretch ourselves in our agility training; and to go over and over our game plan so that we knew it in our sleep. The boys who were reporting to training needed to feel that they were going places and that we had progressed because that is how it had been from the start.

We had to feel that we were advancing. But more often than not the phone would ring as I was on the way to Ballybofey with reports of a new injury. Colm rolled his ankle just before the Ulster final, for instance. And the doctor was assuring me that he would be grand; he would sit out this session but he would be ready. But deep down you're thinking: They might be available but they won't be rested. They aren't rested. They haven't trained properly. They haven't been allowed to build to it so we can peak together, as a unit, as a team. It felt like being in a race against time every single night. Could we get everybody back to full health before we were beaten?

———

On 23 June we played Down in Breffni Park. That was the day I felt it slipping away. Standing on the sideline and watching the boys faltering, weakening. Had there been another ten minutes in the match we might have lost it. The golfer Paul McGinley and his father Mick were in the dressing room that evening. Later, Paul told me that he had met the players and how taken he was by how humble and gracious they were. The boys would have been delighted to meet him but they didn't really get that he was pleased to be meeting them too. He was talking about the match – how it wasn't perfect but we got the result and we'd live to fight another day. And I just kept zoning in and out. I couldn't concentrate. Because I knew right then that we were in big trouble. Everything, everything we had spent the last two years building up, night after night, was just evaporating in front of our eyes. We were in our third Ulster final in a row and instead of being excited, I had this heavy feeling of dread.

The players sensed that it wasn't right. They knew that training was not the same as in the previous two years, when we were all out on the field, locked into something. This time, it was interrupted. We had a skeleton squad out on the field pushing themselves to the edge while the other boys tried to get fit again. I was trying to behave as if everything was exactly the same, staying positive at training and ignoring the obvious, which was that half the first team wasn't with us. And it was wearying. It sucked energy from me. Even when I was training, I was fuming at the thought of what the county board had done, at how wilfully and thoughtlessly they had undermined the boys' chances of keeping what they had won. Did they want this? Was it easier to handle when Donegal were just another football team, never too bad, rarely much good? Just existing – did they want a return to that? Winning Ulster titles and going for All-Irelands was demanding and it was expensive. Maybe that was the problem. I didn't have the answer. I couldn't for the life of me understand it. And the only way to respond to it was to keep winning games.

So on the same Thursday evening we found Lucky, this was the scene at training. No breeze, a warm evening, and we are trying to get a handle on who will be fit to play. The medical team had put together a report for us. It was a light session but, even so, half the squad were over on the sideline. Adam Speer had three stationary bikes over by the dug-out and some of the boys were doing sessions on those. Dermot Simpson was doing recovery with some of the others. The concept was that even though they weren't able to train, it was good for the entire squad to be on the same field. But as the weeks went on, the numbers on the sideline grew and the group that was training became smaller. It was having a negative effect. Dermot gave us a sheet that laid everything out. It was like the book of evidence.

In 2012, we had completed one hundred training sessions.

In 2013, from 1 January to 1 August, we had completed 66.

Of those, Anthony Thompson had missed 53 days and 17 sessions or 25% of our total training season.

And the list went on.

Colm McFadden: 50 days, 17 sessions, 25%.

Daniel McLaughlin: 75 days, 23 sessions, 34%.

David Walsh: 135 days, 44 sessions, 66%.

Frank McGlynn: 66 days, 20 sessions, 30%.

Karl Lacey: 150 days, 46 sessions, 69%.

Mark McHugh: 83 days, 26 sessions, 39%.

Neil Gallagher: 110 days, 45 sessions, 68%.

Neil McGee: 36 days, 10 sessions, 15%.

Paddy McGrath: 70 days, 22 sessions, 33%.

In all, ten players had missed 270 sessions, and many of these guys were on the sideline five days before we played Monaghan. Anthony, both Neils and Frank McGlynn had returned to play club games against medical advice. It was understandable: they would have been under phenomenal pressure to do so. I ended my county career playing for the club in the same circumstances. We found out later that Michael had rolled his ankle in a club game but had said nothing. He just trained injured.

That is when we reached the point where we weren't managing a team in any meaningful way. We were just managing a situation. The reason we only organised sixty-six sessions that year was because the boys were released to their clubs immediately after a Donegal game. We couldn't get our hands on them. We didn't know what kind of training they were doing with their clubs, but we could see that they were losing sharpness and losing power by the week. I stood there on the field reading the report and thought about the final twenty minutes against Down when the power drained out of

us. This was why. We didn't have the work done. It had been
taken away from us. I knew Malachy O'Rourke, the Monaghan
manager, would have been in the crowd that day. And if I were
in his shoes, I would have been very heartened by what I saw. So
now, for the first time, I began to do something I hadn't done
since I took charge. I started to rely on hope. We had to hope
that things went our way. We had to hope that we could scrape
past Monaghan and then buy a couple of weeks and hope that
our injuries might clear up. I didn't know if the people on the
county board couldn't see what was happening or if they just
didn't care. Day after day felt like an unsolvable puzzle.

Jimmy came into the office one evening before the Ulster
final to say that dinner was ready. We had just been told that
Colm and Michael wouldn't be fully right. I was trying to get
some kind of rehabilitation plan right in my head. Jimmy
called down three times, saying, 'Will you come on, Daddy?' By
the time I got up to the table everyone else had finished eating
and the kids were angling to go and watch a cartoon, and I was
conscious of how much I was away, but here I was sitting at the
table and my mind was absolutely vacant because I couldn't
stop thinking about whether we were going to be ready. When
I was around the house, I seemed to spend all my time staring
into space. That's how it was that evening. Half an hour later
I was picking up the bag and kissing everyone good night and
leaving for training and then for Glasgow. And it wasn't fair on
the family. I wasn't really there. The weeks seemed filled with
emails to be answered and phone calls with fresh problems.

So the drive over to Ballybofey was like a sanctuary. No radio.
It gave me a bit of time to try to sort things out and think about
training and our strategy and about the players, but most of all
about the dumb politics of it all; how this situation had been
inflicted on us. The only way to respond was to ignore it and

fight through it and hope, just hope, that we could buy time. The only way through it was to grind my teeth and say nothing.

Ulster final day was on 21 July, bang in the middle of a cloying heatwave. There is no breeze in mid-Ulster on days like that. We had asked the county board to find us somewhere near the ground so that we could go through a proper warm-up. Waiting in the dressing rooms in Clones is pointless: you're cooped up and the officials let the teams onto the pitch at 3.40 and 3.42. You have twenty minutes in which to do a warm-up, meet the president, parade the field behind the band and stand for the anthem. In other words, there is no warm-up. But we ended up in this place on the side of a hill about a mile away from the town. The ground under our feet was rock solid and uneven. It was treacherous to run on. You could see the marks of beasts imprinted in the clay. We had to walk this back road just to get there and some of the Monaghan fans arrived to park their cars. We must have looked like a mirage. We had to walk back to the dressing room among them, in our training gear. There was a really ominous feeling about the day.

After sixty seconds of play, that feeling deepened. Monaghan began to attack at the throw-in and we dispossessed them easily, but once that happened, all fourteen Monaghan outfield players simply turned and sprinted back into their half as hard as they could. Something about the way they moved made my stomach sink. They reminded me of ourselves. And we didn't have the work done. Someone had sent word down from Monaghan that all football had ceased in the county since their semi-final. This game was paramount.

After ten minutes one of their players, Stephen Gollogly, clattered into Mark McHugh when they were both running for a ball. It was always going to be Mark's ball but Gollogly didn't slow his momentum in the slightest. Mark had his eye on the ball and had it in his hands when Gollogly arrived at speed. It was a ferocious hit and Mark was totally exposed. He lay there crumpled. It looked like he had been deliberately taken out of the game. Anyone who knows football would recognise that straight away. When two players are going for a ball in any sport, they make adjustments and judgements and decisions in the blink of an eye. That didn't happen here. The Monaghan player just kept going, even though Mark had his hands on the ball. Gollogly was still a few metres away when Mark made contact with the football, but he just hurled himself into the contact. Gollogly had hurt himself, as well as Mark, in the collision. But he had initiated it. He had kept his eye on the ball but turned his body and allowed his momentum to take him into Mark like a sledgehammer. People still praise it as a brave challenge. But that ignores the fact that it was a dangerous foul. And it worked. Mark was stretchered off and spent the night in hospital with concussion and a perforated eardrum.

This set the tone for the match and left us without a key player. Mark was capable of giving exceptional cover in front of Conor McManus and Kieran Hughes in the Monaghan full forward line. He had this uncanny talent for reading the break of the ball and arriving at the perfect moment, and the speed with which he translated defensive cover into a counter-attack was crucial to us.

Monaghan came with a plan and executed it perfectly. They defended with a ferocity we recognised only too well and banged over a few long-range points, but the quality of their diagonal ball going into the two full forwards was of the highest order. Hughes made Eamon look like an average defender, but the truth is that the ball going in made it impossible for Eamon to do anything but shadow his man. What sickened me wasn't that we were going to lose the match. It was that I could see the boys were giving it everything out there. Their desire hadn't dimmed one bit. But it was a match in which a very hungry and highly prepared team was playing against a team doing its absolute best. They dominated us defensively, just shut us down and played a cagey, smart game in attack. They hit five points in the first half hour. It took us thirty-two minutes to register a score. Rory turned to me: 'Well, at least we're up and running.' I shook my head. It was embarrassing.

The dressing room at half time was an impossible place. We were 0-05 to 0-02 down and the boys were still willing to absolutely crucify themselves for the county and they were looking for a message, for anything that would help them turn it around. But they knew we hadn't done the work. They could feel it in the first half. They just weren't travelling right. And they made a match of it in the second half. They gave the Donegal crowd a glimmer of hope. But it wasn't really there for us. We just weren't in a position to be able to go and win the game. It finished 0-13 to 0-07. It was Monaghan's day. We had been taken down. There wasn't exactly bad blood between ourselves and Monaghan; but there wasn't good blood either. It was a tetchy afternoon. We watched them lift the cup. The Monaghan people were delighted: they had waited twenty-five years for this, even longer than us. I felt nothing, watching their celebrations. No disappointment. No anger. No bitterness. Just this curious detachment as if I wasn't there at all.

I felt blank, as if I couldn't fully process what was happening. After the last two years, it was through the looking glass for us. How come the Monaghan boys were up in the stand? What were they doing with the Anglo Celt? On the bus, the boys had a few beers. I decided not to. I needed to face this down. When we got off at Donegal Town, a few supporters came over to us. They had been out all day and they just wanted to say

'Hard luck'. I couldn't look them in the eye. It was as if we had betrayed them. I felt guilty. I hauled my bag out of the back of the bus and saw the scaffolding for a stage over at the corner. The planned homecoming had been abandoned at five o'clock. I remembered what it was like the year before.

When I got home, myself and Yvonne sat in silence in the living room for a long while. It was like that feeling when you are a youngster and you come out of a nightclub: the silence after all the noise. It is disconcerting. Yvonne was wrecked; it was after midnight. I sat there for hours and eventually went into the office and took out a piece of paper and a pen. There was nothing. There was no train of thought to bring me anywhere. It was as if the day hadn't happened – or as if the previous two years hadn't happened. I was stuck. We were stuck. There was nothing I could find to get us moving again. We had no way out. And I knew what was coming down the track. It was three in the morning and the thought of sleep was depressing me because the reality of Monday morning was too much. There were no answers coming. I kept thinking about the players. Where were they? What were they doing? Were they okay? What were they thinking? I knew what I had asked of them. Their sacrifice was massive. And for me to square that away, the rewards for them had to be massive as well. If we had the opportunity, we could have at least shown our best. And we didn't get to do that. That was the hard part. There is no shame in getting beat. If you give it everything and lose, there is purity in that. But the opportunity to do that was taken away from us.

Then it struck me.

What the boys were being forced to do, an animal couldn't do.

That is when I started to feel angry. But there was no time to change anything. We just had to see this out. Six days later, we played Laois in Carrick-on-Shannon. All of a sudden we were perceived as vulnerable; as a wounded thing. Laois would try to replicate what Monaghan had done to us; it was the smart thing. A huge Donegal crowd showed up. Mark McHugh had been in hospital until Tuesday. I was bothered by that collision because it sent out a message that this was how to beat Donegal. Stop their runners. And early in the match, Laois were doing just that: third-man tackling and obstructing us and body checking all over the field. It was the only time as a manager that I began to communicate with the linesman, but I had to get the point across or we were going to lose the game. Every time one of their players blocked one of ours, I was over to him. In the beginning, he waved me away. He kept saying they were both at it. I had to keep explaining: We have the ball. We are attacking. Our players are trying to get free. Why would they want to be pulling at the guy who is trying to mark them? After a few minutes, the Laois management got involved. Justin McNulty, the Laois manager, came over and hit me with a shoulder. I knew Justin from his days playing with Armagh and was used to it. But this was different. He was a senior manager now. He was supposed to be setting some kind of example. Then he shouldered me again. I looked at him in disbelief. It was like being in some sort of stupid dream of a football match. The frustration of the entire year was very close to the surface now. And I had to counsel myself: Just keep your dignity here. I had a sudden image of the boys looking across at the sideline to see me boxing another manager. It would have looked pathetic. McNulty shouldered me again. I kept looking at him. A few yards away, Rory got caught up in a shoving match with Fergal Byron, one of the Laois selectors. It wasn't how we conducted ourselves. It was nasty and petty.

We got on with watching the game. And the boys found some reserve of willpower or energy to get them through. It finished 0-14 to 0-08. Football ability and pride got them through that evening. But we were in freefall. It was just a matter of when. It was a matter of hoping.

We were paired against Mayo in the quarter-finals on Sunday 4 August at four in the afternoon. Some Mayo fan had draped a green and red flag on one of the footbridges over the motorway outside Dublin. He had printed 'Not today, Jimmy' on it. For some reason it stayed in my mind. Somebody had gone to a lot of bother to hoist that banner. They were hungry. That evening we held a meeting in the hotel. The funny thing was that of all the times we sat together to talk about the games, the boys were more focused than they had ever been. You could see it. They wanted to win this so, so badly. They were proud. They were All-Ireland champions and they would give anything to preserve that. And they were positive. We all still hoped that maybe we would take the field and discover that we had a performance in us. It was blind faith and old-school defiance. You are sixteen years old in the dressing room and someone shouts, 'C'mon the fuck, boys!' and you have this instant surge of adrenaline. But that only carries you so far. We had this internal optimism that we could get ourselves back to a good place.

Mayo had played London on the same day as we played Monaghan. They were rested. Last year's final was a backdrop to this match. And in the first few minutes you could see that our boys were giving it everything. They didn't have the energy and they couldn't turn the ball over, couldn't make the tackles or cover the space, but in their minds they wanted the game as much as they ever wanted anything. Even after we went two goals behind, you could see how desperately hard they were trying. How could you not love a team like that? But Mayo just left us standing. They seemed to effortlessly move into a different stratosphere. There was nothing to do in the second half but stand there and watch as they just cut through us. We were twenty points down at one stage. And the score might have been anything. If this was a boxing match, you'd throw in the towel to save your fighter. But we didn't have that option. Mayo kept on coming. They were entitled to. They were in an All-Ireland quarter-final. They were trying to win an All-Ireland for the first time in over half a century. If they needed to bury us in the process, so be it.

It was strange because even as the game was going on, I didn't have to think about it any more. Recurring thoughts kept presenting themselves. This was a big blow. It was a blow to Donegal football. It was going to be very hurtful for the boys. It was going to be damaging to them, damaging to everything we believed about ourselves. But I had to take it on the chin. Whatever happened, I had to accept it. With every point and every goal, that was all I could say: We have to take this one. Absorb it. The Donegal people were very quiet. But they did not leave. And they were on my mind, too. They had been everywhere with us. We all knew how expensive it could be, travelling to these games, buying tickets, taking their children. They didn't deserve to see this. And they should never have seen this because it wasn't a true reflection of us. Not getting beaten: there is never anything wrong with that. But we had been stripped of the very thing that we took for granted about ourselves. We were denied the chance to be ready. So we had to accept this embarrassment. I took a look at the scoreboard just before the whistle went. 4-17 to 1-10. It felt like a joke. When I shook hands with James Horan, I told him that I hoped Mayo went on to win the All-Ireland. I meant it too.

On the way down in the bus, all I could think about was
the fact that we had been humiliated by sixteen points in an
All-Ireland quarter-final, even though our heads had been in
the right place. I had looked into the boys' eyes. I knew they
were keen. That was the part I couldn't stomach. They had
been betrayed. And none of us could believe the season was
ending like this. The bus pulled into Donegal Town and the
streets were quiet. The boys pulled their bags from the back of
the bus in the Diamond and they could hardly look people in
the eye because they felt ashamed of the way they had played.
We muttered 'Good luck' and headed away to our cars fairly
quickly. The boys felt as if they had done something wrong. But
it wasn't their fault. It wasn't their fault.

———

That was echoing through my mind for a full week in
Glasgow. I wasn't sure whether to continue as manager
or not. On the journey back from Croke Park, Rory had
been trying to convince me that we needed to rebuild from
the beginning now and that a lot of the senior boys had had
their day. Word came through a few days after the Mayo game
that the Donegal county board had decided to cancel the club
championships for five full weeks. They wanted to be able to
give teams an opportunity to prepare properly. I had to smile.
It was the ultimate insult.

But it clarified things. I wouldn't go back unless we could do
things in a way that gave us an honest chance.

In the weeks afterwards, I met the players twice. I needed
to know that they wanted another season. They had to drive
it – I would facilitate it. That was always the dynamic. I wasn't

convinced when we met that they had fully bought into that. The response was positive, but it was vague. So I held off on making a decision and the players organised a meeting independently of me and when we met again I felt happy that they were willing to give it another shot.

Taking on the county board was the next task. Just because the players were in didn't mean I could go back. So I sent out a request asking to meet the club delegates directly. I met them in Jackson's Hotel on the same evening as our twins, Bonnie and Aoibh, were born. Yvonne had given birth a few hours earlier and I drove down from Letterkenny and just told the people in the room how I saw it. I told them how angry and frustrated I felt. I said that the boys had been hoodwinked and had been denied a chance to properly defend their All-Ireland and I couldn't countenance putting them through the sacrifices I asked of them for another winter if all their work was going to be sabotaged in the summer. I reminded them of what had happened in 2012, when I had requested that they postpone the club games because I felt we could do something special. The opposite had happened in 2013. I wasn't issuing an ultimatum. I just said that I couldn't manage the team under the circumstances that had prevailed over the summer. Maybe someone else could, but I wasn't the man for the job. I told them that a thoroughbred horse couldn't do what had been asked of each of our players over the summer. I said that we were beaten before we started. I couldn't put them through that again. I couldn't take on a project that was doomed before we even started. I left it up to them. Then I drove back to the hospital.

The clubs assented. They voted not to hold the club championship in tandem with the Ulster championship. Finally, I decided to change my back-room team. I hadn't been happy with the way things were going with Rory. So many of the qualities that I had hoped he had when I invited him in were there: he was very sharp and analytical and had a terrific knowledge of players from all over the country. And he was hungry. He came from Fermanagh and he was keen for success. Over the first couple of seasons, we used to hash things out on the phone. We would talk for hours about tactics or about players and where to use them. Both of our opinions counted and sometimes I would end up shifting my viewpoint and sometimes he would. We would always reach a resolution that we were happy with. But over this season I felt our conversations were becoming more fractious. It was as if he had his mind made up on things and wasn't going to change, no matter what. It weakened the bond between us.

Rory was a very visible and vocal part of the set-up. We ended up hosting a lot of media nights and he was a natural at talking away and giving an interesting perspective without ever saying anything he shouldn't. So I was stunned when, just before the quarter-final, he gave an interview to the *Irish News* in which he spoke about Mayo and Monaghan being in 'collusion' to try to beat Donegal. This could only serve to provoke Mayo – and they were still smarting from the previous year's All-Ireland final. He tried to tell me afterwards that the conversation had been off the record. I found that hard to believe, so I spoke to the journalist involved and he refuted the claim. I couldn't figure what Rory's thinking was.

I decided that if we were to continue, I had to assume absolute control. There would be no more lengthy debates or joint decisions. When I met him, he was hesitant about that proposal. He asked me if he could think about it. I said to him that I didn't know why he needed to think about anything: he hadn't had to think about it when I asked him in two years ago and when nobody knew who he was as a coach. So why now?

I knew in my heart after that meeting that I would be making changes. It just wasn't going to work. So I rang Sean Dunnion, the county chairman, on Tuesday morning and told him that I was letting Rory and Maxi Curran go. Francie Friel was already working with Maxi in the U-21 squad so it didn't make any sense for him to stay. Then I called the three boys. The conversations were fairly quick and forthright. I thanked them for their time. I told Rory that I felt he would make a better number one than a number two. Then I phoned Michael Murphy to tell him of the changes.

I wanted to draft a statement explaining that I was making changes to the back-room without revealing that the boys had been dropped from the set-up. But while I was at home composing it, reports were circulating that both Rory and Maxi had quit. It made it seem as if everything was falling apart.

So I rang Sean Dunnion and told him to state what had really happened; to state the facts. I needed them to release a statement confirming that I had made the decision. But by then it was too late. What should have remained a private meeting had degenerated into a public event. By midnight, Rory was still arguing that he had quit and was refusing to concede that he had been let go. It was a farcical and sad way to end three years of working together. We had been through a lot and had lived through many extraordinary moments together. But the division between us became permanent that day. We haven't spoken since that phone call.

Over the following weeks, I began to make plans for 2014. I asked Paul McGonigle to come in as a selector. Damien Diver, a brilliant servant to Donegal football, was my next phone call. John Duffy, a fabulously talented player from Ballyshannon whom I played alongside for years with Donegal, came in as well.

That Christmas, our house was full. In life, the arrival of Bonnie and Aoibh made 2013 a year to remember.

In football, it was a year to forget.

2014

'We are not living at all, lads,' the Giant declared one evening. We were sitting in his Passat outside the front of the house. It was around October, when the football is over and the leaves are on the road and it is getting darker and darker every evening and the world shrinks. Because Glenties is inland we don't get the same battering as the coastal towns in Donegal, but you can still feel the winter closing in and the sky gets black dark and the town is deserted and there is the feel of everybody hunkering down.

— What are you on about?

This was John O'Boyle. We'd been having a good evening's craic.

— This place.

The Giant nodded his head towards the street. It was the same street we had been walking up since we started school.

— This place would depress you. We need to get out and see the world.

That gave us something to think about. This was a time when everyone our age was either thinking about going somewhere or had already gone. It was very restless. During the first summer I was in Boston, everyone was applying for Morrison visas. I put in five hundred for myself and Mark. You could apply as often as you liked – I knew of one boy who put in thousands of applications and still didn't get one. All it cost was the price of a stamp. Both Mark and myself ended up getting one, but we had friends who probably wanted it more than we did who weren't successful. It was literally a lottery. But a lot of people were hopping back and forth across the Atlantic to Boston or New York or San Francisco, not quite sure of what to do with themselves. 'Sure there's nothing at home,' was the refrain you would hear over and over. The more you heard it, the more true it seemed. But it meant that people flung themselves into a strange existence, taking up jobs in painting and construction and bars, regardless of whether they were any good at them or not. Some stayed and made lives in America. Some didn't. I sometimes wonder if I would have stayed if I hadn't got the tap on the arm from Brian McEniff that Christmas. Others were caught in between and I suppose that's how the Giant felt on this evening. So a big conversation got up then about whether we were living or whether we weren't living and what's life all about anyway. It was very earnest and philosophical and we solved a lot of the world's problems, as we did many evenings sitting in that car and idling with the radio down low until it was time for dinner.

The following evening, I was walking back to the house after being down the town and as I was going in the front door of the house, John happened to be coming out of his.

— Well, what kind of form is the Giant in today? Did he get over his bout of depression?

— Do you know where the Giant is?

— No.

— You don't know where the Giant is?

— No.

— The Giant's in New York.

— He is like fuck.

— I'm telling you now.

— He is like fuck.

— Come in and ask the auld doll if you don't believe me.

John's jaw dropped.

— He was up this morning and got the ticket booked first thing. Packed the bag and was driven up to Dublin and he should be landing in New York as we speak.

John shook his head and processed all of this. That was exactly what had happened. Mark woke up and just decided he was taking off. It was a wee bit out of character, but then again he was always impulsive when it came to going places. Travelling meant meeting people and I think that meeting people was the chief enjoyment that Mark took from life.

He was a rambler, in the true sense of the word. We came to expect a disappearance around All-Ireland final time. So when Clare won the Liam McCarthy after their eighty-one-year famine, the Giant hit Ennis. There was no way he was missing that. It was the same when Derry won it in 1993. That stuff was just manna from heaven for him. But he was able to make an occasion out of days that most of us would just consider to be work. He often drove the buses for Frank. Keadue Rovers football team were regulars and their boys often told me that they were always over the moon when they saw Mark coming to collect them. They knew that Mark would go with the flow. Sometimes he would be driving them to a match just twenty-five miles down the road but they still wouldn't land home until nine the following morning. John Roarty told me about this time he headed down to Lisdoonvarna with the Giant, who was driving the Glenties Folk Choir down for the Fleadh. They were all booked to stay in bed and breakfasts about fifteen miles outside the town. While the choir was singing, Mark and John knocked about Lisdoonvarna. The craic was only starting by the time the boys were meant to drive the choir home. The festival was in full tilt and the thought of driving away from that was a form of torture for the Giant. So he improvised. He turned the emergency stop on so the bus wouldn't start. When the choir arrived back, he made a big show of checking the engine. He had arranged for Charlie McNamee, who was driving another gang from Donegal, to take the choir back. Not knowing any different, Charlie rolled the window down.

— Ah God, Giant, that's wild. Sure I'll run these people out in my wagon. It'll not take long.

The people in the choir were fretting over Mark and worrying about how he'd get home and he said, 'Don't be worryin', now. We'll be grand. We'll get an auld mechanic and she'll be good to go.'

Then himself and John Roarty headed into the night.

People who hung around with Mark always ended up with stories. One year Martin Doherty – 'Doc' – headed over to New York to visit Mark, who was living with our aunt Mary, Uncle Jim and grand-aunt Teresa in one of those brownstones out in Brooklyn. Tess had been there half her life and she was great value. Every so often when we were children, the postman would haul this massive parcel through the front door. Mum often used to dress Mark and myself in identical clothes when we were kids and there would be awful rows when these parcels arrived. The older ones would always ransack the box and get the best stuff first. Mum would be pulling out these striped jerseys and shirts that were gorgeous but were too fancy for the likes of Mark and myself. So the debate would start.

— Oh, boys, this is beautiful.

— It's not beautiful, Mum! And you know it's not!

— Och, it's lovely on you, Mark.

— It has stripes, Mum.

Auntie Tess was great fun. She sat the two boys down when they landed out to her. The Doc was doing a line with a girl at the time and was thinking about getting married. The two boys were ruminating about this and life in general when Tess suddenly asked the Doc what age he was.

— Twenty-six.

— Twenty-six! Sure I have bras aulder than that.

When Charles died, Mark and I became very close. Because Frank was the eldest, he was at the forefront of the family business from a very young age. Frank was out driving from the moment he could get his licence. He worked so hard – and still does. Nobody really knew how much the whole family was hurting after Charles died, except ourselves when we shut the door every night. But I suppose Mark and I had each other for refuge. We would always be fighting, but he would call it 'toy fighting' because he was that bit older and bigger than me. We had great fun. When we were teenagers we had this Christmas Eve tradition. Money was tight so we were always scheming about how we'd buy presents. We came up with the idea that we would give each other a twenty quid note as presents. It became this ceremonial trade where we would hand the money to each other at the exact same time. The craic was that he would try and grab mine before letting go of his. So it became this tug where the notes were in danger of ripping.

— You let go.

— Naw, naw. You first.

— Right so. Together on three.

— One. Two. Three.

And neither of us would let go ...

For all his roaming, Mark stayed local. He thought there was nowhere like home and no gang like the crowd of boys he kicked about with. After he left school he was on a group scheme in Killybegs and then worked in a factory in Fintown. He fit in anywhere and everywhere. Mark was a person with a lot of love inside him. When he heard people's stories – and for some reason people were instantly comfortable talking with him – he had this very easy empathy with them. The boys used to like heading off on trips every few weekends, maybe to Strabane or Galway or across to Glasgow or just to Donegal

Town. It was always spontaneous. We might all be sitting about the living room and then Mark would suggest a place and go around each one of us.

— Are you on the trip? What about you, young fella? Are you on the trip?

They would pile into one car and take off. Once they passed the speed limit sign on the edge of Glenties, they were 'on the trip'. I got away with them the odd time if we had a break from Donegal training. Mark's habits used to drive the boys spare. We'd no sooner be in a bar than he'd see some auld buck at the counter and he would edge over and start chatting and soon the pair of them would find common ground and that was it. Doc would get wild impatient.

— Will you get over here, Giant, will you? What are you at?

And Mark would signal that he would be over in a second. I could see why the boys were impatient because they were waiting for him so we could have the craic ourselves. But he would never make that move. Eventually, the call would go out again.

— C'mon, Giant. We need to be hitting the road.

We would get back in the car and Mark would be quiet for a minute or two and you could put your house on the first thing he would say.

— Jesus, wild sound fella that.

Mark was a taxi man too. The cars he owned in his life were a white Toyota Carina and a black Volkswagen Passat, which was the car he was eventually killed in. You'd see him about the town in the evenings. The boys took to calling it the Confessional Box because of the number of people who would jump in just for a chat. Mark called everyone 'young fella', even if they were a couple of years older than him. So the greeting was always, 'Yes, young fella, what's the craic? Sit in there.' And the conversation was nearly always about the Glenties senior team or young players coming through or the usual question: Do you think Donegal will do anything the year?

Mark always had an interest in the football. But it was a dream for him when I became involved with the county. It was like a gift. Glenties wasn't producing county players at the time, so it was a little bit unreal for him to have a family member so close to the scene. I imagine 1992 was absolutely fantastic for him but I don't honestly know because I was so absorbed in training and what was happening that I wasn't paying much heed to what was going on around me. It is a funny thing about playing county ball. Players tend to switch off the moment they walk through the front door of the house and family members will chat to them about anything other than football. But Mark and I talked about 1992 all the time. And once I became established as a senior player, Mark was there for every single league and championship game. He never missed a game I played in, and in Ballybofey, especially, I always knew where to look for him. He was a constant presence in my life. He was a big brother. And I have to say: At that time in my life I loved Mark more than anything in the world.

———

Over Christmas 2013 and into the New Year, that same question was bouncing around in everybody's mind. Will Donegal do anything the year? Within the county, I got the sense that people felt it was over: It had been a fantastic couple of years but now we were done and dusted. And the supporters would probably have accepted that. They loved that team. There is an inherent modesty about Donegal people and maybe sometimes we accept things more easily than we should. Nationally, the view was that Donegal were a wreck. You could hear it and read it everywhere – and it was being expressed without much regret.

There was no doubt that we were starting from scratch again. We had been stripped bare by the previous season. I had waited for a few weeks to give the boys a chance to figure out if they really and truly wanted to go for it again. There was no point in me coming in and giving speeches. I had to stand back and they had to drive it. I never phoned one of them, even Michael.

I felt good that Christmas. We had a lovely few days at home. Bonnie and Aoibh had come into our lives and brought so much warmth and excitement into our home at the end of a difficult year. Toni-Marie had just turned six. Mark Anthony was four and Jimmy was just two. So in the space of six years, Yvonne and I went from having no children and so much time on our hands to having five young children. And the energy and joy that children bring to families and grandparents is a kind of power. That it happened to coincide with what was happening with Donegal made it a very fast and exciting and uplifting time for all our families. Christenings and birthdays and Christmases became full-on occasions once again. We had dinner at home on Christmas day, then headed into Glenties to visit Mum and Dad, and travelled up to Creeslough to the McFadden home that evening. That was probably the first time we became conscious of how big the family had become. Seven is a big gang to be landing at anyone's door. Christmas was short because Celtic's season was in full swing. But it cleared my head. I was very clear about how we would approach the season.

We had been deconstructed over the past year so we were vulnerable. We had Karl, David, Neil Gallagher, Paddy and

Patrick dealing with long-term injuries. Christy Toye was back in the panel after a year-long facial nerve affliction that had left us all wondering if he would ever play football again. It was a desperately bleak time for him and just the thought of him back in the dressing room was heart-warming. Christy's a big part of who we are. So we would build slowly and gradually and we would taper our minds and bodies to be ready for the third Sunday in July.

I had looked up some old faces when I was putting a back-room team together. They were all boys I had played with. I got to know Paul McGonigle in my last few seasons with Donegal and found him to be a very steady lad with a really shrewd read on the game. Damien Diver is a man that everyone in the county respected because he gave so much more to the Donegal team than he ever got out. He just never let us down. Damien was an Ardara man and I heard about him before I really knew him, heading over to county training and hearing about this youngster scoring 0-7 from play from half back. The Ardara–Glenties thing is a very weird dynamic. The passion between the clubs is very high and it nearly boiled over to hatred a few times. We had players who relocated to Ardara and lined out for them and if we met in the championship the air was always very tense. Glenties could never beat Ardara, so they were the enemy. When I was young, I couldn't stand losing to Ardara – even though I had plenty of practice at it. Now that has turned on its head. But the odd thing is that there is a good respect between the players. In 1996, when we drew four times in the championship, there was tea and sandwiches in the Highland after the first match. There were a few of us then having a pint in Leo's and the next thing Patrick Larry and Niall Campbell and a few of their boys came in. We were surprised to see them. This big cheer went up in the pub. Next thing a few more arrived and within half an hour, the two teams had gathered in Leo's. And from four in the afternoon until two in the morning it was a full-blown siege. So we were capable of that. When I joined the Donegal panel, Anthony Molloy went out of his way for me. Martin Gavigan was the first player I roomed with, and he is an absolute gentleman. It is a paradox between Ardara and Glenties – there's an immediate antipathy but a broader respect. So it was very easy to go into Ardara to ask Damien if he would be interested in joining up.

John Duffy from Ballyshannon was one of the most talented footballers I had ever laid eyes on. When he was a teenager, John was known all over the county, and he was feared because he could win games on his own. He could make the football sing. We went way back to the county U-21 team. I can still see one particular game where Donegal were awarded three penalties, and he scored each of them in a different place. He made the game look deceptively easy and never seemed in a hurry. He would look at the posts and someone would go in to block him and he would pull back that little bit and then strike it with the outside of the boot. He had a style of playing that was all his own. And John is great fun. He was never precious about himself or about the game. He was good to have about the place.

What we each had in common was that we had shared too many dressing rooms after big, heavy defeats. We had lost league finals and Ulster finals together and we had known that hurt. And I knew that even though these boys had finished playing, that lingering hunger would still be alive in each of them and that they would be excited about coming into our set-up and tasting what a winning dressing room could be like. And it was really enjoyable for me, in the first few weeks, to see them walking in the door, just like when we used to play together.

The crucial thing was talking to them about the culture of the group, making sure they knew that they were there to support the players and get the most out of them. And they would get the same in return. We were all lucky to have had people who put time into us when we were kids but the idea of how to coach was different then. Growing up, we would have heard it harsh: Don't do this! Fuck sakes! Pass it!

No. No. No. We didn't operate like that. The boys had to be indoctrinated into the whole thing of positivity and energy and respect. They had to get that concept. And there were a few situations where one of them would shoot the odd negative comment and then we'd just say: Hang on – just say it positively. And they got it. They all got it straight away because that's how they had been when they were footballers: positive and expansive and imaginative. Our way was that we could be very hard on the players in order to push them to greater achievement and effort, but only in a manner that was respectful.

Finally, I asked Pat to come back in for another year. He said yes straight away. And I felt that no matter what happened over the season, I had a loyal crew around me.

If we had a theme in the first weeks, it was about being questioned. We were being held up for examination and discussion. The belief was that Donegal were gone and we weren't coming back. We had had our day in the sun. We had run ourselves into the ground and we were crocked and we had won our All-Ireland and that was that. We began to talk about that. When you broke it down, the national conversation about Donegal wasn't really about football. It was about people. It was about us and it was about our character. The implicit message contained in the general opinion about Donegal was this: You don't have the fire. You don't work as hard as you did two years ago. Why? Because you have your medals now. So you have become soft.

We had to confront that and prove it incorrect. And the only way to do that was to go and win football games.

We met in the Station House in Letterkenny on a winter's evening to talk about that. It wasn't about trying to manipulate the boys. This group had been questioned all their lives. Now, three years later, they found themselves listening to the same doubts. I thought back to our first meeting in Downings. That room had been filled with nascent energy and promise and anticipation. This was different. The boys had won two Ulster titles and had been All-Ireland champions. They had lost all that. So this was a different mood. We were a different team and different people. I wrote two sets of numbers on a flip chart and asked the boys if they knew what those numbers represented. For a full minute there was silence before Frank McGlynn figured it: the number of days to the Ulster final and the number of days to the All-Ireland final. The clock was ticking. We had to make every single one of those days count.

It was a funny thing. All of the faces were there and I knew those boys. I knew the reserves of moral strength they had. I trusted them. And I could tell that their intentions for the season were pure. But I didn't sense any belief in the room. Not really and truly. Not that old raging, unquenchable belief. The effect of what had happened against Mayo that afternoon in Croke Park was with us in the room, like a shadow. We had to get rid of that. I turned it over and over in my mind as I drove home that evening. This was going to be a bigger test than anything we had done before.

———

After winning an All-Ireland medal with Donegal in my first year on the squad, I played on teams that lost Ulster finals in 1993, 1998, 2002 and 2004. It was a strange experience, going from that unreal high point of having seen the glory to gradually slipping and slipping to the stage where we seemed to find new ways of losing those hugely important games. At the same time, I was in my twenties and trying to figure out what to do with my life. When we won the All-Ireland, it was the era of 'jobs for the boys' and a few of us got positions with Eircom. It was good money for work that wasn't at all demanding. The big thing I learned at Eircom was how to play 25. I went from being clueless about cards to being fairly handy. And it was nice to have a steady pay cheque coming in and hours that made it easy to get to training. But I had a nagging feeling at the back of my mind that I wanted to do something different with my life. The notion of PE teaching was appealing to me but only as a very vague dream. I might as well have decided I wanted to be an astronaut. I didn't even have my Leaving Cert. So I had a conversation with my mother about it. I couldn't go back to the comp in Glenties. I just couldn't face that. But someone told me about an adult education course in Letterkenny. I was hesitant. I had no confidence in myself at all when it came to academic work. Mum put it very simply.

— You know, Jim, there's boys up the town there and they're walking about doing nothing. By the time you've finished that course and are out on the other side, they'll still be walking about doing nothing.

And that rang very true for me. I decided to do it there and then. Within a few months, at the age of 22, I was back in a classroom. Except this time, I was excited about it and I was open to hearing what was being said at the top of the room. It opened up an entire new world for me. Going back to school was easily the best thing I have done in my life. I devoured the course. When I phoned my parents to tell them my results, they thought I was winding them up.

That summer I found myself going through the same dilemmas that most students have in their teenage years. I had hoped to go to Jordanstown, but I wasn't accepted. And that was a crushing setback. Then I got a call from Tralee. At the time they were looking to recruit students who played football and I was eligible because I was on an access course as a mature student and was classed as an elite footballer. I drove down on a Sunday evening in the autumn of 1997 and my head was filled with doubts. My first class was the following morning and walking onto that campus was one of the most intimidating moments of my life. Everyone looked so young and they were all very confident. They seemed to know precisely what they were there for and where they were going. And they seemed to know one another. I stood at the door of the main entrance hall and there was this sound of voices and laughter bouncing off the walls and the notice boards were crammed with bits of paper, and all the students were carrying bags and folders and they were going places while I felt paralysed. And I had the exact same feeling that I used to have in school in Glenties. This voice telling me: This isn't for me. I don't belong here. This is for other people. So I turned on my heels and I sat down on a grass verge and imagined myself driving back up the road home. It would be easy. It was very appealing. I didn't even have my suitcase unpacked. I could be home for dinner. So I was having this conversation where I was consoling myself. Look: You did the Leaving and you did well to get it. But this is too far beyond you. There's no shame in that. And as I got up to walk to the car, this guy who ended up becoming a friend, Joe Dunne, cut across my path and said: 'You're Sports Science, aren't ya?' He must have known me from football or something. 'C'mon, I think we're in this room down here.' I followed him through the corridors and sat down at the desk and got through my first lecture. Within a few days, I had met the other football players and had settled. But I would have been away up the road had it not been for Joe and I doubt I would have come back.

I did two years in Tralee and then got accepted for Jordanstown on a scholarship. And again I went through the same cycle of doubt. Jordanstown was a university, and that held different connotations. But it provoked the same fears. No way would I be able for a university. But I made myself go along and one of the lecturers there, Mary Margaret Meade, opened my eyes to the power of sports psychology and that led on to a master's at John Moores University in Liverpool. Even then, it was the same voice: Jim McGuinness, who couldn't sit still in school, doing a master's – who are you codding? And Liverpool turned out to be the most enjoyable experience of all because the lectures were inspiring. By the end of those years, I was left with an unbreakable conviction in the power of education. I went from being someone who didn't lift a book to someone who loved reading and just wanted more and more information. Education empowers people. It can actually make you a different person – more rounded and cultured and self-confident. If I ever met someone in those years who mentioned that they were thinking of going back to school or college, I would do everything I could to try and convince them to.

So I felt I was moving through two worlds: education and Donegal football. I drove up and down the road to Tralee in a clapped-out car, weekend after weekend. Donegal had good teams and we started every year with general optimism that we could do something, but then each year we seemed to be moving slightly further from the epicentre of 1992. And every year we began to lose more and more players from that team. Noel Hegarty, a great, great player from Glen, retired after we lost a qualifier match against Kildare on a hot evening in Newbridge. We all knew he was finished and when Noel sat down we were all looking at him half expecting this big emotional speech. Noel just spread his arms out like a priest and shouted: 'Hal-le-fucking-lu-jah!' I thought it was one of the best things I ever heard. He had got through: he had put in his time with the county and he could walk away now with his head held high. And that was Noel. Teams are funny like that. The change is so gradual that it is almost invisible, but it seemed like no time at all had passed from my being a kid on the substitutes' bench when we beat Derry in the Ulster final of 1992 to being a midfielder when we played them again on 19 July 1998.

———

In a way, my life revolves around that Ulster final. Declan Bonner was manager that day. Damien Diver played right half back. John Duffy was right half forward. I was at midfield with Martin Coll and I felt strong about my game. I remember standing on the field in line waiting to meet President McAleese and feeling a weird sensation under my foot and when I lifted my heel, I saw that there was a stud missing under the ball of my foot. So while the president was coming through the tunnel surrounded by GAA dignitaries, I went bolting past them to our dressing room. I actually found the stud on the ground near where I had changed, but when I tried to screw it back in, it snapped. I was panicking now. It was just a few minutes to throw-in. Nothing like this had ever happened to me before because I was so meticulous about being ready. On Saturday nights before big games, I always polished my boots and redid the laces and checked the studs. Now here I was with no boots minutes before the biggest game I had ever played in. I had another pair of boots in my bag, but they had long studs and weren't suitable; the pitch at Clones was hard that day. So I reappeared wearing a stud boot on my right foot and a moulded boot on my left. I was marking Anthony Tohill, who was the pre-eminent midfielder in Ireland at that time. And for ten minutes after throw-in, he took me apart. I think I was still shocked about what had happened.

We lost the match by 1-07 to 0-08. In the seconds after the final whistle I knew I would remember the game for the rest of my life – but I didn't know why. We had played so well, all of us. We had the game won. I had actually got to grips with Tohill. Myself and Martin were going well at midfield and even though we were two points up in the last minutes, both teams knew we should have been up six or seven. I remember winning a ball at midfield and then slipping a pass to someone and thinking: That's it, we have it. I was absolutely convinced that we were Ulster champions. We were pushing the ball forward looking for a point to kill the game and we got turned over and Geoffrey McGonigle, the Derry forward, nudged Noel McGinley and won the ball to put Joe Brolly through on goal. He delivered this dagger of a goal and that was that. The whistle went. And the feeling at that moment ... It wounded us as a county, I think, that day. It wounded us all deeply. I know that I carried that defeat with me right through until 2011, when we won it back. We had a decent team in 1998 and our sense was that if we got through Ulster, then we could win an All-Ireland. As it turned out, Galway, the eventual winners, were an outstanding team; but at that moment, in mid-July, there was no clear-cut

contender. Galway had actually surprised everyone by beating
Mayo in the first round. Kildare was the other team that made
the final. So it was a very open summer. And we were out.

We stopped in Lisnaskea and boys were swamping pints.
Inevitably, we ended up in the Abbey Hotel and it felt like
everyone who had been in Clones ended up there. On Monday,
we spent a long time in McGroarty's bar. And there's good fun
and plenty of laughter, but it is all on the surface. You know
everyone is sick at heart. Then we moved on to Ballybofey
and we were gradually making a trail to Letterkenny because
we knew it was the only town in the county where we'd get a
nightclub on a Monday. There was nothing to hold us back. No
training. No All-Ireland. We ended up in the Golden Grill. Half
empty and the lights going and songs you've heard a thousand
times before and everyone sombre underneath the laughter,
and then the Doc and Mark and a few of the Glenties boys
showed up.

Next thing it was three in the morning and we were out on
the street with nowhere to stay. When I was doing the Leaving
Cert, I had lived in the apartment above Mac's Mace for two
years and the fella I lived with, Adrian Doherty, was still there
at this stage. So he got the call and, fair play to him, he said
we could crash for the night. There must have been twenty of
us: players, Glenties boys, a few hangers-on. Everyone found a
corner: the sofa, under the table, in the hallway, on the sitting
room floor. Everyone was pure exhausted. You set off Sunday
morning to win an Ulster final and you finish up in the early
hours of Tuesday morning on a carpet in Letterkenny town.

I couldn't sleep. So I got up and stood in the living room.
The apartment is on the first floor and it has a huge window
where you can see out the Port Road all the way to the Clanree
roundabout. It was around five in the morning and beginning

to get bright and the final was fucking haunting me. I stood there and I could see fragments of it and hear the players around me and my heart was beating faster and the excitement of knowing we were champions welled up inside me again, and then I would remember where I was and realise how far away from it we were. As far as ever. Further, maybe. And I just wanted to turn the clock back and allow us to do the few small things differently that would have changed everything. All of the others were asleep. It was very strange. So I stood there and the silence was absolute and dawn wasn't far away. Mark was lying on the floor in front of me. I stared out the window and every few minutes a lone car would head out the Port Road with its headlights on and all the time I was replaying the game in my mind. Then for some reason I looked down on the ground at Mark.

And I just stared at him. To this day I have that picture of him in my mind so clearly. I can see his black hair and I can see the silhouette of his forehead and his eyebrows and his nose as he slept. He had a goatee beard then. I knew he had come over from Glenties because he knew how much we were hurting.

I understood that. And I remember thinking: Jesus Christ, I love him so much. If anything ever happened him ... I would die. That would kill me. That is what I thought. And it was the pain of the defeat that made me think it. At least I had him. He was there for me. And I am so happy now that I had those minutes with him. It is a difficult thing to convey but it is a very precious moment and I feel as if it was given to me.

The Ulster final was on the third Sunday of July. I got an offer to go to America shortly afterwards. I phoned Mark the night before I was to fly out and asked him to run me to Dublin. So we left Ard Patrick in the Passat early the next morning. We stopped at Kee's filling station in Laghey. I went in and bought a bottle of 7 Up, a chicken salad sandwich and two packets of cheese and onion Tayto. He had half the sandwich and I had half. We had a bag of crisps each. We shared the 7 Up. Kildare had beaten Meath the previous day and we were chatting about that. Mark said: 'If them bucks could play the game today it would be a different story.'

We went through Lisnaskea and came upon a minor accident – a tractor had tipped into the back of a car. The RUC were patrolling the road and the traffic was backed way up and we were stopped. I said to the Giant, 'Do you want to swap over and I'll drive a while?'

— No, you're all right. We'll leave it until Cavan.

About a minute after that, we pulled out around the accident and went up the road about two hundred metres. It is a long, straightish road. This lorry was coming and as it went around a wee bend, it took a twist. We both saw it.

— That lorry's out of control.

Giant said 'I know' and took a firm grip of the wheel. I said: 'Watch yourself.'

We were doing about thirty miles an hour and Mark pulled right into the grass verge on the side and the lorry seemed to straighten up. Then, as it was coming to us and we were just about to pass, it came straight across the road and into us.

It hit Mark's side and lifted our car clean off the road and spun us like a matchbox three or four times. It sent us back up in the direction the lorry had come from because it hit us at an angle. Then we hit a tree and that stopped us. And we fell and the car was shuddering. And an otherworldly thing happened then: as soon as we hit the tree, the noon Angelus bell began to chime. The radio hadn't been on in the car. But the collision must have turned it on and it must have been twelve on the dot and you could just hear:

Donnnng.

Donnnng.

Donnnng.

Donnnng.

Nothing else.

I thought about that often because we were told in our house that Mark was born on the bell of the six o'clock Angelus. So I could hear these bells sounding and I still couldn't understand what had happened. Something like that knocks you out of your senses. The noise of the smash was just like a sledgehammer, so loud and violent and close. I turned off the radio and turned to Mark. 'Are you all right?' And I could see then that he was badly hurt. I pulled off my belt and jumped up onto my two knees and could hear footsteps fading. It was the boy driving the lorry. It turned out that he had no insurance for the lorry, there were sixteen faults with the lorry and it wasn't roadworthy. He shouldn't have been in it. It felt like forever before someone arrived. But the RUC men were only a few hundred metres back the road and they were with us in minutes. I put my left hand on Mark's left hand and told him that I loved him. I kept telling him not to die.

Someone told me later that when someone is dying, their hearing is the last sense to go, so he could probably hear what I said. I stayed in the car with him and kept trying to get him to come around. It was just us in the car. Reality was banging on the door outside and I wasn't letting it in. Medical people appeared. They were saying words I couldn't really hear. They were asking me to get out and I didn't want to. I didn't want to leave Mark. But I needed to let them do their job. So I moved away from the car and there was a long line of cars behind us, driving by in slow procession. I was on my knees on the grass praying to God not to take him and I could see faces looking through the car windows as they drove slowly by, looking in at Mark. And I was back making pleas.

— Please don't take him now.

— Please let him live a bit longer.

I got up off my knees and walked to the car. Medical people were working and then the guy on the left moved away from him and I looked into his face and I saw the same look that Neilly Bonner had when he walked away from Charles in the bedroom. Why was he doing that? Why was he stopping? He needs to keep going. Mark is going to be all right.

The medic walked over to me and put his hand out and said the words I was trying to push back.

— I am sorry about your brother.

No. No. No.

This was the very worst thing that could ever happen. A priest had materialised now and he was anointing Mark and another ambulance arrived. I was numb.

My brother.

My best friend.

Giant.

This was all happening around me. And I was shaken too because we had got an awful bang. I was cut all over my face and it must have been about an hour later and I was starting to get very sore. The medics put me in an ambulance, but I wouldn't leave until Mark was leaving. So my ambulance followed his. That journey from Lisnaskea to Enniskillen was the longest of my life. I was on my own in the back of this ambulance and the shock was overwhelming. It was just a huge wave pounding down and down on me. As they were checking me out, I started to understand that Mark wasn't here now and I got very sad. I couldn't stop crying. Then I began to fall asleep and I knew they had drugged me. When

I woke up Frank was sitting there with my uncle Seamus. I couldn't talk. I couldn't say what had happened. And then they took me home to my mother and my father and Mark wasn't with me. That was the most difficult thing of all. The thing that kills me to this day is the thought of the Gards knocking at the door to tell my parents. And I think of our own children and then I think of my parents and it is just the saddest thing.

So all the thoughts go through your head: Why did we have to lose the Ulster final? Why did I decide to go to America? Why did I ask Mark to drive me? What if we had changed seats then? You have to live with the answers you come up with for the rest of your life. There were many times afterwards that I wished I had been in his seat. I wanted us to have swapped.

In the hours afterwards, I knew what was coming down the track but now I was an adult. I wasn't a child, as I had been when Charles died, and I was thrown into this other deep reality. You are never going to see this person again. That leaves a permanent void inside you. That void is Mark. You struggle with that for years afterwards. I was fragile and I was broken from that moment. I will have that vulnerability inside me until the day I die.

Things were in motion. The numbers coming through the house for the wake were staggering. Many were those people he had chatted to, people he had given an hour of his life just to ask them about themselves. 'I only met your brother the once but I feel as if I knew him all my life.' We heard that so many times. There were so many people and most of them were young. So it was a strange atmosphere. There was a lot of laughter and fun in the talk about Mark. We waked him for two nights. On the second night I spent the hours from about four in the morning until daylight with him, alone in the room in our house while the others were asleep. For a few hours it was just me and him. So I spent that night just talking to him as if he was sleeping.

The Giant had been playing reserve that year. The senior team would often arrive at the end of the first half of the reserve game and I used to stand on the verge and watch him play for a while. A few weeks after the accident, we were playing a league game down in Burt. I threw the bag in the dressing room and headed over to look at the game. And I was scanning the field looking for the Giant. Where is he? I can't see him. So I turned to the fella beside me.

'Where's — ?'

For a second or two, I completely forgot that he was gone. And then your legs buckle beneath you and you feel dizzy and the freefalling feeling is back, worse than ever. It would take about ten years before I could accept what had happened. Football helped, but my game fell apart. We played Fermanagh in the first round of the Ulster championship the following summer. At the end of the national anthem, I looked for him standing at the usual spot and he wasn't there. And I just felt very heavy. For the first time in my life I couldn't understand what I was doing out on the football pitch.

———

Not long after Donegal were beaten in the 1999 championship, I got a call from Christy Ryan about going out to Philadelphia to kick football. I told him I would go if Glenties were knocked out of the championship. Then we played St Eunan's and they scored a last minute goal and the following day I was in this pub in Philly signing up for their summer championship. It felt like the NFL draft because this was the final day of registration and the place was absolutely packed. Myself and Brian McLaughlin landed in and it was as if the team we were signing for had pulled some kind of stroke by getting us at the last moment.

That was the day I first clapped eyes on Gogie. He is one of those people who suck you into the chaos of their life and you are happy to go. Within weeks, Brian and I knew the stories about him – how he had broken a bone in his neck on the pitch and checked himself out of hospital. He did all kinds of repair jobs and took us under his wing. He would do roofing jobs and offer to check for broken tiles just in case – and he'd take a hammer up the ladder with him in case he could find none. My summer was spent driving around DC in a pick-up with Christy Ryan, talking about football. We would just drive from site to site. Every so often Gogie would have some Saturday work out of town and we would set off at 6.30 for a day trip. 'A wee job upstate' he'd call it. We often had to put steel frames down on the roofs of houses to support the felt that would get tacked down. On one particular day we drove for about two hours and arrived at this house and worked solidly for about six hours. There was a group of Hispanic carpenters and they were chatting away and sort of gesturing but we were paying no heed. When we got finished, we packed everything away and we were sitting in the van, wrecked. Gogie took out a box of Marlboro and was puffing away when all of a sudden he started staring at the house and then he was squinting.

— What are you looking at?

No response.

— What are you looking at, Gogie?

Silence.

— What are you looking at?

And he was silent for about ten seconds.

— The number on that house. We should have been next
door.

My hands were raw from the steel and I just said, 'You're
having a fucking laugh, Gogie.' I always remember what he said
because he was so serious: 'Jim. Nobody wants this to be a joke
more than me.' I asked him what he was going to do. He just
shrugged. 'I'm going fucking home.' He was over it by the time
we were back in Philly.

Gogie was a very funny guy to be around. He has this stutter
sometimes but he made it work to his advantage. We were all
in this bar the day after the Philadelphia county final and it
was square-shaped, so you could see everyone who was sitting
there. This conversation got up where people told each other
how they ended up in America. Some were American, others
Irish. When Gogie was asked, he took the floor.

— I was g-g-g-going to be a j-j-j-ockey.

And this group of girls started laughing and Gogie made a
show of being annoyed, so they were all apologetic. And now
he has everyone's attention. And he tells his story.

— I was all s-s-s-s-set. I was brilliant. And I got a chance to
ride at the C-C-C-Curragh ...

And he describes the day and taking the horse around
the paddock and the crowd and all the money on him and
they get into the stalls and his heart thumping and then the
starter shoots the gun. Everyone in the bar is really drawn in.
Eventually someone says, 'What happened?' And Gogie shakes
his head and there's a pause. He keeps us hanging for a full
thirty seconds.

— By the time I said 'g-g-g-g-g-giddy up' sure the race was
nearly fucken over.

And then he actually fell on the floor, he was laughing so
hard. He had sold every single person in the bar.

We got to the Philadelphia final. The referee was down on us. If you were a county player you were going to get singled out and I was busted all day long. Eventually the game stopped and a big brawl broke out. The match was abandoned. It was never replayed – they just awarded it to the other team. This old man from Termon, who had been out in Philly for years, used to sit under the shade of a tree and watch the games, so I trotted over and sat down beside him. When I got home a few weeks later, Declan Bonner phoned me. I was in Belfast in college. Declan wanted to know what I was at in Philly. I hadn't a clue what he was on about. It turned out I had been given an eight-week ban for bad language, even though I'd surveyed proceedings from under that tree. The message was clear: don't be coming back to Philly.

There was a whole gang of boys from home out there that year. Boys who had never held a paintbrush talking about bonuses worth five thousand if they got a job done on time. Nobody gave much thought as to why we were out there. We just were. A crowd of eejits from Donegal let loose. We decided we'd head to Wildwood one weekend. The plan was to get a train to Atlantic City and then get a bus. Myself and Hugo Daly had a few beers at the bar in the station and left it late for the train. The bar girl told us to run straight down the tunnel and hop on the 22, so that's what we did. We sat down feeling pleased with ourselves and I turned to Hugo and said, 'Jesus, Hugo, it's a fine train, this.' It turned out we were in first class. It also turned out that we were on the New Jersey transit non-stop going the wrong way. I will always hear the conductor when he looked at our tickets. 'Awwww, man. You are waaaaaaay off.' There was nothing to do but sit back and enjoy the spin. The conductor was great. He took pity on us and let us sit in first class drinking Bud Light. Four hours later we were back at the bar in Penn station. By the time we got to Wildwood we had no idea where the others were. We found out later that they had actually been in the same night club as us. We found a bar called the Celtic that opened until six a.m. and we persuaded the owners to let us sleep on the floor there. The next morning, at around eleven, Gerard McBride and Joe Brady wandered in for a casual drink. They didn't even seem surprised to see us. We didn't know what we were at.

And that was the point. For me, that summer was just about getting away. And every single day was hard. It was fun and the weather was hot and we had money and I was laughing hard. But I was hurting so much. I was in freefall and there was nothing I could do. Mark was on my mind all the time and I had this pain way down that never went away and I felt as if my body was shutting down. For years, I got these electric shocks for no reason at all. Shooting, lightning pains. Philadelphia was about pretending that life was still normal. But nothing worked. All I was doing was trying to distract myself and to dodge things. I was back in the circus again.

———

I t took a decade of grieving.
   About ten years after the accident, I was able to have that conversation with myself: Mark is not coming back. Until then, I had been drifting and doing the best I could. But minor problems and little obstacles were magnified by ten. You turn small issues into big things. Something as trivial as a parking ticket can floor you. It is as if you are codding the world that you are okay. Maybe around the time I got the U-21 job, I was starting to think about the future in a coherent way. I was starting to ask:

What am I going to do with my life? How is the rest of my life going to pan out?

Asking yourself that doesn't make things okay and your reality is still the same. But for the first time you are not drifting and drifting and drifting without any meaning. I can honestly say that life meant nothing to me for a fair few years.

That changed after I met Yvonne. We started going out after that day in Croke Park in 2002 and we married in 2006. She slowly and steadily helped me to rebuild a sense of who I was and to get some focus in my life. I am not sure if I would ever have got there without her. And we were both blessed with the children we have. I had wanted a boy so badly and a part of me probably felt that it would make things okay or change things. But, of course, life doesn't work like that. Toni-Marie was our first child and I was delighted she was a girl because I realised within seconds of first seeing her that she was her own wee person. As all the children are. I had been pretending, or hoping in some mad kind of way, that having a wee boy would change the dynamic and make things the way they had been. When Toni-Marie came into our lives, I understood that could never happen. Then we had Mark Anthony and I understood that he was a unique individual in his own right.

Now, I always look at the parallel between winning football games and my own belief system. When things aren't going well you have to believe you are going to win. It is never over. You keep playing.

And I feel I am going to meet Charles and Mark again. I believe that absolutely. I never lost my faith in God in all of this. I questioned it deeply but never lost it.

The thing about death and bereavement is that people assume it is okay after a year or so, but the reality is that people are never the same again. It is a constant daily struggle. The family were grieving Charles for years and years when people in the town might have forgotten that it ever happened. With Mark, we lost a really, really good person. I love him more today than at any other stage in my life and I am closer to him now as well.

Mark and Charles: I carry them with me inside me and the way I feel about it is that whatever I see, they see.

Whatever I experience, they experience.

———

By my late twenties, one question about Glenties was beginning to preoccupy me. Why do other towns win but we never do?

I was sick of it: of Ardara, of Kilcar, of Ballyshannon, of Killybegs, of Donegal Town. Our town was like a compass point for all of these places and yet we were always out in the cold looking in through the window while they won championships. That drove me mad. We were trying our best but never in a deliberate, orchestrated way. It was like when you're a child playing snakes and ladders and you always land on the boy that takes you right back down to the bottom of the board. After every season we were back at the beginning again.

It was around then that I began to look outside of myself and at the club. We were edging towards competitiveness but each summer seemed to contain a new life lesson. We met Aodh Ruadh in 1994. Our attitude was: Crowd of fuckin' townies – we'll get stuck into them. And we went out onto the field and they absolutely battered and dominated us. It was like a lecture: This is senior football. The four games we played against Ardara in 1996 were locally famous and we finally beat them after extra time. Then we played St Eunan's in the quarter-final and they beat us. Another year, we played Killybegs in Kentucky and lost by a point. The year I went to Philadelphia, St Eunan's knocked us out with an injury-time goal. So we were close but a million miles away too.

The 1990 intermediate championship was the first men's championship that Naomh Conaill had ever won. At the time, I felt we were a very slick, serious outfit but as I recall now, a few of our lads would have been having a smoke in the huddle at half time. Our team talk was designed to encourage discipline without compromising our social life. So the night before a big Sunday game the message was something like: 'Don't do anything different, now, boys. Go up the town and have your few pints and be home at half twelve. Don't break your routine. No point in sitting in drinking minerals and then freezing up tomorrow.'

But football was a wild big deal for Glenties. We could lurch from division three to division one. We had no tactics. We had no strength and no conditioning. Occasionally, we imposed a drinking ban on ourselves but it was like a game of who blinks first. Everyone was waiting for the other man to crack.

We had a lot of good people who gave untold hours to the club and to coaching. And we had some good footballers. We had five Donegal U-21 players; by 1990 John Gildea, myself, the Cat, Doc and Big Roarty had made the squad. Paddy Campbell was coming through. So we knew if we could keep that group of players together we would improve. And it took such a long time. We had to wait until the winter of 2002 before we won the league. There was a cavalcade through the town to celebrate it.

It was around then that I took a notion that Glenties would win the Donegal senior championship. Martin Regan, the minor manager, had guided a team to an A title for the first time in forty years in 2003. We won it again the following year.

So by 2005 we felt we could make a strong push.

My Donegal career ended a week before we played Antrim in that year's Ulster championship. The club was playing Killybegs. County players weren't supposed to play, but I was asked to tog out as a substitute, so I did. By half time the game was going away from us and Joe McKelvey asked me to go in. I felt under fierce pressure. I knew I'd be in trouble if word went around. But I went on at the beginning of the second half. Within three minutes, I had scored a goal and finished my career. I caught a ball in the middle of the field, turned away from the midfielder marking me, took a solo and looked up. I saw Leon Thompson, one of our forwards, making a run from the left to right corner of the field. And I went to deliver the ball. As I kicked it, my left foot was coming up while at the same time John Ban Gallagher, the Killybegs man whom I had often partnered at midfield for Donegal, came across me with his shoulder, straight into my quadriceps. My leg kind of doubled around him like a U. It snapped at the knee joint. The pain was like nothing I had ever experienced. Both cruciate ligaments were gone and I did my lateral collateral ligament at the back of my knee. There was nothing left to support the knee. I knew I was in serious trouble. Some of the boys were trying to carry me off the field and I could hear the panic in their voices. The leg was swelling up something serious. Yvonne was at the match and she ended up driving me to the hospital. That was the day I realised how bumpy the Donegal roads are.

I should never have played. I was 32 years old. In the *Democrat* that Thursday, Brian McEniff said that the injury could be 'the death knell' of my career. If he was saying it, I knew I was finished. I read that and a wave of sadness washed over me and I felt sick and numb.

I could still hear him asking me that day in Ballyshannon, 'What do you think?'

All those evenings down at the field chasing a football in the half dark. For it to end like this seemed like a waste.

The following months were just a miserable joke. I had an MRI scan and the notes got lost and I had to have it done again. I was told to run on it after seven weeks, which was the result of a misdiagnosis. I ended up having to have a second operation in Manchester and I paid for it myself. It came about through happenstance: Roy Keane was at a function in Mayo and someone there told him what had happened to me. He gave this guy the number of the Manchester United surgeon and told him to have me call him. That message was passed on to me. It was so classy of Keane to try to help out someone he didn't even know. So I rang the surgeon, not sure if anything would come of it. I phoned on a Friday evening and was in the operating theatre the following Wednesday for a scope and then booked in for an operation a week later. The surgeon was wonderful. He explained everything. He ended up using one of my hamstrings and the middle third band of my patellar tendon to replace what I had severed. There are two pins in my leg to this day. It felt great, even if it cost me thirteen thousand pounds sterling – a lot of money and even more when you are a student.

The operation took place the same night that Liverpool played AC Milan in the Champions League final. The hospital staff knew I was studying in Liverpool and when I was coming round after the operation a nurse told me that the game wasn't going well. Liverpool were three goals down at half time. Then a wee while later another nurse came in, saying, 'Big celebrations in your town tonight!' For a few days I didn't know if it was true or if it was just the morphine.

So I ended up coaching Glenties that summer. We had a very young, very strong team. Leo McLoone played, even though he was still under sixteen. Leon was just out of minor. We got to the final against St Eunan's, who were teeming with county players. The game ended in a draw and we had performed fairly well. So I came up with this game plan for the replay which involved getting our boys behind the ball, closing down space and not allowing St Eunan's to play the way they wanted. That was the first manifestation of the system I would put in place with Donegal five years later. It made the other managers nervous. I was convinced we would win with it. And the funny thing was that there was no tension at all in the town before the replay. Everyone had been edgy before the drawn game, but now we weren't so fixated on the occasion. We had marched behind the band. So it became all about football and we relaxed. A good few of the boys had a few hundred quid on themselves at 6/1. They drove over to Ardara to place their bets just to make the collection that bit sweeter.

On the Tuesday evening at training before the replay, we were taking a session and Hughie Molloy, the manager, turned to me and said: 'Jesus, Jim, it's wild altogether. The only thing that's making me sad is that you're not there yourself, having played for the club all your life.'

If Hughie hadn't said that, I would never have asked, but I was feeling really apprehensive and excited, and I asked him if he would put me in for the last few minutes of the replay if we were five or six points up. Hughie thought about it for a few seconds and said he would. It was dangerous because this was only about four months after the operation and the knee was still very fragile. But I was like a child at the thought of it. And now I wasn't just coaching the team to try to win the game. I was coaching them to try to win it well. Nobody knew about the plan except Hughie and my brother Frank.

The final was on 9 October 2005. The boys played out of their skins and Eunan's were struggling to get any kind of joy out of our defence. Right enough, we were six points up with about five minutes left. Hughie and John Molloy were standing at the river end of the ground and I was across the pitch at the stand side. So I trotted back towards the dug-out. Frank was in the stand with Mum and he turned to her.

— That's Jim now away round to go on.

She didn't believe him. There were about three minutes left and the score was 1-08 to 0-05. Hughie just said: 'Are you ready so?' I felt like I was playing my first ever game. And I wasn't on the field thirty seconds when St Eunan's scored a goal and you could feel the whole mood shift. We were anxious. They sniffed a chance. And I was on the field with a knee that could buckle at the slightest contact. We held on. The boys held on. How it ended was that John Gildea won a free and I made a diagonal run out towards the stand and took a pass from him and won another free. I had the ball in my hands when the referee blew it up. The first man over to me was Frank. He had jumped the fence.

People talk about the once-in-a-lifetime exhilaration of those few seconds after the whistle in an All-Ireland final and it is all true. But I think that minute or so in Ballybofey may have brought us into a miraculous place. Nobody in Glenties ever thought we would get to live this day. Full decades had passed when you would only talk about Glenties as county champions if you were telling a joke. And here we were now heading home with the Dr Maguire Cup. Words were needless. I ended up just looking around me a lot for the next few days, the same as in the early years. The town was mental that Sunday night. A few friends of mine were staying in the house and Mum made a big fry-up for us. It was one of those damp, bleak October Monday mornings, but to me the day was beautiful. We got into Leo's at about eleven in the morning and the place was already packed. And when you scanned the tables you could see the different teams scattered around the room. The 1990 team were drinking together and a few of Leo senior's compadres from '65 were knocking about. I remember taking my first pint and having a very clear thought: This is going to be one of the best days of my life. I sat down at the table and the conversation was about when we had started playing football down at the field.

We probably sensed that day that the club had entered a different realm of existence. The following autumn, seventy-six lads showed up for reserve training. Men were rummaging around the attic to haul out football boots that hadn't seen daylight for twenty years. Watching what the senior team did made them want to play again. They just wanted to kick a football again. They were excited. We built a new pitch and dressing rooms at the cost of €400,000. And it made me proud even though I was smarting that the club board had voted against paying for my operation for an injury I had suffered while playing for the senior team. By 2006, I was back playing for Glenties. My Donegal days were over and what I had often heard was true: once you are finished with the county, it is as if you never existed. You just never hear from them again. The ship disappears over the horizon and that's that. I was player-manager in 2009 when Glenties were beaten by St Eunan's. We won our second senior title in 2010 and became established as one of the strongest clubs in the county.

So that morning in Leo's was a moment when we got to pause and look at who we once were and who we were becoming.

Emotion is such a powerful thing. I'd stick my head up from the table every so often and just scan the room to see these faces who had lived and breathed Naomh Conaill football for as long as I could remember: Pat Ward and Daffy and Red Joe and John Bacon and John Block. The younger boys were all together just having the craic. Leo was behind the bar, master of ceremonies, taking phone calls from Highland Radio every so often and describing the scene. As the beer kicked in you would see one of the older boys actually welling up. One phrase was repeated over and over: 'I never thought I would see this day.'

But here we were.

———

Donegal played Laois on 2 February. It was the first day of the national league. We had spent the previous few months back where it began, running through the salt air and the dunes in Dunfanaghy. The effort was there and the enthusiasm was back and the sense of fun was still there. And I was unhappy. We didn't feel right. It felt as if something was restraining us. And I knew I was going to have it out with them. After dinner on the Saturday night we all sat down. And we talked. Certain truths were established. We agreed that we needed to stop living in the past. But we needed to become what we used to be. We agreed that we were working hard. But we weren't possessed. We were just hoping to have a good season. That's a million miles away. For forty minutes, we left the players alone.

When we came back, we were struck by the players who spoke. Rory Kavanagh stood up and he spoke very directly and powerfully. Leo McLoone and Patrick McBrearty followed.

These are quiet enough boys who usually sit back and observe, but there was a bone-deep honesty to their words. And they wanted us to get back to the rawness and hunger with which we had played through our first season. In 2013, we were targeted because we were All-Ireland champions. Now we needed to forget about all that and think about taking other teams down again. There was nothing to stop us from overwhelming teams. The mood was very solemn and the meeting went on close to midnight. Our schedule went out the window. We could see the boys reaching a resolution between themselves and they walked out of the room in a different frame of mind. Damien Diver shook his head after the players left. He said: 'Laois are in for some pasting tomorrow.'

In the dressing room the next afternoon, that was the message. The boys were getting ready and I was asking simple questions aloud for them to answer to themselves.

— In or out?

— Truth or lie?

— Black or white?

— You need to decide now. You're being questioned. This is the moment it starts. Whoever is going now, go with it. And you need to decide now. In or out? Black or white?

And once the game started, their intensity was off the scales. They were supporting in twos and threes and breaking through tackles and making lung-busting runs on the off-chance that they might be needed. They were just fizzing with energy. We won 2-19 to 0-10. But the result wasn't important. There was a chance we could have won the game anyhow. The significant thing was that they had played true to themselves. The purity of intent was there and they knew it. They had rediscovered it themselves. That is the magic of team sport. People need to be striving for new things and to feel that they are moving forward. Once that starts, the group can begin very quickly to move at frightening speed.

We found ourselves again that day in Portlaoise and didn't look back. We spent much of our time on the training ground developing our kick-outs and putting pressure on the opposition kick-outs and slowly getting the energy back in our legs. We played games without showing how we intended setting up over the summer, particularly if we were featuring in games that were on television. We were promoted to division one and went on a training camp to Portugal a week before we played Monaghan in the division two final in Croke Park. Before the season began, I had phoned Donall Barrett and asked him to head a fundraising committee for the team. He liaised with Seamus Carr in London, who did untold work for us. People from across the world donated money to the training fund. Their only stipulation was that the money did not go to the county board. These training camps gave the impression that huge resources were being channelled into the senior team. But people were working like demons to make that happen for us.

The boys trained three times a day in Portugal. They got to live like professional athletes for a week and they got to spend a bit of time together. They are always great fun to be around. We all liked to have a good time and we enjoyed one another's company. There was always some kind of prank going on. The best one in Portugal was the one with Oreo cookies. Colm and Frank and a few of the usual suspects bought a packet of Oreos for the cup of tea in the evening. Some of the boys had developed a liking for them out in America. So they scraped the filling out and replaced it with toothpaste and then were really careful about putting the biscuits back in the tray so it looked like the packet had just been opened. They laid it out with a few other packets on the table. Four or five of them sat around and waited until the others came along for a cup of tea. A few boys didn't bother with any biscuit but finally big Neil reached out and grabbed an Oreo. And the boys were trying to stay casual when he bit into it. But the thing was, Neil didn't react. He was just nibbling away and chatting. Eventually, he looked at the packet and shook his head.

— Jesus. They're wild minty, aren't they?

We came back and trained hard on the Tuesday and Thursday before the league final, with an eye on the championship. On Sunday we played the league final in Croke Park against Monaghan and we hit the wall after twenty minutes. We would have liked to win the game, but not at the expense of championship preparation. And the boys heard plenty about it from the Monaghan team. Dick Clerkin told Rory Kavanagh, 'You've never beat me in your career.' And it was the same over the field. 'Youse can't beat us. Youse'll never beat us.' I was happy to hear about all that. It was tough to swallow that evening but I felt it would do us good. Leaving Croke Park, I got a text from a Donegal supporter. I didn't know the number and didn't know how the sender had got mine. It was very sharp and reproachful and said that we were going nowhere and that we had fallen back so much since 2012. And it cut me to the quick because at that point in time I knew that was how it looked to everyone outside. We lost 1-16 to 1-10 and the defeat conformed to the national view that we were finished. But we didn't feel like that. Not inside.

My only concern was that the boys would subconsciously absorb the dismissiveness. Nobody feared us. There is only so much you can hear and read without taking notice. We spoke about self-reliance and about only ourselves mattering. Still. Shortly before we played Derry an article appeared in the *Derry Journal* – which would be a big paper north of the Gap in Donegal – that wasn't so much scathing as degrading. It referred to us as a so-called mythical team that could be broken into three syllables. Don-e-gal. And the old question came back: Would they write this about Kerry or Dublin? Would they write about Tyrone in those terms? They felt they could write anything they wanted about us. The author queried whether we had anyone to cope with Mark Lynch. Nobody, he reasoned. That jumped off the page. Lynch is a terrific all-round player but it was an issue I was happy to put to our players when we met. I asked Neil McGee if he felt he was up to it. Then I went to Karl Lacey. 'How many All-Stars have you, Karl? They don't think you are up to it.'

We had our work done, but it was an awkward game because Neil Gallagher had an ankle problem and only lasted a half so we ended up rotating him and Christy and Martin McElhinney. Celtic Park was packed out. There was a feeling that we were there for the taking. When we left the dressing room, which is behind the posts at the city end of the ground, the stewards were supposed to open the double gates to let us out. But they were giving instructions to the boys to trot over and go through this narrow single-file gate at the far end. Neil McGee and a few of the boys were shaking the gate. They were frothing. Your man wouldn't shift. But our boys were so pent up that I had a good feeling about the afternoon.

That game got us up and running for the summer. Leo finished a really slick goal move after half time and we saw it out comfortably. We were drawn against Antrim in the semi-final and were able to win it without showing too much of ourselves. And one year on, we were back in Clones, back in an Ulster final, back against Monaghan. We were where we wanted to be.

The previous year was still very vivid in our minds. A lot of things that went on in that match we had carried with us throughout the winter. Mark McHugh wasn't with us now: he had decided in May that he wasn't enjoying the game and was spending the summer in the States. But we hadn't forgotten that tackle on him. And there were words thrown about like salt on wounds from that time. In the hotel before the game, I stuck a photograph on the wall that someone had taken seconds after Monaghan won in 2013. Michael Murphy was on his knees. He was distraught and he was trying to disappear into his own world. Four or five Monaghan boys were around him and, rather than celebrating their moment, they were jeering at Michael. Word came back to us that the Monaghan boys had told people that they didn't fear us. They considered some of us to be soft. They considered some of us to be yellow. I got a phone call from someone who had heard this being said and I repeated what I heard verbatim at training. I repeated it night after night. I confronted the boys with it when we were in the huddle.

— They are walking around the place calling you cowards.

— You a coward, Paddy?

— You a coward, Neil?

I knew the men that they were. But it was no good me knowing it. They had to go and show it or else Monaghan were right. That was going on every single night. They were becoming more and more edgy. Michael and Paddy McGrath sparked one night and there is a big disparity in size between the two boys, but Paddy wouldn't yield an inch. That was a week out and if I could have fast-forwarded time I would have.

I had asked Pat Shovelin and Joe McCloskey to do up the dressing rooms in Clones before the squad arrived at the ground. People forget that St Tiernach's is Monaghan's home ground. So before the boys went in to change, we had Donegal flags hung on the walls and their jerseys hung up on the walls and water bottles beside their gear. We had a commemorative name card folded and sitting on top of the gear. We had spent hours a few nights earlier trying to work out where each of the boys usually sat so we could have it perfect for them. And it looked picture perfect when the boys walked in. It wasn't like a normal dressing room. It was just a small touch to help them feel that this was a big day in their football lives. After they had changed and were comfortable, I began talking them through the game plan. We had deconstructed Monaghan's patterns of play to a very detailed level and were confident we had them figured. We knew we could compete physically this time because we had the work done. And we had devised a game plan around a double-switch, where we moved the ball to one wing and then worked it quickly to the other side of the field and looked to hit a left-footer on the right side and a right-footer on the left side. We staggered our forward line along the 21 and 45 and out at the 50. But it wasn't about the game plan. It was about character.

— This is about you. About each of you. As people. They think you are weak. That you are soft. That you can't look this challenge down. That you are going to break. This is about you as men. They don't fear you. They think you are yellow.

Michael was on his feet before I had finished.

— I'm fucking sick of listening to this. I don't want to hear any more of this.

— Sit down, Michael, good man. You might be sick of listening to it but you haven't proved anything different yet. Because as you stand here now it is the truth. As we stand here now, they beat us in an Ulster final. As we stand here now, until we prove them wrong, it is the truth. Now, everyone, get on your feet.

And then Michael spoke. He didn't take long, but by God, it gave you the shivers. And out the door they went. I turned to

Pat and said: 'If Monaghan are able to beat us today, then good luck to them.'

This time, we were ourselves from the very first minute. It was the only game in which I let the opposition manager know our intentions by shouting out instructions to the boys. I wanted Monaghan to know what we were at because there was nothing they could do about it, in a single game. And I wanted to try to spread confusion. Even if they figured out what we were doing they couldn't make any meaningful adjustment. The boys were primed. When Ryan McHugh was tackled high three or four of our players were over pushing him and pointing him out to the referee. We were controlling the game this time. And we got touched by bad luck when Eamon and Frank clashed heads going for a ball and Christopher McGuinness finished a goal chance in fine style and Monaghan were alive again. The great thing about the match was that they came really well prepared and were on their game too. It was a true contest. But the boys kept doing the simple things well, over and over. I wasn't interested in the final whistle. I just wanted to watch them drive as hard as they could for as long as they could. Whenever the whistle went, it went. I wanted to see Donegal making a statement and they did that. That was why it was probably the sweetest day of the lot. All of the qualities that we valued about ourselves shone through that afternoon of football.

On Monday, we got to have the Anglo Celt at home for the night. It's funny: we invest everything trying to win these cups and once the parades and homecomings are over, we don't even know where they are half the time. We had the Sam Maguire for just one evening in 2012. So it was special for the family to have the Anglo Celt so soon after the team won it. We were out in the garden and the weather was fine. The twins were almost one year old, which was hard to believe. The day made me feel good because I felt they hadn't seen anything like enough of me. The schedule was very intense on the family. I was usually home on Mondays but would fly back to Glasgow first thing on Tuesday morning and go straight to work at Celtic. Late that afternoon, my father-in-law, Colm, would collect me at Belfast airport and drive me to Ballybofey for training. We would leave for Belfast again afterwards. Knowing that home was just a half hour down the road and thinking of what they were doing, but having to drive away, was the worst part. It would be close to midnight when Colm dropped me off and then he would head to Creeslough. I'd get an early morning flight back to Glasgow and then repeat the journey on Thursday. I don't know how many evenings myself and Colm would be chatting in the car and the next thing I'd wake up and we'd be outside the hotel. I was so grateful to have him that summer. Seeing the cup in our home made a bit of sense of it. Yvonne set the camera on delay and we sat on the sleeper steps and got a lovely photograph of that moment. It felt like the first time we had sat still in a fair while.

———

A few days after the Ulster final, Pat Shovelin dropped into the house just for a chat. I was down in the office and he popped his head round the door and asked me what I was up to. I laughed. 'If I tell you, you can't tell anyone.' I was just finishing off the last couple of lines of a plan about how we were going to beat Dublin. I wasn't fully sure we were even going to meet them because we had a quarter-final and whatever else to play. But I knew that if we hoped to beat them, we needed to plan for it well in advance.

They had owned every team they met over the summer and they appeared to be getting stronger with every game. You regularly heard the word 'invincible' mentioned in radio discussions about them. It is a dangerous word, that. There was history between Dublin and Donegal. The 2011 semi-final had been central to people forming their opinion about us. And the league match in Ballybofey when we were All-Ireland champions had had a really dark atmosphere. But we had drawn the game. That seemed to have been forgotten.

Normally, you would like to have three weeks to prepare for a team but I knew in my heart it wouldn't be enough for Dublin. I spent all my spare hours – between working and preparing for the quarter-final – watching recordings of Dublin games. I was studying as deeply as possible. It meant that once we reached the All-Ireland semi-final and the boys began to turn their thoughts to Dublin I could say to them: I know what Dublin are about. I know what they are going to do and how they are going to do it and that's all you need to know.

So Dublin were floating around at the back of my mind when we played Armagh in the quarter-final. It was a day that showed us just how easily planning can fall apart.

I always look for good match-ups before games and on this instance we had six defenders suited to their attackers. Paddy McGrath was assigned Kyle Carragher, Neil would shadow Jamie Clarke, Eamon McGee was on Stefan Campbell and so on. But when the ball went in, Eamon stayed at full back even though Campbell went out to wing half. We ended up making quick positional shifts all through the defence, so we only had one of the match-ups we had planned for. And it was disorienting. It took a few minutes to work out what had happened on the sideline and we could sense that it was causing confusion through the team. Nothing was quite as it should be. So we were trying to fix it as the game went on, but Armagh were constantly rotating anyway, so even as we tried to get our shape back, the puzzle changed. We were thrown. In addition, Armagh were really well set up. Paul Grimley had assisted Kieran McGeeney for a number of years at Kildare and now, the roles reversed, back at Armagh, they were well organised. They were playing with clarity and intensity and we were in a game. We had asked Christy to man-mark Aaron Kernan whenever he came forward into our half and to play as a sweeper whenever he remained in his half of the field. But Kernan was very busy and Christy ended up giving him too much attention, so we didn't have the cover we had planned.

It was as if there were little fires starting all over the pitch. To outsiders, it just looked like a good half of football – and it was that. But we were completely addled. It took us most of the half to get it fixed. The match was taking shape during all that and it narrowed into one of those unflinching Ulster derbies that can look unruly in Croke Park. There was a lot of pushing and shoving going on and at one point Kevin Moran, our doctor, was flung to the ground by an Armagh player. There was some holding and even headlocks going on off the ball. It was like the old Armagh. They were very intimidating and they were determined. But none of us on the sideline truly felt at any moment that we were going to lose the game. It was tough stuff and it was a gripping match and when it reached the hour mark, Michael just stepped up and Patrick kicked a couple of excellent points, which won it for us. We got there. It was a victory based on experience. The boys knew how to win these games. So we were back in a semi-final and we all felt as if we had managed to do so while flying blind. Nobody noticed. And it meant we won without revealing anything of where we were at.

So now I could take out the folder on Dublin for real. It wasn't that I had been taking the earlier games for granted. The truth is that I was hedging my bets because of the enormity of the challenge that Dublin presented to all teams. On the bus on the way home after the Armagh game, all I said about Dublin was: 'I know what they are about. I know what they are going to do and how they are going to do it and that's all you need to know.'

We sat them down on Tuesday night and went through it all. Then we coached it. So it was an instant switch. I was talking with conviction and they knew it.

Our theory was this: we are going to beat Dublin because they are going to give us a chance to. If we follow our plan to the letter, not only can we beat them – we can destroy them. And I believed that one hundred per cent. Dublin were excellent at what they did so they weren't going to change for us. Why would they? They were 10/1 on to beat us. Their attacking game was wonderful to witness and they seemed to have options all over the field. The consensus was that they had no real weak link.

I am not sure how many hours of my life I gave to watching Stephen Cluxton taking kick-outs. Match after match, restart after restart, play and rewind, night after night. I was looking for patterns. I would watch the same game several times over and write notes. Each match might take four hours to watch. And for a long time, I was concluding that Cluxton didn't have a pattern, which was spooky. I came to believe he was just ad-libbing these clairvoyant kick-outs which managed to initiate Dublin attacks while simultaneously turning opposition defences. His deliveries were always sympathetic to the runner, falling into their path, guiding them into space and never asking the receiver to break stride. The quality of his play was admirable. But eventually I saw what I felt was a consistency of habit. If you don't push up on his kick-out, then he goes short. If you do push up, he will chance the odd kick straight down the middle, but more often he will look to hit his half backs dropping back for the ball. If you succeed in shutting that down, then he looks for Paul Flynn and Diarmuid Connolly. And both of those players like to get up to speed before he pings it to them so that when they catch the ball, they're off. They give their marker just the slightest wee push before they move and have the power and speed to sustain it. As they move, the half back begins to move on the inside and either Flynn or Connolly will look for him and slip the little reverse pass. So now they have the ball and are carrying at speed and the defence is stretched.

Everything Dublin do revolves around not crowding their full forwards until the ball is passed inside. Once that happens, you have two and three men cutting through at good, strong angles and it becomes a nightmare for defenders because the Dublin player on the ball seems to have three or four options. Straight away, that gives the opposition a very simple and unpromising choice: take them on or don't take them on. I needed to know the pros and cons of both. If we didn't take them on and conceded the short kick-out and let them come on to us, it would invite a deluge of scoring chances. But stepping up would be an extremely difficult task. Studying them gave me some appreciation of the work they must do on their kick-out alone. And even before we played them, I admired where they were at.

But it wasn't as if Dublin just ignored their opposition. What they wanted was for other teams to play stupid. They worked out that if they pressed really aggressively on opposition defences and around the middle of the field, they could dictate the terms on which other teams attacked. Their big advantage was that their full back line is very physically strong and fast. So they programmed their forwards to hustle and harry like crazy and their half backs to push up. Just getting the ball out to the halfway line became an ordeal for teams. And this is where the Dublin management and team gambled on human nature. Think of it: you're in Croke Park, in that sea of noise, and you are on a team that has been harassed again and again just to bring the ball out to centre field. You look up and you see that they have left their full back line open, just three backs marking your three forwards – or two if you are playing two up front. And you see all this space in front of you and you reason that if you give it in, your forward has a good chance of winning it. And that is the illusion Dublin presented all summer. They had their full backs playing two and three metres in front of their men on whatever side the ball happened to be on. And they were expecting these long, hopeful passes in; everything Dublin did invited them. So they inevitably won the race for the ball. And it looks great: Dublin defenders storming out and cleaning up and the Hill crowd cheers and all of a sudden the pressure is back on the other team. Another attack has broken down and Dublin are full of movement and running and you are reeling. It is demoralising. It is only a matter of time before somebody cracks and before a goal goes in and then the entire stadium is rocking. So our big question was: Do we give them their kick-out or do we take them on? And we decided to take them on. We did so much work on practising against their kick-outs. As it turned out, we only won three of twenty-three, but we got 1-1 from those possessions. We decided that our full forwards would mark their men. Our half forwards were also to mark – but they were to stay on the outside of the Dublin half backs so they could block out the little chip to the wing from Cluxton. It was the same with the midfielders: we needed to mark tight but stay on the outside of their midfielders. Frank was detailed to mark Diarmuid Connolly. We put Anthony on Paul Flynn.

The trick for us, when we got inside the attacking half, was to not kick the ball directly towards our forwards. Instead, we would keep the pass away from the Dublin defenders. So when we were attacking, we weren't looking for the Donegal jersey; we were looking for the sky blue shirts of Dublin so we could play a pass fifteen to twenty metres left or right of that jersey. Then we worked on it: bombing through the ball from the half way line and a 'Dublin' full back marking our forwards. We practised kicking it around the corner to force defenders to turn and adjust so that Michael or Paddy or Colm, or whoever was inside, would be facing the goal when they got possession. It was up to our forwards to read the pass and because the Dublin defenders were no longer certain where the ball was going, it became a more even battle for possession. We also spent hours and hours working at getting the ball out while under pressure and avoiding contact in the first and middle third. We put a big defensive press on them and got them to work the ball through it. Our hope was that breaking down what Dublin did into segments would make it all clearer.

Then we worked on our kick-out. We absolutely knew that they would go man-to-man on us when we were restarting because they had destroyed Monaghan in the quarter-final on that alone. They had scored 2-8 off Monaghan's kick-out. So we began working on this drill where we would pull everyone into our own half and alternate between Michael and Neil Gallagher as the target man for our delivery. Paul Durcan has an incredible repertoire of pinpoint kick-outs that he has worked exceptionally hard to perfect. The boys had total confidence in him. So as Paul kicked, our half forwards were sprinting towards our half. But once we hit the 45-metre line,

Ryan McHugh would slam on the brakes, turn and run the other way. It gave him two or three metres on his man and that is all Ryan needs. He is lightning quick and he is the smoothest ball carrier you could ask for. So we told Neil and Michael not to even bother trying to catch it; to just flick it into the path of our runners. Then we had a situation where we could carry the ball straight at their full back line and give the ball when and where our forwards wanted. It should create overlaps for us. We got two goals in the second half from that alone.

If we found ourselves in a situation where we were attacking and Dublin's defence was established, we imposed a condition on ourselves that none of our offensive players was allowed inside their 21-metre line unless the killer pass was on. We played these little games of ten versus ten inside a half just to get used to keeping the ball out of contact in congested space. We got our second goal from that: Anthony made a strong run towards the Dublin goal in front of the Hill and Ryan timed his run so that the pass was definitely on. We planned to double up on their full forwards because we respected them so much.

The final and most important thing we worked on was this idea that we called 'anticipating the anticipator'. The more you watch Dublin, the more you see that it is not the guy on the ball you have to worry about as much as the guys coming through. You could see it again and again: a midfielder wins the ball and plays it to Alan Brogan. Once he takes possession, he has a runner coming through alongside him. Sometimes, when they are at their best, they have three men coming through. It is close to impossible to mark that – and they know it. So you have to be diligent and track those runs, time after time. The trouble is, it is not the same players making those runs. The entire Dublin team is capable of doing it.

We spent five days in Johnstown House at a camp and

watched so much film that we came to know their patterns off by heart. We could talk through the move: ball is won, James McCarthy takes it at speed, lays it off, and the ball goes inside to Bernard Brogan. Nobody is watching McCarthy, who continues his run at three-quarter pace and then bombs through once he sees that Brogan has clocked him. Another slip pass. Point. By the time we left the camp, we were confident we knew their game well.

We used the final week to burn the game plan into their minds. By the end, they were sick of listening to me. They were finishing my sentences for me and cutting across me. They knew it. They had it off. They were getting cranky at hearing the same thing over and over. That made me feel good because then I knew we were prepared.

At our last meeting, I wrote Donegal 3-16 Dublin 0-12 on the blackboard. That was the final score we were banking on. It actually ended 3-14 to 0-17. It wasn't too far off the mark because Dublin did kick unbelievable points in the first five minutes of the game. That was no surprise either. We had identified that danger before the game. We figured that if we do this, this and this, then the only option available to them will be long-range points. So on the basis of that, our last tactical decision was to set our defensive line outside our 50 by about five to seven metres. But we played too deep for the first five minutes. I think it was because of the start that Dublin made and the power and the crowd and noise. We were blown away initially and dropped into a siege mentality for a bit. We were as vulnerable then as any other team they had played. If you don't deconstruct Dublin in your mind before you take the field against them, you are entering a different world. It doesn't matter how good a footballer you are; you cannot cope. And we were just about coping in the first few minutes. It was a barrage and it was relentless. Dublin got their goal chance and Papa made a brilliant save. If that had gone in, it would have been very difficult for us. And we went 0-09 to 0-04 down. Standing on the sideline, we were so disappointed. We felt that there was a possibility that we could implode here. Maybe this is a bridge too far. And if that happened, so be it. That's the game. That is why we play.

The big screen happened to show Jim Gavin, Declan Darcy and the rest of his back-room team sitting in the stand together and laughing about something. It was probably unfortunate timing for them, but we noticed it on the sideline. They had just moved into a five-point lead, 0-09 to 0-04, with not even twenty minutes on the clock. So you stand there expressionless and you have these little debates. If they keep up this rate of scoring, they're on to break thirty points. And you scan your team and you see men with real substance. We had some very tough characters out there, guys who had persevered through dark seasons and hateful losses and had come through all that. The incremental pressure that Dublin apply is incredible to stand so close to. But the minutes went by and we could see that the boys were beginning to turn small things. Dublin's scoring rate slowed and we were starting to play through their press and then it became about a series of little things. Can we force them to do this? Can we just get that pass down to Colm? One or two little things from the training field began to work for us and we became emboldened. Odhrán Mac Niallais floated this lovely point to make it 0-09 to 0-06 and that was the first time I felt a real jolt inside: this is on. Other things were happening. Dublin claimed a ball at midfield but Christy chased down Michael Darragh MacAuley and made a brilliant steal. The McGee brothers were getting out in front of Brogan and Eoghan

O'Gara and we were starting to dominate that sector. Then Michael won this long ball that only Michael could win and slipped a ball to Colm and there was Ryan coming through, all alone. We had our goal. Paul asked me what I wanted from the second half. I told him that I wanted to see Jim Gavin out of that fucking seat in the Hogan Stand and down on the sideline giving his substitutes a rub on the back when he was sending them in.

When we played St Eunan's in 2005 our boys had us backed. Now our boys had us backed to beat Dublin. We were available at 10/1. They had a few hundred euros on themselves. And we knew leaving the hotel that we were going to win.

It was one of those rare days when everything you talk about and plan for and work on happens. I remember seeing Neil Gallagher watching Ryan and moving to his left before reaching for the ball and setting him in motion. Neil had become a vital figure in our game plan. He was a leader and a towering old-fashioned midfielder with a deep game intelligence. Neil reads a game so well. So much flowed through him and he was the conduit for the attacks we created in the second half. In some ways, it was unreal to watch because Dublin are a phenomenal football team. Their goalkeeper is probably the best in the history of the game. Their half forward line is the best I've ever seen. The only glitch in their system was the one we took them down on. So as unbelievable as it was, it also felt inevitable. It had to happen. And once the Dublin players lost their sense of certainty, they became as fallible and vulnerable as any other team.

Sometimes you can play in front of eighty thousand people and it can feel no different from Ballybofey. The only time I was aware of the atmosphere was close to the end. We could see all the Donegal supporters beginning to wave and make noise.

We couldn't figure what was going on and then we spotted it. They were waving goodbye to the Dublin fans leaving the Hill.

———

Somebody showed me a photograph of Michael Murphy on the field in Croke Park after Donegal had beaten Meath in the 2002 All-Ireland championship. He was looking straight up at Brendan Devenney. He wasn't quite twelve years old and he had this shine in his eyes. You could see in the light of them how much he wanted all this.

When I started out with Donegal, I had no relationship with Michael. I'm not sure how many hours we spent over the four years on the phone and sitting down talking. He is unlike anyone I have ever come across in terms of his focus. A standard rule in psychology is that focus is a connection between two things. And Michael has this fierce connection between his day-to-day life and his football life. When we started out, I got the impression that he was watching and evaluating and working out what he felt was going to happen. Once he was happy that there was substance behind the talk, he just went through the roof. He led. This is a guy who has played senior county football since the age of seventeen and has carried this constant expectation on his shoulders since then. He wears it lightly. Our group often feel as if we have the best footballer in the country in Michael and yet he is the one driving himself to the edge at training. He trains with ferocity. He is acutely aware of his position and responsibility. He gives a hundred per cent in every tackle drill and training session. And he may well be the best footballer in the country yet he is driving himself harder than anyone in the group.

That leaves everyone else wondering. He has an exceptionally intelligent football brain. He is out there playing games, but he can read games too.

We ended up on the phone for hours each week in the winter of 2011 after I told him I felt we could win the All-Ireland. We spoke about what was needed and we worked through different elements of the game plan I wanted. What I wanted was economy of effort. We couldn't have fifteen men dropping back and then fifteen going forward. So we spoke about how we would operate at a very high level but keep players fresh to bring the transition to attack. Economy of effort was crucial. If we had twelve behind the ball, six could go and six could stay. A corner back could end up at full forward with Michael Murphy. These were the concepts. But they had to be validated by him and we talked it through as we played: that worked against Derry, this didn't against Kildare, and so on.

Michael was sixteen stone ten pounds at U-21. He ended up fourteen stone twelve pounds. The work that went into making that change of body shape was frightening. He went from a traditional big man full forward to a really high-level athlete. He dropped weight while increasing muscle size and became faster and more powerful. He did this by giving every aspect of his life that same level of attention. I think one of the reasons he went to DCU was so he could train as a professional athlete.

He had a hernia at one stage and he was working with Eugene Ivers and JD McGrenra in Dublin on his rehabilitative gym work. But on the night before his operation, he did a session of one-legged cycling. He just wanted one more work-out where he could blast it. When we were in a huddle and I talked in the centre I often noticed his lips moving and he would be repeating whatever I was saying so that he would take it in. He followed instructions verbatim. He was very particular and needed to know precisely what was going on. 'Just go through that again'; 'Just go back on that.' And we would go through it until he was satisfied.

The general consensus in the country was that if you stopped Michael Murphy you stopped Donegal. It was something I was very aware of. We constantly heard the complaint that we should put him on the edge of the square. We didn't do it all that often for one simple reason: it was very predictable and managers would work out how to double- or triple-mark him and make it impossible to get him the ball. To us, it was a nonsense debate. Michael had very good discipline but he got physically hammered in every single game he played. He got no protection because he is so strong. You would see boys hanging out of him and referees just ignored it. If you are Peter Canavan or David Kelly, you will get seven or eight frees a game. I have often heard referees say to Michael: 'You're a big strong man; you can take it.' Or if I went to the linesman to complain, I would often get: 'There's two of them at it.' And I would think: What are you talking about? Michael is the fucking forward. He just wants away from his man so he can score. If he was a different type of player, he would be protected more.

I believe that the penalty miss against Dublin in Breffni Park made him stronger. He didn't look for excuses or blame anyone. He just took the disappointment and absorbed it and became a better player. I had seen him practise penalties afterwards at training and he didn't shy away from going high with that whipped power kick if he wanted to. If the team he was on in training wasn't winning or going well, Michael wasn't happy. He wants to win in-house games so badly. His intensity and commitment level at training was always on the limit. When Michael is on song he is very, very difficult to hold. The only time we fell out was over injuries; he tried to play through them and insisted that he was all right. It was almost as if he had this idea that as captain, he wasn't allowed to be injured.

As a person, he is a very well-mannered young man. He has a lot of humility and a lot of grace. He is respectful and has great patience. He wants a happy squad and he enjoys the fun in the group. One night during the early days of training, we were walking away from the pitch in DCU. We had had a really good session and we were walking up towards where the cars were parked. There was an old man standing there and he saw us and he just shouted out: 'Michael Murphy! The Donegal man!' There was real joy in his voice. Michael nodded at him and we walked on to the cars, just chatting. And Michael stopped suddenly and said: 'I'll ring you later, Jim.' He turned on his heels and headed back towards the pitch. And I knew he was going back to the old man because Michael knew that the man had wanted to speak with him. Another evening, after we had won a big championship match, I mentioned that I had a load of texts I needed to reply to. I asked him if he got many messages like that. He laughed and just said, 'I do, aye.' He had received over one hundred after that game alone. I asked him if he tried to get back to the people who sent them. His face became serious and he said: 'Aw, I respond to every single one. I couldn't not.'

———

I often felt that if what the boys gave to Donegal football was a gift for the county, it was also a gift for the family and for Mum in particular.

It is only now in adulthood and as a parent that I can begin to comprehend the hardships that she went through in losing the two boys. I sometimes feel sad when I think about her because I feel that she didn't get the opportunities from life that she should have. I know that a lot of her generation worked themselves to the bone just to raise their families as best they could. That was so true of Mum. I don't know how many mornings she would leave for the café at seven and it might be eleven at night before she would be turning off the lights there. She wanted us to have the best of everything, to be the best we could. I suppose that wasn't uncommon.

But on top of those everyday pressures, she had to endure a series of terrible personal hardships. Over the course of 1983 and 1985, she lost her mum, her brother and her son. My grandmother was going on eighty-five when she died, but uncle Liam was only thirty-eight. Losing Charles pitched us all into another world of sadness but Mum had to keep on going through all that. She was always there for us and was able to influence our lives in a very positive way. She has taught us all so much. She has a very acute perspective on life and has a lot of empathy for people. Sometimes you see her well up if something really tragic comes on the radio or on the news because she can instantly appreciate what it means for the families involved. She has never lost her faith and is always stealing out to mass when she gets the chance. But I'm sure there must have been times when she asked herself why she had to go through such tragedy.

Football became her escape. She enjoys the whole excitement and the chat as well as the games. She used to accompany Mark to games the whole time. I think she was only beginning to feel she was back on her feet after Charles when Mark died. In calendar years, 1984 and 1998 might seem like a long time ago but everything is still very close to the surface for all of us. And Mum has had to carry that.

She loves to have family around her, but at Christmas at home she could never relax until dinner was over. She is a gifted cook but she always wanted the run of the kitchen and needed us out of the way. She would only be happy when she was pouring gravy on the plates and even then she wouldn't sit down to eat herself for about an hour because she was too busy making sure everyone had enough. She can sometimes make a show of Donegal toughness – a kind of no-nonsense briskness. But it is easy to detect the softness underneath. I think that when our children came along, they gave a lot to Mum and Dad as well. And then the All-Ireland year was something that she couldn't have expected. It wasn't so much the fact of winning it as the joy and sense of well-being that filtered through the town and county afterwards.

She has never changed and whenever I'm with her or even when I think about her, I see someone with extraordinary grace and personal resolve. We all admire her so much. She kept our family together through the darkest times. We will never be able to thank her enough.

———

In our history, Donegal have played in two All-Ireland senior football finals, both within living memory. None of us knew what it was like to lose our grasp on those days. Maybe we believed those days were only for winning.

Planning for Kerry began on the way down the road the evening of the Dublin game. We were on the phone, organising tapes of their games and beginning to think about how they would negotiate playing us. The back-room staff had given exceptional commitment all through the year. The day we played Antrim coincided with the first communion of John Duffy's child Oisín. He never said anything. He just turned up. I was speechless when I heard about it. But that was John. His enthusiasm all through the season was brilliant. Paul was taking a day off work every week at this stage and he would call around to my house and we would run through everything. We went on a training camp to Lough Erne and the team sat down for two video analysis sessions per day. In the evening, we would take a long walk around the perimeter of the golf course and go through everything. Are we missing anything? What's going to beat us? After we broke it down and looked at the match from every perspective, we couldn't see it. We knew how Kerry would set up and we knew their kick-out strategy and how they would go man at the back and have that eight-man press along the middle. The way to beat that was either a dink ball over them – if we went from the left wing to the right wing – or just to come through with the ball and speed punch a hole and take six or seven players out. We knew we had players capable of doing both. We understood we had to play under pressure in the middle third but also play with our heads up. We knew we wanted to push up on their kick-outs. These are the things we worked on in our preparation for the game. We felt that if we did everything to the letter, we could win the game by five or six points. So we travelled to Dublin extremely well prepared and focused.

The county was feverish about this final because our win over Dublin was being spoken of as a sensation. And we were back in an All-Ireland final. People couldn't believe it. But we kept ourselves away from the fuss. The suit-measuring took place over half an hour in the dressing room. Only a few of the players were involved in the press day. So the build-up was like any other championship game and there was no feeling of pressure. We just needed to go and win.

We named the team on the morning of the game and went through the tactical stuff again. But I got this odd feeling in the dressing room that we were a little bit quiet in ourselves. People were just a bit subdued. So I addressed it.

— The game needs to be played now. You have to play the game now. You can't play it tonight and you can't play it tomorrow or next month or next year. You have to play it now.

Why I said that I don't know.

But that mood carried through to the field. It was plain to see. Our intensity was missing. We looked lethargic and burdened. Instead of the usual clarity of intent and ruthlessness, it was as if the collective thinking was: We should win this as long as we don't make any major mistakes. And that made us conservative and cagey instead of just going full-blooded to win the match. Straight away, we were in trouble because if a team has that mindset, it is very difficult to switch out of it during the game. And it took its toll.

Ryan McHugh and Odhrán Mac Niallais were one of the main reasons we were in the All-Ireland final. They brought legs and a work rate that were new assets to us and they are both very classy, instinctive footballers. After twenty minutes both were struggling. Never for a second did I think that might happen, because they both have temperaments as cool as a breeze. I took it for granted that they would deal with the occasion. And I was looking at Ryan and he was running up and down in the one spot. He couldn't support the ball and couldn't get back. But Ryan is such an athlete that I knew it wasn't lack of physical fitness. Ryan's struggles just mirrored the struggles of the entire team. Something else was happening. The work rate wasn't there. The energy wasn't there. The backs weren't marking as tightly as we had spoken about. We wanted to be as tight as a vice and then knock the ball away and stretch the pitch and drive the ball at them and ask questions. We were not doing that.

But we were playing a game within the game. When we got the ball, we hesitated or took a solo or passed the ball laterally and allowed them to make tackles. On the last day we met, myself and Paul had debated for close to an hour on whether we should have Paddy marking Paul Geaney. In the end, we decided we were happy to go with it. The concern was that Paddy ceded height: Geaney was six foot plus and decent in the air. But not once was Paddy isolated in the semi-final. We had a very solid defensive shape all the time, with two sweepers in front of our man-markers. We never allowed that situation to develop. So the only way that could happen was if we were caught on the counter. Also, the alternative was to put Frank in on him but then we would lose what Frank gave us out the field. We wanted Frank going forward as much as possible. Plus, Frank wasn't a whole pile taller than Paddy. Eamon was always marking Kieran Donaghy. Neil was on James O'Donoghue. Then you are looking at major switching and we decided that Paddy was the way to go. Now, we also knew that Éamonn Fitzmaurice knew that this would be our dilemma and that he would be looking to exploit that. But these are the decisions you live by and I would do the same thing again. So we said to Paddy: Just break the ball down if it comes in high. So we were caught on the counter attack and Kerry sent in a long ball that was deflected and fell perfectly for Geaney. He took his goal well. There was little Paddy could have done because of the trajectory of the ball. But that set the tone. We tried to be cagey and ended up playing Russian roulette.

We had a few guys pushing to the maximum – both Neils and Leo, for instance. And the funny thing was that in the huddle at half time, Leo spoke for the first time in four years – with real passion. 'What are we doing here, boys? Get stuck into the game plan here.' This was the first time in our four years together that this circumstance had arisen. We were playing with inhibitions. We weren't giving everything and we acknowledged that to ourselves at half time. We weren't supporting the ball. We were trying to do it a different way and we paid a huge, huge price for that. Aidan O'Mahony was shadowing Michael and sticking close, but if we had gone at Kerry, things would have opened up for him. All we had to do was move the ball and shift their defence and Michael would do his thing in the chaos. He was just waiting for the gaps, but we couldn't make them materialise. Then Kieran Donaghy got the goal off our kick-out early in the second half. It went down as Paul Durcan's error, but Paul's mistake had zero to do with Paul Durcan and one hundred per cent to do with the collective – including me. I was the manager. I put them out onto the pitch. Don't try and tell me that that goal would have happened if we had savage defensive shape, if we put our bodies on the line, if we were scrapping for every ball and breaking hard and driving at them asking questions. It wouldn't have happened. It was a negative energy being pushed down the track because every time we didn't do something there was a collective question: Why aren't we? And every time they got a shot off and we didn't put pressure on, it was the same. That is what the boys were thinking – in unison. It was inevitable that someone was going to make a mistake that would highlight that collective mindset. It happened to be Paul. And then the boys woke up and reeled off three points. Neil McGee got us back in with this inspirational score and for that minute it looked like we were alive. But it was not a light switch. We were in a fugue state, and even that just couldn't lift us out of it.

Kerry did nothing in the game that we didn't flag. That's what was so disappointing. They didn't catch us on the hop, even for that goal. They set up as we expected and their kick-outs went where we knew they would. We just didn't deliver our normal purposeful performance. The game went into a melting pot and it was one of the very few times we allowed that to happen. For four years, when we were at ourselves, we were so disciplined and controlled and played with such intensity that we controlled the game. Now this was just an ordinary game of football that could go either way. And that was contrary to everything we had done up to that point. We controlled the terms. We asked the questions. The players are the most intelligent element in the group. They knew that they weren't being true to the game plan or to themselves but they didn't know how to lift themselves out of it. We hadn't been here before. It was as if they were feeling that we didn't have to go out and win it, we just had to not lose it.

So I'm standing on the sideline and I have this ominous feeling the whole way through the match. It is a bad feeling. It is not about winning or losing. If our boys had been living it and playing with abandon and Kerry were just that bit better, you could walk away with a clean conscience and think: Wow, that's a great team we met. There are ways to lose. Kerry were the better team on the day, but our performance was not there.

I wasn't blaming the boys for this. I was the manager: I sent the team out to play; I was responsible for their mindset and their approach and it wasn't right. We were just off colour. They were trying their hearts out but it looked like they were moving through water. They were heavy. In the final few seconds, I turned to Paul and said: 'We are going to get a goal chance here.' We were three points down and we needed a goal and all of a sudden I recognised a movement pattern – one with urgency and intent. It was a kind of collective sign that I had seen over and over at training. When certain people move with purpose and shape their runs in certain ways, they can move the ball so slickly and at such pace that they create chances. Standing on the sideline in that moment, I had this sense that we would conjure up a goal chance.

So it is sometime after five o'clock in the evening now on 21 September 2014 and there are 84,000 people in Croke Park and Lord knows how many watching on television around the world. And the boys work the ball up in front of the Cusack Stand. It is in the square and it is loose and Colm is diving for it. And then a moment comes when I am standing in Croke Park on my own. The stadium falls away. There is no crowd. There is no All-Ireland final.

That second felt like an hour. Everything – your football life, all those decades – can be compressed into that second. Colm is my brother-in-law and my former teammate. He was stretching for a goal and I felt very far removed from it for that second. I might well have been back on the pitch in Glenties, climbing over the padlocked gate and carrying a fishnet bag of footballs on my shoulder and feeling like I owned the place.

Colm is reaching and I have one thought.

I don't want the goal.

I didn't want it because it would have felt shallow. Nothing we stood for was in our performance. We would have been sneaking something out of it. We didn't deserve it. Kerry deserved it because they came with a plan and made it happen.

Colm dives and he is stretching and he bats the ball with his right hand. It hits the post. The Kerry players scramble the ball clear and the whistle goes.

Over.

I went onto the pitch. Éamonn Fitzmaurice walked over to me with his hand extended and as I shook hands with him I thought: Youse did more than us in the game, so fair play to you. I said to him: 'Enjoy the week.' In those first minutes, I just felt very sorry for our players. I walked around them and I knew they were crushed. And I knew it wasn't because Colm had hit the post or that we had been beaten but because they realised that they hadn't shown themselves for who they are. That would be the hardest thing to take from the day. And we had to take it.

For once, everyone was still in the dressing room after the television and press interviews were over. I told the boys that we had played Russian roulette with the final and lost. If there was one lesson to take from the match, that was it. We do things the way we have always done things.

And about an hour or so after the final whistle, the pain becomes truly intense. It becomes something else entirely. It took a grip on the boys and it took a grip on me. What happens is that you are being propelled further and further away from the All-Ireland final with every passing second. You can do nothing to redeem it. Time is pushing you on. Your world has stopped but the world goes on. The underground of Croke Park is so mundane after matches. The caterers are leaving and the stewards are beginning to close up. The match is over and you are left to deal with the hurt. When we got on the bus we had to wait because the Kerry team bus was blocking our way. We sat there and a few of the Kerry boys came down from the lounge with beers. The odd Kerry supporter was wandering over to have a photograph taken with them. James O'Donoghue and Anthony Maher were standing in the tunnel with the cup beside them. They looked so carefree. They looked sated. We all knew how they felt. It is blissful, that hour or so after you win. We just stared out at them. That was all we could do. This was our reality now and we had to accept it.

Eventually our bus moved out into the evening and onto

Jones Road. We went down O'Connell Street and flashes of the evening in 2012 came back. And the pain was intensifying all the time. It was like a physical wound, as if I had been hit a blow deep inside. The questions began to come. How could this happen? What could I have missed? What did I not do? The boys were very quiet and everyone was in their own private hell. It was very silent and remorseful. I think we would have been content to have sat there and let the bus drive all night. Instead, it pulls up outside the Citywest Hotel and the realisation comes that we are obliged to see this day through. There is a banquet with 1,800 people attending. We all just want to disappear into our beds. Nobody wants to talk. Nobody wants condolences. We just want to vanish.

They give the manager this room that must be a presidential suite. It is like a luxury apartment. I got the key from reception and went up, and there was a suite: a sitting room, a kitchen, an office and a gymnasium. It was completely disconcerting. The pain was bad. I kept thinking: What is this all about? Colm and Marjorie, my parents-in-law, were there; Yvonne was putting the twins to bed. The older ones were looking at me and they knew something was wrong but they couldn't figure what. I kept saying: 'I don't know what happened. I don't know what happened.' It all felt distorted and wrong. Losing an All-Ireland final is the most incredibly miserable feeling you could imagine. You have this acceptance that it is over and that we didn't play. We lost by three points and we didn't really show up. When we lost the All-Ireland U-21 final, it hurt too but it was different because the boys had left part of their souls out on that pitch. There was no bad feeling then; just pride in what we had given. But this was different. This was hard to live with.

We spent the evening having a few beers but really just whiling away the hours and turning it over and over in our minds. I began to wonder what all the people at home in Donegal were thinking now. They had sat down to watch that final and they had an expectation or faith as to how we would deliver on the football field. And they knew we hadn't done that. We had failed them. Food was served and speeches were made. We just wanted to get home.

———

It becomes a ghost journey.

We left Dublin on Monday and we were coming back to Donegal without the cup. And it was a devastating feeling. You would hear the same question murmured, 'What happened ya?' It was fair enough. I didn't know the answer. I wasn't sure if it would ever come. The boys were having a proper drink now and I was happy about that because it might kill the pain for them. We stopped at the Kilmore in Cavan. Two years earlier, there had been a wall of people waiting for us and this guttural roar went up when we walked through the main doors. Now it was like visiting a party that had finished. The dining room was so quiet we could hear our cutlery against our plates. There was just the odd straggler about and even that was too many people.

We headed towards the border. This phrase I always loved came through my mind. Paddy Campbell, who played for Glenties and Donegal with me, had an uncle Charlie who came home from America after about forty years. Charlie got involved with a group who organised day trips for the elderly people's society. One year they had a Christmas party which involved a lunch in Glen and a dinner over in Bundoran. It turned out that the party included quite a number of bucks who were seasoned campaigners of the high stool. So they kept dodging off and it became harder and harder to shift them from the tavern. Charlie had this wonderful accent which was half American and half Donegal. And after about the tenth detour to collect this crew from whatever pub they had found he shouted: 'This is not a social trip! This is a torture trip. Drive on, Frank. Drive on!'

That was ringing in my ears because it felt like that's what we were on now. A torture trip.

See, in 1992 and 2012, the joy of knowing what was ahead of you was what made the experience so special. You become like a child on Christmas Eve. The anticipation is so wonderful that it becomes almost unbearable. Now, we knew there would be a big crowd waiting for us and the thought of it was weighing heavily on me. We stopped in Pettigo and the welcome was, as always, humbling. The bus moved on to Donegal Town. The boys had agreed to meet at the Forge, a little bar behind the castle on a street called Waterloo Place. But we had the homecoming to attend first. The bus driver took us around the back of where the stage was so the crowd didn't see us come through. I was off the bus first and I was escorted by the stewards up to the back of the stage. The boys were filtering off the bus in ones and twos, stretching themselves and getting their heads right.

And they were kind of hanging back. One of the boys had become emotional. He started crying. The man nearest went over to him and the rest gathered around and within seconds, it was as if it all hit them as a group. I stood and watched them from about ten metres away. They were all together, by themselves. Over the years, I have told the boys that I love them and meant it. I've said it in dressing rooms before and after matches. I never felt as strongly about them as I did at that moment, watching them helping each other. I stood and

watched with one of the stewards. I knew him: he was Leo
Calhoun from the Four Masters club and I would have marked
him in reserve games when I was fifteen years old. He signalled
to me wondering what to do and my face remained blank as
though to say: We wait for them. However long it takes.

I walked over to where Damien and Paul were and I said,
'We are ready to play the final now.' And we were. But I was so
happy to see that moment. The darkness lifted because there
was an unbelievable purity surrounding them at that moment.
We really, really cared about the fact that we had missed our
chance. I knew that they would probably have reached that
point of clarity at some stage but I was glad it was happening
now rather than at three in the morning with the music blaring.
And it brought the whole thing back to the group.

We made our way onto the stage and as soon as we stepped
into the lights we got this huge, heart-breaking cheer. Neil McGee
couldn't stay. He walked off. He said: 'I can't fucking take this.'
That was fine. I had to say a few words and as I was speaking,
I was thinking about this same place in 1992 and in 2012 and
about all the lives who are wrapped up in this and who love this
team. I knew this was it for me. I knew my time was up. So it was
a strange moment. I was trying to say the right things and figure
out what it was all about. I hoped the boys were feeling okay. So
many faces were flying through my mind.

We exited the stage through the back entrance and we
walked around by the old cinema and over the bridge. And it
was absolutely lashing; that heavy clean late summer rain. The
streets were deserted and the rain was hammering against the
road. So we ended up ducking into doorways and then running
a few metres and taking shelter again. It was just ourselves, just
the team. There was nobody else about. We made a run for it
across the bridge and got into the pub. The boys had arranged

to have a guitar there. We got our seats and ordered pints. Christy took hold of the guitar. We began to see the night out.

I knew now that the end was hours away. Once I left the pub, that was my time over with the boys. We would speak on the phone the next day trying to make sense of where we went wrong. I would sit up until it got bright trying to figure it. I was the manager and I was responsible for how they performed. Something wasn't right. The worst part was feeling that we had let everyone down: yourself, your family, the team, and all the people in the county. Past players. Everybody. And there would be chat over the next few weeks. The boys were saying that we all need to go back and sort this out and put it right. There was a moment when I was reconsidering. But I was thinking: We had our opportunity and we didn't take it. That was why the final had to be played then. It was the appointed hour. We couldn't rectify that. We couldn't change that. We would be trying to go back and right a wrong. You take your chances when you are there. And afterwards you deal with something that I think we will all be carrying for a long time, which is this pain that becomes part of you.

I knew I would miss them so much. We had a once-in-a-lifetime experience together. I had seen them grow up together and some of them become fathers and we had success and holidays and a fair bit of pain too. These are all very elemental life experiences. The players are like immediate family, but then you have all their families around them and it becomes a sprawling group of people who are going through this intensely binding passage of time. Letting go of that wasn't going to be easy. But I had always known it wouldn't be forever.

When we started out, the most I could say was that I didn't know what was going to happen. I just wanted to give it a blast and hoped that the boys could retire with an Ulster medal. That was something that all the players I came through with never got. And they had wanted it badly. John Duffy, John Gildea, Damien, Brian Roper, Barry Monaghan, Niall McCready, Aidy Sweeney: these were boys who had hurt a lot for Donegal. They would have given anything. And in the beginning, winning one Ulster was the totality of what we wanted to achieve. So I just wanted us to give it our all so that, no matter what the sacrifices and what the results, we could walk away with a clear conscience.

It turned out that the hunch I had had that day in Crossmaglen was right. The boys taught me so much. They are exceptional people. They are special. Never in my life did I demand as much from any group of people as I did those boys. And they accepted it all and embraced it and took it with good humour. And they knew it was edgy and extreme and that we were pushing boundaries. They knew that what we were doing was making us become something different. They were incredibly honest and so dedicated to what we were trying to do. And that wasn't lost on our supporters. That was the really special thing. There was a union between the team and the Donegal people which you could feel on match days. It felt alive. People could see just how much of themselves the boys were giving to this.

I think we created something out of nothing. We gave the people of Donegal a surprise when they weren't expecting it. We used that energy to bring everyone in Donegal together and we made ourselves become a team to be proud of. We helped to remind ourselves of place. The more we were criticised, the more the supporters got behind us. There is a magic in all of that. The boys did that.

You could dispute how we played the game and how we set up the team. But you could not dispute the purity and the honesty and the togetherness with which the boys represented

Donegal. We left it out there. That was why the 2014 final was an aberration. It just didn't happen. But that's the game. I will always remember our first game when I was U-21 manager, against Armagh, and walking out of the dressing room knowing that if we lost I would never be in charge of another Donegal team again. And if we had just won that lone Ulster title in 2011, then I would have achieved all I wanted for the boys. But we went further.

If someone had told me when I was running around the pitch in Glenties as a child that I would get to be involved in three senior All-Irelands and that I would win two, well ...

I am very proud of that. And I owe everything to the players. They showed up, night after night. I have said it to them. When you can stand before Gweedore lads and Creeslough men and tell them you love them without them narrowing their eyes and thinking: Is this boy all right in the head, I think you are in a good place in terms of what you are able to create.

On one level, Gaelic football is not important. When I was young, I approached it in a very surface manner. I wanted to win because I wanted to be the winner. When I lost I hated being a loser and all of the connotations that held. That is not important. What is important is not the result, it is the people you have about you. Two weeks after the All-Ireland final, I would send a text from Glasgow to the boys wishing them all the best and thanking them. That was the last thing I did as Donegal manager.

The funny thing is even when you are training at your hardest and there is frost on the windscreen or it is lashing rain, you understand that while the seconds are moving slowly, the whole thing goes by in a flash. You have a little run of time when you all have a chance to do something and then it is over. The boys will always be a team, long after they have finished up playing. I am sure of that. We may not see each other so much but we are bonded now and when they meet each other in twenty or thirty years' time they will remember what we did. And we didn't do everything right. But we went about it with the right intentions.

It must have been after two in the morning when I took my leave from the pub. I didn't want to leave but I couldn't stay any longer. The music was still going strong. Pauric Kennedy came to pick me up and drive me over to Glenties. How many championship days had ended in this trip from the Diamond to Glenties in the small hours? When I woke up we were outside the house. I was never as happy to see home in my life.

The whole county was asleep.

I closed the door quietly so as not to make a sound.